Arthur Cawston

A Comprehensive Scheme for Street Improvements in London

Accompanied by maps and sketches

Arthur Cawston

A Comprehensive Scheme for Street Improvements in London
Accompanied by maps and sketches

ISBN/EAN: 9783337012052

Printed in Europe, USA, Canada, Australia, Japan

Cover: Foto ©ninafisch / pixelio.de

More available books at **www.hansebooks.com**

A

COMPREHENSIVE SCHEME

FOR

STREET IMPROVEMENTS IN LONDON

ACCOMPANIED BY

MAPS AND SKETCHES

BY

ARTHUR CAWSTON, A.R.I.B.A.

"*Humanity may endure the loss of all things—all but the possibility of improvement.*" — FICHTE

LONDON: EDWARD STANFORD
26 AND 27 COCKSPUR STREET, CHARING CROSS, S.W.
1893

To my Fellow Townsmen

PREFACE.

LONDON is often described as ugly, but it is not past redemption. Though ill-proportioned and shapeless, it has a noble river, unrivalled parks, a few fine buildings; and it may be possible to evolve out of the chaos of its streets a city which will be a worthy capital of the world. The literature relating to London discloses no practical method for effecting this, and the object of the present work is to attempt to indicate in what way our metropolis can best be remodelled without placing an intolerable burden on the shoulders of any of its inhabitants. Why this has hitherto been impossible is due to the fact that London has never possessed a real municipality, and has consequently lacked the unity of purpose and common pride that effective self-government alone can give.

Nearly sixty years ago our provincial towns received corporate life under the Municipal Corporations Act, but it was not until the present Session that there has appeared any near prospect of disjointed London sharing in the benefits of municipal government. A Royal Commission is now actually formulating the method by which the ancient and exclusive Corporation of that square mile in our midst called the City, can be expanded to take in all London. It therefore appears probable that for the first time a prospect of improving our street system in a statesmanlike and comprehensive manner will be afforded, and if this book can furnish any practical help, however small, in this great work, the author will be amply repaid for the labour bestowed upon it.

In sending it forth he tenders his thanks to those writers whom he has laid under contribution in its pages.

13 QUEEN ANNE'S GATE, S.W.
May 1893.

CONTENTS.

CHAPTER I.
REASONS FOR IMPROVEMENT.

Combination and harmony necessary before improvement possible—Paris in 1750—London in 1700—London's decline—Benefits from improvements to health, traffic, labour, generally 1

CHAPTER II.
THE EXAMPLE OF PARIS AND OF OTHER TOWNS.

Paris the pioneer of adequate city reforms—Principles of Parisian improvements—Vienna, late Emperor's decrees with reference to improvements, present progress towards completion—Berlin, a city without a slum—Land laws in Prussia—Glasgow, extensive improvement inaugurated in 1865—Birmingham, central area splendidly transformed—The lesson from these leading towns .. 13

CHAPTER III.
THE POWERS NECESSARY FOR LONDON TO REGENERATE ITSELF.

The progress of municipal socialism—Impossible to regenerate London until full powers are given—Advantages and drawbacks of Parliamentary interference—Lines on which regeneration might proceed—Urgency for reforming our present system of compensation—Powers over land which are necessary to the municipality 27

CHAPTER IV.
THE ADVANTAGES OF ADOPTING A GENERAL SCHEME IN MAKING IMPROVEMENTS.

Present difficulties have arisen from want of general scheme of improvement—Advantages of general scheme: 1. For discovering causes of present inconveniences; 2. For producing best improvements: (a) complete utilization of every district for most valuable purpose; (b) creation of judiciously placed continuous arteries; 3. For producing improvements speedily; 4. For producing improvements cheaply; 5. For æsthetic reasons: (a) avoiding interference with ancient monuments; (b) raising municipal enthusiasm 38

CHAPTER V.

SUGGESTIONS TOWARDS THE FORMATION OF A GENERAL PLAN FOR IMPROVING LONDON.

Six general principles—1. *Open out parks*—2. *Open up crowded districts*—3. *Create more main arteries (a) sufficiently wide (b) straight and uniform in width (c) without steep gradients (d) each an integrant part of whole scheme (e) with convenient and safe street junctions*—4. *Provide additional bridges*—5. *Facilitate approaches to railway termini*—6. *Open out public buildings* 49

CHAPTER VI.

THE APPLICATION OF THE SUGGESTIONS, AND THE SEQUENCE IN CARRYING OUT IMPROVEMENTS.

Formation of draft improvement plan—*Details of some proposed new streets and some difficulties*—*Description of Ordnance sheet*—*Criticism of Council Broadway*—*Description of map of Paris*—*Two methods of advancing improvements*—*By increasing width of present thoroughfares*—*By avoiding interference with existing thoroughfares until others are formed*—*Reasons in favour of each method* 65

CHAPTER VII.

THE COST, AND HOW TO MEET IT.

Cost the final test—*Extravagance of borrowing*—*Unjustifiable for street improvements*—*Various sources apart from rates from which money might be raised, gas, water, trams, docks, municipalization of land*—*Impossibility of poorer ratepayers contributing*—*Suggested rates (1) graduated death duty on land (2) on buildings (3) graduated improvement rate on occupiers*—*Minor sources, from nation, from omnibus and cab companies, from railway, gas, and water companies* 77

APPENDIX I.

EVIDENCE OF THE RIGHT HON. JOSEPH CHAMBERLAIN, M.P., GIVEN BEFORE THE ROYAL COMMISSION ON THE HOUSING OF THE WORKING CLASSES, JUNE 1884 91

APPENDIX II.

PRIZE COMPETITION FOR A GENERAL IMPROVEMENT PLAN OF THE CITY OF VIENNA 121

INDEX 129

LIST OF ILLUSTRATIONS.

MAPS.

Central London, to the 25-inch scale	
London from Kensington to Whitechapel, to the 6-inch scale	In pocket
Paris within the walls, to the 6-inch scale	

PLATES.

	TO FACE PAGE
Sketch for suggested retail market	11
Place de la Concorde, Paris	13
Place de la République, Paris	18
Franzen's Ring Strasse, Vienna	19
Maps of the inner city of Vienna, 1857 and 1887	20
Elizabeth Bridge and Fruit Market, Vienna	22
Municipal buildings, Glasgow	24
Municipal buildings and art galleries, Birmingham	26
Specimens of London lamp-posts, 1870 and 1890	32
Sketch design for opening out Gray's Inn, London	39
Sketch design for opening out St. James' Park, London	51
Sketch for opening out Hyde Park, London	52
Sketch for opening out Lincoln's Inn, London	54
Sir Christopher Wren's plan for rebuilding London	56
Pont de la Concorde, Paris	57
Plan of Trafalgar Square as lately altered, and as it might have been improved	60
Plan of Regent Circus	61
Griffin Street, Waterloo Station, as it should be	62
Palais de Justice, Brussels	63
Sketch design for opening out the Temple	67
Sketch design for completing the southern embankments of the Thames	69
Sketch design for completing the southern embankments from New Bridge	70
Rond Point, Champs-Élysées, Paris	73
Place de la Bastille, Paris	83
The courtyard of the Privy Council Offices, London	90

A COMPREHENSIVE SCHEME

FOR

STREET IMPROVEMENTS IN LONDON.

CHAPTER I.

REASONS FOR IMPROVEMENT.

Combination and harmony necessary before improvement possible—Paris in 1750—London in 1700 - London's decline—Benefits from improvements to health, traffic, labour, generally.

NONE of us really know the great capital in which we live. In some ways magnificent, it has more squalid streets, more regions destitute of hope, than can perhaps be found within similar limits in any other part of the world. London is so large, so shapeless, that no one person can really know its wants or the needs of its people. Working amongst its poor is an army of Samaritans and Reformers, and from time to time a voice is raised for some improvement in the environment of the masses. Moved as we may be at the moment, we soon fall back into our old groove, taking no steps which will permanently benefit our people or our town. If we could only combine, the energy that is now largely frittered away in individual effort might then become potent for good. There seems to be no absolute reason why millions of our fellow beings should continue to live in the miserable squalor that now surrounds them—other towns have to some extent regenerated themselves, and if the right path leading to the regeneration of London can be indicated, doubtless many will gladly take up a work so vital to the welfare of the whole community.

A century ago Paris was even in a worse position than London, and Voltaire expressed the common feeling of shame so powerfully that his words incited the Parisians of his day to a combined effort for the improvement of their city. Voltaire wrote :—" We possess the wherewithal to purchase Kingdoms, we see every day what is wanting to our Capital, and we content ourselves with murmuring. . . . We rush to the *theatres*, and are indignant on entering them in a manner so inconvenient and so disgusting, to be so uncomfortably seated there, and to leave them with

B

more trouble and confusion than when we entered. We blush, rightly, to behold public markets established in narrow streets, spreading dirt and infection. We have only two fountains in good taste, and they are far from being advantageously situated; all the others are worthy of a village. Immense districts require open spaces, and the centre of the town, obscure, confined, hideous, represents a period of the most shameful barbarism. We say this without ceasing, but until when shall we say it without remedying it? . . . The meanness of ideas, the fear, still more mean, of a necessary expenditure, rise up to contend with those projects of grandeur which every good citizen has made to himself a hundred times. We are discouraged on thinking what it will cost to raise these necessary monuments, the greater number of which, becoming every day indispensable, must be executed in the end, whatever they may cost, though, in the main, it is very certain that they will cost nothing to the State. . . . What! shall it be only at the last extremity that we do something great? If half Paris were burnt down we should rebuild it, rendering it superb and commodious, and we are not willing to give it, to-day, at a thousand times less cost, the accommodation and magnificence which it needs! Yet a similar enterprise would redound to the glory of the Nation, would be an immortal honour to the municipality, would encourage all the Arts, and, far from impoverishing, would enrich the State. It would, moreover, accustom to work a thousand worthless loafers, who sustain a miserable life in the infamous trade of begging, and who still contribute to dishonour our Capital. . . . May Heaven send some man, some statesman, sufficiently zealous to undertake such projects, with a mind sufficiently firm and enlightened to carry them out; and that he may have trust enough reposed in him to make them a success! If, in our immense City, no one can be found to do this, if we are contented to talk of it at table, to utter useless vows, or, may be, impertinent pleasantries, 'il faut pleurer sur les ruines de Jérusalem.'"

Substitute the word "trains" for "theatres" in this despairing appeal, and one might almost suppose the words were put together to describe the London of to-day. Contrast with Voltaire the following description of London, as given by Edward Hatton in 'A New Review of London,' published in 1708 :—" London is the most ancient, *spacious*, populous, rich, beautiful, noble city that we know of in the world. Tis the seat of the British Empire ; the Exchange of Great Britain and Ireland ; the Compendium of the Kingdom ; the Vitals of the Commonwealth ; and the principal Town of traffic that I can find accounted of by any of our Geographers."

Clearly, in Hatton's time, London was commodious and its streets well adapted to the needs of those days. Then its citizens must have been men of breadth and intelligence, who clearly saw their necessities and determined to fulfil them, and if this spirit had been maintained with London's growth, Voltaire's words would never have been applicable to it. But the reverse of this has been the case, and many an attempt has been made to suggest how the inadequate street system of London can be transformed so as to meet the expanding requirements of the present day. The remedy apparently has not yet been found, and the probability that London is now for the first time about to acquire a satisfactory and powerful Municipal Government, seems to make it desirable that yet another attempt should be made.

It will be well first to consider both the losses caused by inadequate streets, and the benefits to be gained by improving them. This can best be done under the heads of Health—Traffic—the Labouring Classes—General benefits.

1. HEALTH.

"Life in a modern city should not be an evil or a misfortune for any class. There should be such sanitary arrangements and administration as to make the death-rate of a great city smaller than that of the nation as a whole. There should be such educational facilities as to insure to all the young people of a city the most suitable physical, intellectual, and industrial training."[*] We in London are rising to some faint perception of these truths, which are being gradually brought home to us by the improved material conditions which exist in many of our more energetic and progressive provincial towns. No doubt some works have also been accomplished in London, reducing its death-rate; but the death-rate of those districts of London where the population is most dense is still far greater than the death-rate in any of the principal cities in Europe. In the whole of the central districts, for instance, the death-rate in 1891 was 27·6 per thousand, whilst, according to a report to the London County Council, the death-rate for the year 1890 in portions of the crowded district of Bethnal Green, is stated to have been 40 per thousand.[†] It is just in these districts that one of the greatest dangers to the health of London lies. They are the spots on which epidemic diseases fasten, and until they are transformed, progress in lessening the general death-rate will continue to be arrested. Not only so, but London, which was once in the van of sanitary progress, has lost her place, and until the remedy be found will lull farther and farther behind cities to which she formerly showed the way.

The following figures are taken from the annual summaries of deaths issued by the Registrar-General since 1874, from which date the death-rates of foreign cities have been included in the summaries.

[*] "How London is Governed," by Albert Shaw, 'Century Magazine,' Nov. 1890.
[†] 'Annual Report of L.C.C. for 1891,' p. 38.

DEATH-RATE IN TWELVE LEADING EUROPEAN CITIES IN 1874 AND 1890-1.

Cities.	1874.	1890-1.*	Decrease of Death-rate.
1. Berlin	32·9 per 1000.	20·9 per 1000	12·0 per 1000.
2. Liverpool	32·0 „	23·6 „	8·4 „
3. Birmingham	26·8 „	19·7 „	7·1 „
4. Hague	26·5 „	19·5 „	7·0 „
5. Glasgow	31·1 „	25·3 „	5·8 „
6. Turin	26·7 „	22·8 „	3·9 „
7. Rome	27·5 „	23·6 „	3·9 „
8. Brussels	23·9 „	21·5 „	2·4 „
9. London	22·5 „	20·3 „	2·2 „
10. Paris	22·4 „	21·6 „	0·8 „
11. Vienna	24·6 „	24·6 „	Nil.
			Increase.
12. Dublin	26·0 „	26·5 „	0·5 per 1000.

These figures clearly show the improvement that has taken place in many large cities, and they also show that no material alteration has taken place in the health of London and Paris during the same period. The reason of this may perhaps be found in the fact that radical changes were being made in those cities which show marked improvement, while in London and Paris little change took place during that period. For instance, between the years 1880 and 1890, Glasgow transformed about ninety acres of slums. In order to give an idea of the beneficial results of this work on the health of that city beyond what is stated above, I cannot do better than quote from that most interesting book, 'Vital, Social, and Economical Statistics of the City of Glasgow, 1885 to 1891,' by James Nicol, City Chamberlain.

"The table of the total mortality of the city in the last ten years exhibits, when compared with the preceding decade, most gratifying, in truth remarkable, results touching the health of the people of Glasgow, and is eloquent testimony to the success of the great municipal work carried out by the City Improvement

* During the years 1890-1 influenza was prevalent in parts of Europe, and affected the death-rate materially. For this reason, where the rate seriously differed in any city during those two years, the lower rate is quoted as being closer to the normal rate.

Trustees in breaking up the dense and fœtid closes in the old and central districts of the city;* of the sanitary conditions enforced by the department on health; and of the drastic measures applied for the arrest of infectious disorders.

"In the decade 1871-1880, with a population averaging
494,574, the deaths per annum were   14,303
And in the last decade 1881-1890, when the population
averaged 537,000, the yearly number of deaths was .. 13,132
Giving a diminution per annum to the credit of last
decade of   1,171
Add for the difference of population   100

And we have an annual saving of lives of ..   ..   1,271 "

Similar good results followed the comprehensive improvements in Birmingham, which were also undertaken during the period referred to. Mr. Chamberlain's evidence on this point, given before the Royal Commission on the Housing of the Working Classes, contains striking testimony to this.†

During this same period, sanitary and street improvements were being vigorously carried out in Berlin, Liverpool, and the Hague. No doubt these great strides in improvement were taken owing to the example of London and Paris. London had, before this period, by the construction of her great sewerage works and other sanitary improvements, reduced her death-rate materially, and Paris, by abolishing her slums, and transforming herself into a city of wide and beautiful streets, had also reduced hers. During the later period above referred to, both London and Paris rested more or less on their onward march, for no one can believe that the London death-rate of 20·3, or the Paris death-rate of 21·6, indicates the ultimate goal of sanitary reform. Many of us, indeed, believe in the possibility of reducing these figures to one-half. That this is no mere dream is shown by the death-rate of Hampstead, which is 14·7, and by the striking experience of the Artizans' Dwellings Company, which is able to boast of a death-rate in its tenement blocks of 12·85.

If then we are to keep pace with what is being done for the health of townspeople elsewhere, the most urgent necessity at the present moment is obviously the adoption of a scheme under which our dense and thickly-populated slums can

* The work of this trust is described in Chapter II.
† See Appendix I., Questions 12,394, 5 and 6.

gradually be transformed into broad arteries and lofty blocks of dwellings. Such a system is undoubtedly the healthiest and most convenient means of accommodating the population of large towns, for the wide roads not only continually change and purify the atmosphere around every home, but at the same time provide accommodation for the ever-increasing traffic. Neither of these benefits can possibly be procured by means of narrow streets flanked by low buildings, which under our present policy are created in all directions. Moreover, although our streets are always narrow, the buildings in them are not always low. The result of this is indicated by the fact that the School Board visitors can tell whether a child lives at the top or bottom of a block of dwellings, so much is it *visibly* affected by living without sunshine in the stagnant and polluted air around the lower part of buildings situated in narrow and ill-ventilated streets.* Assuredly, then, if this policy be continued, not only will the health of our capital suffer incalculably, but the cost of providing a remedy in the future will be vastly greater than that of securing one now.

2. TRAFFIC.

Every omnibus and cab that uses the main streets of the City of London and its approaches is delayed on an average half an hour every day, through blocks and partial blocks. From the same cause, every van that passes through its narrow lanes is delayed on an average at least an hour and a half. The number of vehicles that passed into the City on May 4th, 1891, was 92,372.† Calculating this waste of time on 50,000 vehicles only, the loss in money amounts to at least five thousand pounds a day, or a million and a half a year. In addition to this, there is an enormous loss of time from the same cause to business men and others, the money value of which it is impossible to calculate.

An attempt has been made to find an artificial remedy so far as the unloading of vans is concerned, by a provision in the Metropolitan Streets Act of 1867, which forbids vans to stand for longer time than is necessary to load and unload. This provision, however, increases rather than lessens the blocks in the streets, as the carters walk their horses with their heavy loads up and down the streets, awaiting their turn to discharge. Another clause of this Act attempts to minimise the difficulty by forbidding timber or other lengthy merchandise from being carried through narrow streets during certain hours ; and a further clause prevents traffic

* 'Royal Commission on the Housing of the Working Classes,' Question 2282.
† 'Ten Years' Growth of the City, 1881–1891.' James Salmon.

LOSSES FROM DELAYS TO TRAFFIC.

from the North or East passing through certain streets, while other streets are similarly blocked against traffic from the South or West.

Inadequate streets necessitate an excessive number of constables to regulate the traffic and prevent loss of life. Sixteen constables are daily required to regulate the traffic at the point where Southampton Row and Little Queen Street meet Holborn. Even with all possible care, street accidents are persistently increasing. In the year 1881, the number killed and wounded in the streets of London was 3527, whilst in 1891 the number had risen to 5784, although in the meantime the police force had been increased from 11,699 to 15,038.* Judicious street improvements will obviously remove most of these difficulties, and materially reduce the number of accidents. For instance, traffic, both vehicular and foot, quite as heavy as that of the congested Strand, freely passes through Whitehall without police regulation, and almost without accident.

Not only do many existing streets want widening, but new and more direct routes should be provided for diverting much of the present traffic from overcrowded thoroughfares. For instance, if the northern side of St. Paul's Cathedral were widened and thrown open to vehicular traffic, the present indirect way round the south and east of the Cathedral would not remain the route for the traffic going eastward from Ludgate Hill to Cheapside. Again, if a new street were made direct from Charing Cross to Rosebery Avenue, the omnibus traffic to Islington would probably not make the present detour by Fleet Street and Chancery Lane. If Piccadilly were continued eastwards by a broad street parallel to Covent Garden, as shown on my plan, all the traffic from Kensington would probably no longer find its way to the crowded Strand.

There is another and growing consideration that ought not to be overlooked. Most of our main thoroughfares are absolutely unsuitable for tramways—a mode of conveyance which is undoubtedly a boon to the working poor, and a convenience to most. Although differences of opinion may exist as to whether trams should be admitted into the centre of London, even where the roads are of ample width, there cannot be two opinions as to the advisability of encouraging them from the suburbs to termini as near the centre as practicable. It is true that existing tramways are a danger in many parts, such for instance as those in the Walworth Road; Westminster Bridge Road; Nine Elms Lane; Old Street, St. Luke's; and, of all places, in one of our newest thoroughfares, the Clerkenwell Road! This, however, is no argument against tramways, but is a powerful reason for improving our streets in a sufficiently liberal manner to meet the inevitable growth of all sorts of traffic.

* 'Annual Reports of the Commissioner of Metropolitan Police.'

3. THE LABOURING CLASSES.

We are all used to the cry, now periodically raised, that occupation must be provided for the unemployed; and with that cry most of us have sympathy. It is, however, a question of great import whether or not it is sound policy to create work which is not admittedly of permanent benefit to the community at large, in order to give employment. Any well-considered scheme, on the contrary, would have a healthy effect in stimulating trade and inducing prosperity. I can think of nothing that would have a better effect on the prosperity of a town, and on the well-being of its industrial classes, than the carrying out of a well-considered scheme for its material improvement. Such a scheme could go on uninterruptedly from year to year, with such occasional developments as periods of exceptional depression demanded. It is not too much to say that there is hardly any branch of industry that would not be more or less beneficially affected by it. This must be apparent to any one who will even casually consider the great number of trades which are brought into play by the removal of existing properties, the formation of new streets, and the erection and furnishing of buildings on the new frontages.

Rightly considered, the money actually spent in work of this character is pure gain to the community. Not only does it provide an investment for capitalists, work and wages to industry, and profit to all the many employers who supply the labouring class with the necessaries of life, but the community has usually, in the improvement itself, excellent and permanent value for the money spent. Next to the actual production of wealth from the soil, there is perhaps no form of expenditure which brings greater prosperity, or more lasting benefit, than that employed in the permanent improvement of towns. How much better is this than attempts to create, in times of labour crises, special devices for employing the unemployed; for in these there is admittedly a pauperizing effect which is permanently injurious to the class they are intended to aid.

It may be urged that one of the effects of carrying out improvements on a large and systematic plan in London will be the attraction of labour from other towns, thus adding to the over-stocked labour market of the metropolis. It is true this might be the effect at first, but the general influence on labour would be wholly beneficial, for there can be little question that when London steadfastly begins its work of regeneration all the other towns will surely follow. Emulation will rapidly and inevitably have its stimulating effect, even on the least enterprising, and, as will be shown in the next part of this chapter to have been the case elsewhere, the powerful example of the metropolis will continue to be followed, in the future as in the past, throughout the whole of the country.

In Chapters IV. and V. an attempt will be made to show that the true solution of the question of housing the working classes in London does not lie wholly in the direction of tempting them to the suburbs, nor wholly in the reconstruction of the slums on their present costly sites. It may be found possible to provide dwellings quite as healthy and pleasant as in any suburb, on suitable sites within a mile of those central districts where work chiefly lies. If, in doing this, we can at the same time find work for the worker and employment for the unemployed, we shall be doing that which must be an unmixed good to the community.

4. GENERAL BENEFITS.

Not only local convenience, but national dignity, demands that our metropolis should be improved. A well-known English writer, Mr. Hamerton, has summed up foreign criticism of London as follows :—" Foreign critics are usually so horrified by London smoke, and by the ugliness of our ordinary houses, that they become incapable of perceiving beauty even where it really exists, and confound all things together in indiscriminating, unsparing condemnation." *

After living ten years in England, a very intelligent Frenchman, "Max O'Rell," writes thus :—" If nothing is more sad and gloomy than out-of-doors life in the large English towns, nothing that I know of is more charming than the interior of a well-kept English house. It is a paradise of studied comfort and well-understood luxury." †

In comparison to this, note his remarks on London :—" London has, so to speak, no monuments. The Abbey and Palace of Westminster, St. Paul's—you must not look for much else. A few statues: the great Cobden shivering with cold in a dirty out-of-the-way corner; Nelson stuck upon a Roman candle high in the air; three Wellingtons and a Shakespeare – this last a private gift. At the four corners of Trafalgar Square, the London Place de la Concorde, four pedestals are to be seen. Three are surmounted by statues, the fourth is wanting. Not that there is any dearth of great men in England; it is simply indifference, nothing more." †

Foreign opinion as to the ugliness of London is, indeed, so well known that it will be unnecessary to make further quotations. Few foreigners, or indeed few of us, know the immense areas, especially in East and South-east London, where the streets are narrow and monotonous, and the houses poor and squalid. Miles and miles

* 'Paris in Old and Present Times.' † 'John Bull and his Island.'

of such streets follow each other, unrelieved in any way in their dismal monotony, and it would be impossible to imagine more cheerless and depressing surroundings than those in which hundreds of thousands of our fellow Londoners are doomed to spend the greater part of their lives. To relieve this monotony by bringing through such districts new main thoroughfares is surely desirable. We have seen the beneficial results that have followed the making of such improvements. Charing Cross Road and Shaftesbury Avenue have opened up and brought light and variety to such dismal regions as Soho and Seven Dials; and none who remember what these districts were, and know what parts of them now are, can for one moment doubt the unmixed good that the construction of main thoroughfares brings to such parts. This may not be a matter which appeals equally to all of us, for to some it will certainly be difficult to realise the dismalness of the life of those whose monotonous occupations and crowded homes are far away from busy thoroughfares; but to those whom the duties of either business or philanthropy take constantly into the vast tracts of Darker London, this reason for improvement will strongly appeal.

Another class, higher in the social scale, will also be beneficially affected by the making of judiciously placed new streets. It is notorious that in what are called choice positions, such, for instance, as in the Strand, New Bond Street, or Oxford Street, the rents paid by shopkeepers are enormous, and must form a most serious tax upon the customers who purchase at these shops. Few of us have any conception of the excessive amount of these rents, and that the life of the shopkeeper is often almost one of slavery, endeavouring to win a large income, not only for his own, or his family's benefit, but for the benefit of his taskmaster, the landlord. This unnatural state of things is only made possible by the fierce competition for shops in the very few good thoroughfares that London now possesses. If more of such thoroughfares are made, and especially if they are so planned as to insure a large amount of through traffic, as they certainly can and should be, many additional sites for high-class retail shops would be created. Then, by the natural law of supply and demand, it might be possible for the retail tradesman to obtain good shops at reasonable rental. The same benefits would accrue to many wholesale traders. For instance, before the formation of Queen Victoria Street, iron-founders, stove-merchants, and wall-paper manufacturers were only to be found in the confined warehouses of Thames Street, for which inconvenient and almost inaccessible premises fabulous rents were paid. Now, these wholesale traders are accommodated at lower rents in the spacious premises in Queen Victoria Street, which has become the centre of these trades. If more main thoroughfares were carried through to the City, wholesale clothiers, fancy-goods merchants, and others would gradually occupy the new premises in the more commodious streets, extending the trade area of the City,

Sketch plan of proposed
PVBLIC MARKET & PLAYGROVND
Strvtton Ground, Westminster S.W.

Sketch of Exterior   Sketch of Interior

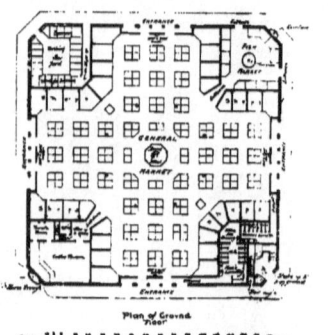

Plan of Ground Floor   Block Plan

ii 1892

and leaving the confined lanes of the central portion for those merchants and others who are bound to find accommodation near their exchanges and markets. It must be remembered that, although the inflated value of some few existing premises may thus be reduced, the development of districts now occupied mainly by property of a poor and comparatively unremunerative kind will be so great, that their rateable value will be largely increased, thus bringing general benefit. Instances of this may be readily found on the Westminster and Cadogan estates.

There is yet another advantage which will arise from the improvement of London. No one perhaps realises the enormous sums brought into some countries by tourists and temporary residents from abroad. London is only beginning to reap a large harvest from this source; but in the past such towns as Paris, Vienna, Brussels, and the chief Italian cities, have done so. The Secretary of the British Embassy at Rome, in one of his reports on Italian trade, gives as his estimate of the sum spent in that country by visitors from abroad, twenty-one millions sterling annually. Since London commenced to improve itself, and especially since it has been provided with its three or four magnificent modern hotels, it has begun to share the enormous annual income derived from the pursuit of pleasure. That it can eventually be made one of the most attractive of cities is without doubt, and owing to the advantage of its position on the highway between the New World and the Old, its improvement will be the means of intercepting some of the wealth spent in pleasure before it reaches the Continent.

To make the Metropolis really beautiful, not only will new streets be necessary, but many new public buildings. For years past we have spoken of erecting new Government buildings for the Departments of War, Trade, Agriculture, &c., and we now undoubtedly need a great central group of Municipal Offices. There are many other architectural buildings, both public and private, that will probably be erected when really advantageous positions are provided. This can only be done in connection with the formation of fine thoroughfares in central districts, and when this is done, London will begin to be the beautiful and dignified city that its wealth justifies. Among the many public buildings from the want of which London has long suffered inconvenience, Retail Markets may be mentioned, but there is now a probability that our Council will supply this want. Judiciously placed, these markets will afford not only attractive features in London's architecture, but will bring light and variety into many of the poorer districts. How this can be done I have endeavoured to show in the accompanying plan and sketches, and it will be apparent that not only would such markets remove a serious reproach from our streets, but would enable both buyers and sellers to transact their business under conditions of comfort and decency.

c 2

Do what we will, it is impossible at once to bring London to the level, in design and architecture, of many Continental cities, as with them the work has been steadily progressing for a long period. But when the turn of London arrives, we shall doubtless gradually succeed, by skilfully-planned new streets, and well-placed public buildings, in largely transforming it from the ugly and shapeless mass that it now is, into a really attractive city. Not only would such a city become a great centre for visitors from all parts of the world, but the interest its improvement would excite in the breasts of its wealthier citizens might be the means of diverting a portion of their wealth to still further improvement. The munificence of Englishmen towards work that really interests them is well known, and beautified London would be likely to attract some of this munificence to itself.

That such a transformation would encourage every trade in the country is undoubted, and it would not be by means of the improvements carried out in the metropolis alone that London would thus encourage the nation's trade. "The majority of visitors to Paris will find comparatively little to interest them in the provinces of Northern France. The towns are merely repetitions of the metropolis on a small scale. The modern taste for improvement, which has been so strongly developed and so magnificently gratified in Paris, has also manifested itself in the provincial towns.... Broad and straight streets with attractive shop-windows are rapidly superseding old and crooked lanes; whole quarters of towns are being demolished, and large regular squares taking their place; while ramparts of ancient fortifications are converted into boulevards faintly resembling those at Paris. Admirably adapted as these utilitarian changes doubtless are to the requirements of a crowded town in this nineteenth century, it cannot but be deeply regretted that the few characteristic remnants of antiquity which, in these quiet provincial towns survived the storms of the Wars of the Huguenots and of the Great Revolution, are now rapidly vanishing." *

When, therefore, London determines to dispense with her narrow streets and lanes, we shall expect to find Brighton at last ashamed of her Western Road, North Street, and East Street; Richmond, of her High Street; and Portsmouth, Chatham, and Swansea, of their unhealthy, inconvenient and inartistic thoroughfares, which certainly have little historic interest to induce us to preserve them. Thus will the example of the metropolis be copied from one corner of the kingdom to the other, to the great benefit of trade and to our national honour and repute.

* Baedeker's 'Guide to Paris and Northern France.'

PLACE DE LA CONCORDE, PARIS

CHAPTER II.

THE EXAMPLE OF PARIS AND OTHER TOWNS.

Paris the pioneer of adequate city reforms—Principles of Parisian improvements—Vienna, late Emperor's decrees with reference to improvements, present progress towards completion—Berlin, a city without a slum—Land laws in Prussia—Glasgow, extensive improvement inaugurated in 1865—Birmingham, central area splendidly transformed—The lesson from these leading towns.

PARIS.

"PARIS is the typical modern city. In the work of transforming the labyrinthine tangle of narrow, dark, and foul mediæval alleys into broad, modern thoroughfares, and of providing those appointments and conveniences which distinguish the well-ordered city of our day from the old-time cities which had grown up formless and organless by centuries of accretion—in this brilliant nineteenth-century task of reconstructing cities in their physical characters, dealing with them as organic entities, and endeavouring to give such form to the visible body as will best accommodate the expanding life within, Paris has been the unrivalled leader. Berlin and Vienna have accomplished magnificent results in city-making, and great British towns -- Glasgow, Birmingham, Manchester, and others"—(alas! London is not, and could not truthfully be included)—" have, in a less ambitious way, wrought no less useful reforms; but Paris was the pioneer. French public authorities, architects, and engineers, were the first to conceive effectually the ideas of symmetry and spaciousness, of order and convenience, of wholesomeness and cleanliness, in urban arrangements." *

The present dignified and convenient modern city has replaced the picturesque mediæval one under a system which embodies certain general principles. A short description of these principles will be useful in showing that such a system, subject to certain modifications, can also be carried out in London with complete success. In these days, for instance, it would be quite impossible—at any rate outside the precincts of the City of London, where ancient monuments have received short shrift—to think of sacrificing our ancient buildings as they have been sacrificed in

* "Paris," by Albert Shaw, 'Century Magazine,' for July 1891.

Paris; neither could Englishmen tolerate the military directness of the Avenue de la Grande Armée and other boulevards.

The work of remodelling Paris was commenced after the Revolution of 1848, upon the lines of a general plan for the cutting of new streets prepared by a "Commission des Artistes." This plan included 108 distinct projects, and although political changes interfered with its full execution, the work of reconstruction has never ceased. The same plan has persistently and continually been advanced, and to-day is still advancing, either by opportunities afforded by fires, by railway extensions and by rebuildings, or, when urgent necessity demands such a course, by the municipality purchasing outright. We can all remember the chaos caused, in the days of the late Emperor, by the driving of new streets through the heart of the city, when during eighteen years (from 1852 to 1870) the net public expenditure on new streets was 2,666,000*l.* per annum. The bulk of the work, however, was not done in that way, and to-day we see little evidence of such wholesale destruction. Still the transformation is going on, and the same comprehensive plan of forty-four years ago is always being carried out. In many districts, indeed, the scheme is fully developed—a standing proof to the whole world of the art, industry, and perseverance of our systematic and thrifty neighbours.

I quote from Mr. Francis Hooper, A.R.I.B.A.,* an account of the laws under which this transformation has taken place:—"Before 1841, the same law as regards frontages which applied to provincial towns applied also to Paris. This *loi d'Alignement* gives powers to municipal authorities to create a servitude or restriction on land bordering on public thoroughfares, which is in advance of the line of frontage laid down on authorised plans of alignment. This servitude, preventing the erection of any new building, or the reconstruction or structural repair of any portion of any old building existing upon it, in process of time secures the rectification of the lines of frontage in old streets, as well as their widening. This law had its origin in the reign of Henri IV., in 1607, when it was enacted that application should be made to the Grand Voyer, or Surveyor to the King, for permission to build along any part of the grande voirie, or highway, thus securing to him power to amend the lines of frontage. About a century and a half later, the need for systematic procedure becoming apparent, instructions were issued that every town of upwards of 4000 inhabitants should cause a preparation of a plan of its streets, together with recommendations as to the future lines of frontage to be adopted.

"The structural repairs which are prohibited by the servitude of alignment are such as would consolidate the building and prolong its duration indefinitely. On the other hand, the Courts have allowed the repair of roofs and cornices, façades to

* "Building Control and Legislation in France," a paper read before the R.I.B.A., 1889.

be raised, and the position of windows altered. *The equity of this 'servitude' is based on the principle that the thoroughfares are public property; buildings erected along them enjoy light, air, and convenience from their proximity, and their owners are therefore held to respect the enjoyment and convenience of the public.*

"When, from whatever cause, the owner of property to be set back desires to rebuild, the new alignment is followed unhesitatingly; and should he not be satisfied with the offer of compensation made to him by the municipal authorities, he can apply to the Prefect of the Département for a consideration of his claims by the Jury of Expropriation at their next sitting, and its award is binding on both parties. unless notice of appeal before the Cour de Cassation is made within fifteen days. In estimating compensation, no consideration is given to buildings on the ground to be vacated, as the owner may enjoy their use until, from decay or other causes, his property becomes subject to condemnation as injurious to the public, and reconstruction is necessary at his expense. In the valuation of the land much depends on the free space in the rear of the house; for, if garden land only, the setting back is not costly; but should sufficient ground not exist for rebuilding a healthy house, the whole site is purchased by the municipality, and offered at a price to the adjoining owner. The adjoining owner may appeal for a valuation by a jury, if willing to purchase; but if unwilling, it is possible for the authorities to acquire his property by the agency of the Law of Expropriation on account of public utility, and to dispose of the two sites as they deem best.

"This Act, not being costly in execution to the community, is applied in many of the provincial towns with manifest advantage, where its exceedingly slow operation is not of great inconvenience. It is also in operation in many of the older streets of Paris, although a general plan of alignment of the city has never been executed, the task having proved too formidable.

"In Paris, however, the necessity for more rapid execution of improvements, to meet the demands of a busy and wealthy city, had led to the application of powers granted by the 'Loi d'Expropriation pour cause de l'Utilité Publique' of May 3, 1841, and it provides for the immediate acquisition of property, by municipal or other bodies, required for varying purposes, such as sites for new public buildings, monuments, streets, railways, &c., as well as of property required for the sanitary improvement of a district. In order to secure the rights of the individual, three operations of great importance are necessary to effect expropriation:—

"1. 'The Declaration of Public Utility,' by the State.

"2. 'The Judgment of Expropriation,' by a Court of Justice.

"3. 'The Award of Compensation,' by a Jury.

"Plans have been prepared, in accordance with certain general instructions, to fully demonstrate the scheme and the relation of the proposed works to existing streets and public buildings, an *enquête préliminaire*, or enquiry, is held at the Mairie of the arrondissement in which the property to be acquired is situate. This *enquête* is announced by placards posted throughout the arrondissement, as well as by advertisements in the local newspapers, and for fifteen days the plan is exhibited, in order that the residents, and others interested, may examine it and record their observations in writing. For three additional days a *Commissaire-enquêteur*, or agent appointed by the Prefect, attends at the Mairie to record all verbal observations made to him with regard to the scheme. These observations may relate either to the questionable necessity for the work, or to the efficiency of the plan proposed. The *Commissaire-enquêteur* also furnishes a full report, giving his own opinion on the scheme, which is forwarded, together with all other documents, to the Town Council ; and, should it be determined to modify the scheme in accordance with suggestions offered, a revised plan is exhibited. The plan and reports are then submitted by the Prefect of the Département, with his observations, to the Ministry of the Interior, where the project is examined in the Office of the Voirie, which controls the whole of the thoroughfares of France ; if approved, the documents are submitted to the Conseil-d'État, and the scheme becomes effective by the signature of the Chief of the State to a declaration of its 'public utility.' The succeeding stage of the procedure is the 'judgment of Expropriation,' which can only be pronounced by the High Court of Justice, after being assured that provision is made for adequate compensation to all whose property and rights are to be acquired on the ground of 'public utility.' A second enquiry is held, which is publicly announced like the first, and extends over eight days, during which time a *plan parcellaire* is exhibited. This plan, with certain additions, is the same as the former, all the properties to be acquired being numbered consecutively ; a list is attached giving the names of the several owners, copied from the *matrice cadastrale*, or official register of property, together with the tenants reported by the *Commissaires-voyers* as having claims to compensation. A general description is given of each property, with its area and the character of building upon it. This enquiry permits the notification of any interests which may have been overlooked, and the correction of any errors in the description of property. The High Court thereupon pronounces 'expropriation'; and, in the case of municipal improvements, a decree of cessibility by the Prefect renders the occupants of the property ' tenants at will ' of the municipality. The judgment of the Court is made public by advertisement, and claimants for compensation must at once communicate with the municipal authorities or other body for whom the expropriation is effected. Should the offers of the promoters not be accepted within eight days, application is made to the Court for the appointment of a jury to settle the claims for compensation. This jury of Expropriation, constituted similarly to that in criminal cases, consists of twelve persons, whose qualifications are that they have reached thirty years of age and are entitled to vote in parliamentary elections. The Court transmits to the promoters through the Prefect of the Département a list of sixteen jurymen and four supernumeraries, whose names are in turn communicated to the claimants. Both the promoters and the claimants respectively have the right of cancelling two names in the list, and the jury will consist of the first twelve persons remaining. A *magistrat-directeur* (being a Judge of the Civil Tribunal) conducts the deliberations ; documents are laid before the jury, and witnesses are examined. The properties are inspected, the decision being by the votes of the majority, and costs are taxed by the *magistrat-directeur*. The awards, which are in the form of a report justifying the valuation, are binding on both parties, unless notice of appeal to the High Court be given within fifteen days ; the jury not being dismissed until all claims are settled in connection with any one scheme."

In order that the Prefect of the Seine may be able to secure independent technical advice on architectural questions, a standing council composed of experts is attached to the prefecture and summoned as occasion requires. Thus it happens that when at length an improvement scheme is submitted to the Prefect for his approval, Parisians can rely that his consent is fortified by the opinions of the leading architects of the country. That Parisian architects become thoroughly competent for the work that is required of them, and that Parisians generally are content with nothing but the best improvements is insured by the excellent higher education provided by the municipality, and by the yearly expenditure of a moderate but regular sum for the promotion of fine arts, by means of the purchase, under a competitive system, of designs for public statues, of pictures, and mural designs for schools and various public buildings,' and of other artistic works. This not only educates the popular taste, but adds to the adornment and beauty of the city.

"*Plan of Paris.*"—The official plan of the Paris streets is a most important feature of the French system. It is in charge of a large staff, responsible to the Directeur-des-Travaux-de-Paris, who, though independent of the three main divisions of the Department of Works, and responsible only to the Director of Works, is closely associated with all the operations of the Division of Public Thoroughfares. Their work is to preserve a correct plan of the city, showing the authorised alignment of every street, for the purpose of determining the lines of frontage to be followed in the case of all new buildings or reconstructions bordering on the public streets ; to prepare plans of all property bought or sold by the municipality ; to elaborate schemes for new streets, and the improvement of those existing.

* The map of Paris, which accompanies this book, is further described in Chapter VI.

"The forethought in matters of street improvement is well exemplified by a work published in 1878 by the Prefecture of the Seine, entitled 'Projets de Voirie,' which is a register of the various schemes drawn up at that time. These are classified by Arrondissement—as street widenings, new thoroughfares, &c. A description of each is given, with details of its length, the ground to be thrown into the roadway, the estimated cost of acquiring the necessary property—cost of construction and selling value of surplus land, resulting in the approximate estimate of the cost of execution. With such a register a municipal councillor or ratepayer can, without difficulty to himself or labour to the authorities, ascertain what improvements are contemplated or have been contemplated in his own locality."

Comparing the aspect of the Parisian streets to our own, Mr. Hamerton writes,* "An Englishman who finds himself in some great Parisian street quite of our own time, such as the Boulevard Haussmann or Boulevard Malesherbes, has nothing to do but simply confess that here indeed is the ideal street, and that his own Shaftesbury Avenue, Bond Street, or Oxford Street, are not yet the ideal. A street should not only be wide for the facility of traffic, but it should be of the same width throughout, that there may be no local obstruction. The causeway for foot passengers ought to be wide also, and there ought to be seats where they may rest when weary. Trees are not an absolute necessity, but, next to space, air, and light, they are the greatest of all luxuries, not only for their shade, but for the delightful refreshment afforded by the green of their foliage in a wilderness of stone and mortar."

All these advantages are to be found in modern Parisian streets, and perhaps the climax of street planning is reached at the Arc de Triomphe; and assuredly there is no more stately arrangement in any capital than the wheel of streets that radiate from that wonderful centre. There are twelve of them, three of which are 300 feet wide, whilst seven of them are more than 1000 yards long, and in five directions there is a clear view of more than an English mile. The grandeur and masterful thoroughness of such improvements seem to prove that—"Paris, as it exists at present, is the model modern city that London is probably destined to copy, as the density of population makes it more and more necessary to pile up many human beings on a square mile without impeding a constantly increasing circulation." †

No doubt "the masterful thoroughness" with which these improvements have been carried out has resulted in an enormous debt. The total net amount of debt contracted for these improvements, and for restoring the damage done by war and commune, is 80,000,000*l*., ‡ upon which the annual payment for interest and redemption is 4,000,000*l*.

* 'Paris in Old and Modern Times.' † Ibid.
‡ 'Westgarth Prize Essays,' p. 269.

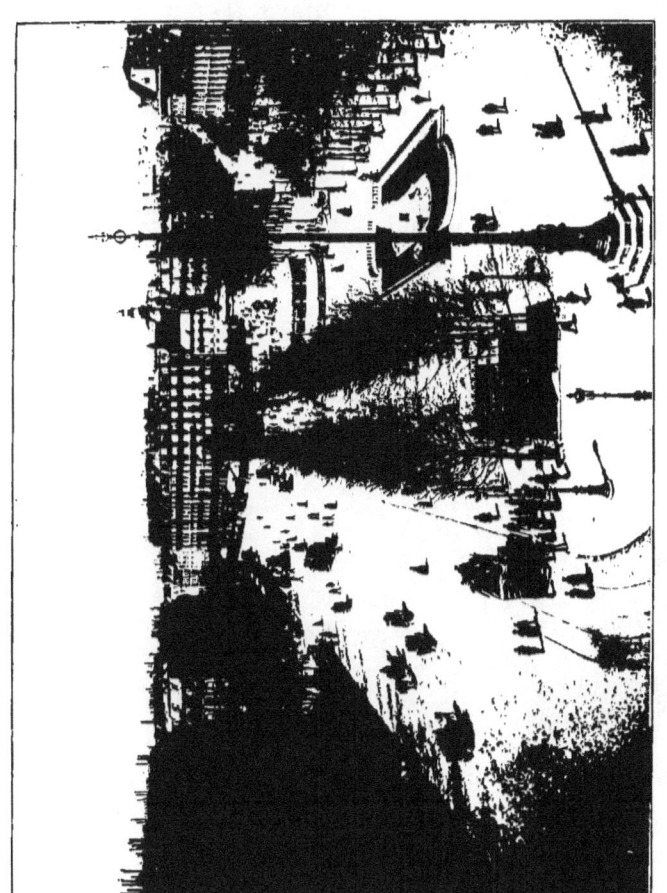

PLACE DE LA RÉPUBLIQUE, PARIS

FRANZEN'S RING STRASSE, VIENNA

It must not be thought that these Parisian improvements form an isolated example of comprehensive town improvement schemes, for Brussels, Berlin, Vienna, Rouen, in fact most of the important towns in Europe, have been or are being similarly transformed. Even some of our own provincial towns have endeavoured to keep pace with the tide of progress, London alone remaining the one great capital with a tangled network of narrow and dark streets unrelieved by sufficient arteries to give it health, beauty, or convenience.

VIENNA.

I will quote part of the history of the first improvements in this city as related by Mr. Frederick R. Farrow, F.R.I.B.A. (holder of the Godwin Bursary), in his paper read before the Royal Institute of British Architects, in December 1887 :—

"Less than thirty years ago the metropolis of Vienna consisted, as does our own, of a small inner city, distinct from and surrounded by an outer town of vastly greater extent, but with this difference, that whereas the division between the City of London and its surrounding town consists for the most part of an imaginary line, the separation between the city and town of Vienna was most clearly defined by the existence of a system of fortifications (see plan) which had successfully withstood the Turks in 1529 and 1683, though they had failed to keep out the French invaders under Napoleon in 1805 and 1809. The inconvenience of this artificial separation of the inner city from its suburbs became more and more felt by the increase of population, and much discussion took place as to the advisability of removing the old fortifications, and the best method of accomplishing the desired improvement.

"At a general conference of German architects, held at Leipzig in September 1842, a plan by Ludwig von Förster was exhibited, showing a proposed enlargement of the city by the removal of the fortifications, a model of which scheme was already in existence in Vienna ; and the question having been thoroughly discussed by the public, matters were at length brought to a head by a Decree of the Emperor, dated 20th December, 1857, and published in the *Wiener Zeitung* on Christmas Day of that year. This decree, which was addressed to the Minister of the Interior, translated into English, reads as follows :—

'DEAR FREIHERR VON BACH,—

'It is my will that the enlargement of the inner city of Vienna, for the purpose of a suitable connection of the same with the suburbs, should be undertaken as speedily as possible ; and also that the improvement and adornment of my residential and capital city should be considered concurrently therewith. For this purpose I decree the abolition of the enclosure and fortifications of the inner city, together with the ditches thereof.

'Every part of the area obtained from the abolition of the fortifications, ditches, and glacis, which is not designated on the accompanying plan for a particular purpose, is to be sold as building land, and the proceeds thereof are to be devoted to the establishment of a building fund, from which is to be defrayed the cost of carrying out this alteration of the public property, the erection of public buildings, and the provision of the necessary military establishments.

'In the preparation of the necessary ground plan, and for my approval thereof, the following points must be attended to in the carrying out of the city enlargement :—

'The removal of the fortifications and the filling-in of the ditches is to be commenced in the space between the Biber Bastion and the enclosure wall of the Volksgarten, so that a broad quay can be formed along the Danube Canal, and the space obtained from the Schotten Gate to the Volksgarten can be partly made use of for the modification of the parade ground.

'The enlargement of the inner city is next to be undertaken, in the direction of the Rossau and the Alser suburb, between these two points, following on the one side the Danube Canal, on the other the boundary line of the parade ground, and taking into consideration the suitable enclosure of the Votive Church now in course of erection.

'In the arrangement of this new quarter of the city, care is to be taken to include the erection of a fortified barrack building, in which also are to be located the great military bakery and the city prison, and these barracks are to be situated in the axial line of the road to the Augarten Bridge, and distant 80 Viennese fathoms* therefrom.

'The square in front of my palace, next the gardens on both sides, is to remain in its present condition pending further arrangements.

'The area outside the palace gate, as far as the imperial stables, is to be left open. Also, that part of the city walls (the Biber Bastion) on which the barracks called by my name abut, is to remain.

'The further enlargement of the inner city is to be proceeded with next the Kärnthner Gate, and thence on both sides of the same in the direction of the Elizabeth and Mondschein Bridges as far as the Caroline Gate.

'Consideration is to be given to the provision of the following public buildings :—A new War Office, a City Marshal's Office, an Opera House, Imperial

* A "fathom," a Viennese measure now seldom used, equals about six English feet.

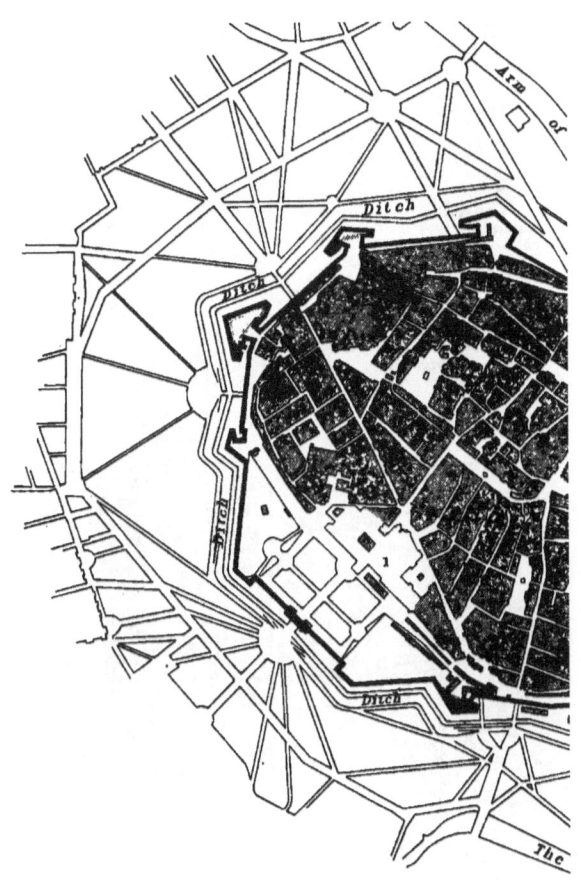

THE INNER CITY OF
VIENNA
PRIOR TO THE REMOVAL OF THE FORTIFICATIONS
1857.

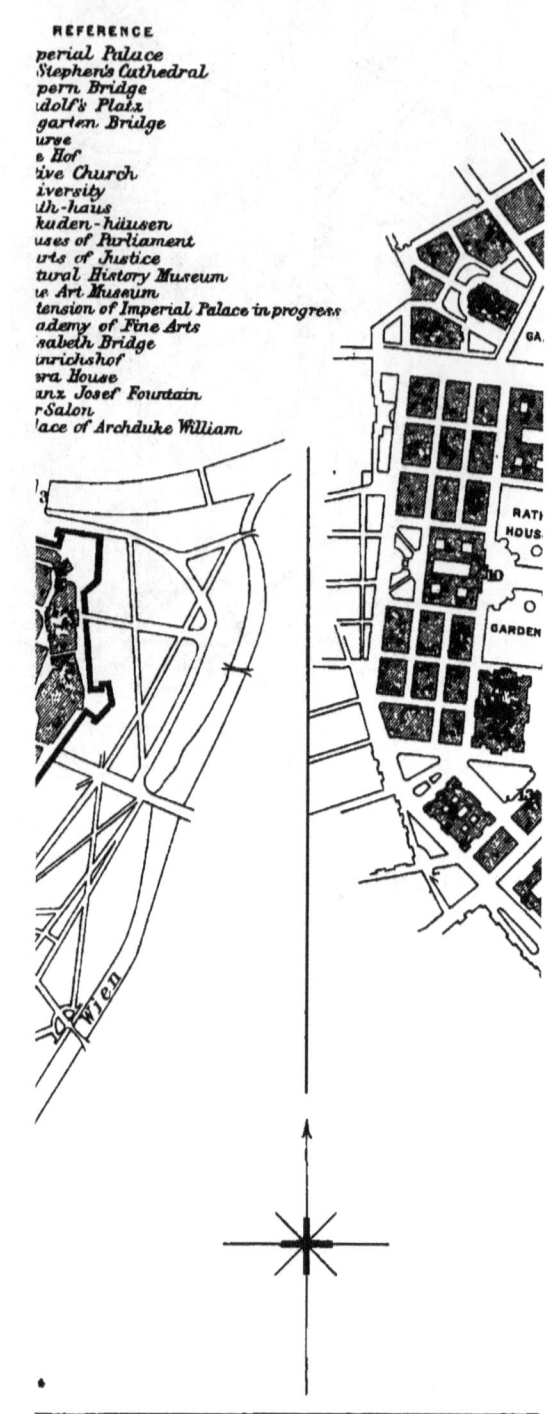

REFERENCE

perial Palace
Stephen's Cathedral
pern Bridge
dolf's Platz
garten Bridge
urse
e Hof
ive Church
iversity
th-haus
kuden-häusen
uses of Parliament
rts of Justice
tural History Museum
e Art Museum
tension of Imperial Palace in progress
ademy of Fine Arts
sabeth Bridge
inrichshof
ra House
anz Josef Fountain
r Salon
lace of Archduke William

THE INNER CITY OF
VIENNA
AFTER THE REMOVAL OF THE FORTIFICATIONS
1887.

Archives, a Town Hall, and the necessary buildings for Museums and Galleries, and sites for the same are to be allotted, as well as for the following open spaces :—

'The area from the Caroline Gate to the Danube Canal shall be left open, to be added to the great garrison parade ground in the neighbourhood of the Burg Gate.

'From the fortified barracks on the Danube Canal to the great parade ground, a space of 100 Viennese fathoms is to be left free from building. Moreover, from the junction with the quay along the Danube Canal a boulevard around the inner city, of at least 40 fathoms in width, is to be arranged on the site of the glacis, including a roadway, with foot and riding ways on both sides, so that this boulevard may include an assemblage of buildings alternately with open spaces laid out as public gardens.

'The remaining chief streets, and also the cross streets, are to have a width of at least 8 fathoms.

'No less care is to be taken in the arrangement to provide for markets, and for their suitable distribution.

'Together with the arrangement of the ground plan of the city enlargement, attention is to be given to the arrangement of the inner city in connection with the main arteries of communication with the suburbs, and the provision of the necessary bridges for these lines of communication.

'For the purpose of obtaining a ground plan a competition is to be promoted, and a programme is to be drawn up on the lines of the principles herein indicated, but, nevertheless, with freedom of conditions, so that the competitors may be allowed free scope for the conception of their designs, consistent with the carrying out of the proposals herein contained.

'For the selection of the plans submitted, a Commission is to be appointed of representatives of the Ministries of the Interior and of Commerce, of my Central War Department and Chief Police Department, a Member of the Representative House of Lower Austria, and the Burgomaster of Vienna, who are to submit the plans to a Committee of Specialists appointed by the above-mentioned representatives and the Minister of the Interior, and by this Commission three designs are to be selected, and premiums of 2000, 1000, and 500 gold ducats awarded.

'The three ground plans thus premiated are to be submitted to me for final selection, so that I may arrive at a resolution as to the further details of the carrying out of the premiated designs.

'You will arrange forthwith the necessary steps for carrying out this my decree.

'FRANZ JOSEPH.

'Vienna, 20 December, 1857.'

"In accordance with the terms of this Imperial command, an open competition was instituted, in which eighty-five designs were sent in. The premiated designs were by Friedrich Stache, Ludwig Förster, and von Siccardsburg and van der Nüll, but none of the three were literally carried out. The final plan, prepared in the Office of Works of the Ministry of the Interior, was approved by the Emperor on the 1st September, 1859, previous to which the work of demolition had already commenced."

"The map of Vienna, as it is at present (see Map), shows that the rearrangement of the area previously occupied by the fortifications consists of a wide boulevard or ring round the inner city connected to the broad quay next the Danube Canal, referred to in the Emperor's decree. At intervals along the line are open spaces—the Stadt Park, the Palace Court and People's Garden, the Rath-haus Garden, and the garden in front of the Votive Church. When these open spaces had been set apart, and sites allotted for the numerous public buildings contemplated, there remained still a considerable area of building land free for the operations of the capitalist or speculator. This was speedily taken up at prices ranging from 150,000*l.* to 300,000*l.* sterling per acre, and thus was provided a building fund which has given to Vienna, during the last quarter of a century, a series of public buildings, such as no other modern European capital has had the opportunity of securing during a similarly short space of time."

At the present moment, the municipality of Vienna are inviting the architects of the world to compete for the remodelling of the old central part of the city, and also to provide for the extension, on a systematic plan, of the outer city into the suburban districts. In Appendix II. will be found full particulars of this competition.

BERLIN.

No doubt many of my readers have learnt through Mr. James Pollard's 'Study in Municipal Government' that there are now no slums in Berlin.—"This is the simple fact. Poverty there is, misery and suffering of the innocent by the ill-doing of others are common enough, as they are wherever frail human beings are gathered together; but filth, which is usually the concomitant of poverty and crime, has no local habitation. For the past twenty years the Corporation have urged constant and successful war against dirt and material pollution among people and dwellings in any form in which those evils menace the general health of the community." This is made the easier because "it is settled public law in Prussia—and it must be owned that the law it distinctly utilitarian in its conception—that owners of property hold it subject to the right of the State or the municipality to take it compulsorily, on due compensation, for any purpose in the public interest. If, then, the corporation resolve to

ELIZABETH BRIDGE AND FRUIT MARKET, VIENNA

carry out some improvement—to cut a new street, erect a new institution, or make an extension of the drainage system, proprietors cannot refuse to sell their property if it be required for such purposes. The town, having obtained the necessary sanction from one or other of the authorities described, has a fixed period within which to exercise this right; or it may, for reasons of its own, renounce its right, or make no use of it. But the owner is always bound, and if the town require his property, he and the town must go before arbitration authorities (not law courts), who have experts to guide them, and who fix the full value to be paid for the property proposed to be taken. Both parties, the town and the owner, have the right to dispute the decisions of the arbitrators by a suit in the proper courts, but it is not often that these decisions are overturned. The full value of the property being duly ascertained and fixed, it must be instantly paid in hard cash. More than the full value is not paid. There is no solatium over and above full value. In this manner the whole of the vast expense with which we are so familiar in this country, incurred by corporations in promoting private Bills in Parliament for carrying out measures of local improvement of the most obvious necessity, is wholly obviated. It is as if we had here in operation a public law, dispensing altogether with the irritating and expensive Parliamentary proceedings at present in vogue, and leaving corporations and individuals precisely where they are after a Corporation Improvement Bill has been passed into law, with the Lands Clauses Act and other public statutes to guide parties to a settlement of whatever difference may be between them." *

GLASGOW.

Between the years 1865 and 1875 the Corporation of this city, with the comparatively small population of 425,000, mostly of the artisan or poorer classes, bought more than 88 acres in the central parts of that town, for which they paid about two millions. This they remodelled, forming twenty-seven entirely new streets and greatly widening and improving twenty-four others; they then sold portions of the new frontages to the value of one million sterling, and still retain property valued at three-quarters of a million. The rate for this improvement was at one time 6d. in the £, but it has been steadily reduced until now it is only 1d.

Other large towns have followed the example of Glasgow, and demolition, street-widening and improved construction under public auspices are no longer a novelty. But Glasgow, it should be remembered, had the courage to lead the way, and the Glasgow City Improvement Act furnished Lord Cross with a model upon which his Improved Dwellings Act was constructed.

* 'A Study in Municipal Government,' by James Pollard.

It is not surprising that in these days, just thirty-eight years after these improvements were inaugurated, we can see where Glasgow made mistakes. The greatest of these was forming the new streets of insufficient width. It is true that a considerable proportion of the space cleared was given up for public parks, but on the ground of health, beauty, and utility, it would have been infinitely better to have provided wide streets, if both parks *and* wide streets were impossible. The streets of Glasgow are so narrow in proportion to the height of its tenement blocks, that enough light and air for health are still lacking to the city. Wide streets are the means by which alone these vital essentials to a healthy life can be brought to the houses of all; while parks, desirable as they are, can after all only benefit those who dwell on their edge or who have the leisure to visit them. The death-rate in Glasgow is still 25 per 1000, whilst it is no uncommon thing to find the rate of other large towns less than 20 per 1000, and it is notorious that the infant mortality of Glasgow is exceptionally high. Moreover, another effect of making the new streets so narrow was that the citizens had little pride in them, and for this reason the improvements never aroused popular enthusiasm. In many directions, however, Glasgow has set an example worthy to be followed by other towns, and especially by London.

At the present moment it may be expedient to call the particular attention of Londoners to one example of Glasgow's enlightened policy. No fewer than four times in the course of three-quarters of a century have the municipal authorities sought new and enlarged accommodation for public offices, and, let it be added, each building they have vacated has at once been eagerly taken over for national offices. In 1810 the Glasgow municipal offices were removed from the ancient Tolbooth to the splendid classical buildings facing the green, now used as a Justiciary Court. Thence in 1842 they were transferred to new buildings in Wilson Street, now occupied as a Sheriff Court and county offices, and again in 1875 the municipal departments were transferred to Ingram Street. Within a very few years this increased accommodation was found to be quite inadequate, and in 1890 the Corporation took over their grand municipal buildings in George Square, which may be expected to suffice for some years. These buildings, which have been constructed by our " canny " friends, regardless of cost, are the delight and pride of all the citizens. Referring to the opening ceremony, Mr. James Nicol writes :*—" Most fortunate have the Corporation been in their highly-accomplished architect and in their contractors. In their hands the work has progressed without let or hindrance, without disputings, and without serious misadventure ; and now the ideal of the Town Council and of their exponent, Mr. Young (the architect), stands embodied in an

* 'Statistics of Glasgow, 1885–1891,' by James Nicol.

MUNICIPAL BUILDINGS, GLASGOW

enthusiasm. As already stated, the Corporation of Glasgow improved the streets of their city cheaply; Mr. Chamberlain, on the contrary, improved Birmingham handsomely. All are proud of the love for Birmingham displayed by its citizens. Mark, in contrast, how the City Chamberlain of Glasgow has to speak of their city improvements, even after nearly forty years, and when the debt is almost wiped out:—"The Improvement Trust in its scope and methods has never been very well comprehended by the general citizens, and it has therefore been the happy hunting ground of the critics of municipal government." *

Assuredly, then, enthusiasm cannot be created by doing things cheaply and poorly. It is only by doing work really well that interest and pride can be thoroughly roused.

* 'Vital, Social, and Economic Statistics of Glasgow,' 1885–1891, by James Nicol, City Chamberlain.

MUNICIPAL BUILDINGS AND ART GALLERIES, BIRMINGHAM

CHAPTER III.

THE POWERS NECESSARY FOR LONDON TO REGENERATE ITSELF.

The progress of municipal socialism—Impossible to regenerate London until full powers are given—Advantages and drawbacks of Parliamentary interference—Lines on which regeneration might proceed—Urgency for reforming our present system of compensation—Powers over land which are necessary to the municipality.

" FROM the extreme of chaos, disorganisation and uncontrolled freedom of individual action, it is not impossible that the great metropolis may, a generation hence, lead all the large cities of the world in the closeness and unity of its organisation, and in the range of its municipal activities. Municipal socialism has a better outlook in London than in Paris or Berlin, although as yet London has given fewer tangible evidences of the trend than has any other centre of civilisation." *

Coming from such an acute and impartial observer of municipal institutions, these prophetic words indicate an insight into the tendency of the more recent developments of local self-government which is almost startling. Many of our most experienced and far-seeing reformers are looking forward to developments in the direction Mr. Shaw indicates. They have long foreseen the growing tendencies of municipal socialism, and the absolute need of increasing dependence upon a developed system of local autonomy. Without this it appears impossible to create that municipal spirit which is the breath of the life of local self-government, or to attract to the work of perfecting our municipal life, men of character, culture, and position. Such men do not care to embark in work where indeed the initiation may be theirs, but where the deciding power is not. They will not give months or years to the work of developing and perfecting schemes of improvement, if the carrying out of such schemes is to be left to the chances of a parliamentary campaign. They will not quietly rest while the work they have been patiently building up is frustrated or undone in a committee room of the House of Commons in the course of a costly and uncertain parliamentary fight.

I freely admit, then, that it will be impossible to improve London in any com-

* " How London is governed," Albert Shaw, 'Century Magazine,' November 1890.

prehensive or satisfactory way until it has been given a full measure of local self-government. While our large towns continue to be compelled to apply for parliamentary sanction to every improvement scheme of more than the smallest dimensions, they cannot be said to have their government in their own hands, or to be able to effect any really comprehensive improvements within their boundaries. London is, of course, in a much worse position than any other city of the Empire, to it alone have been denied the advantages of the Municipal Corporations Act of 1835, and while other cities have their corporate government, with the consequent municipal pride, London has been allowed to grow into a shapeless and disjointed province of houses, with scarcely any cohesion or articulate voice to express its common wants. Makeshift arrangements for its tentative government have indeed been made, and these have perhaps saved it from absolute chaos. For such special purposes as its main drainage, and the embankment of its river, for its education, for its infectious diseases, for dealing with its poor, and for such necessary purposes as lighting, cleansing, and general sanitation, various public bodies have from time to time been created. These bodies are mainly independent of each other, and frequently their functions overlap, and the Londoner has yet to be found who could successfully pass an examination as to what authority is responsible for each of the many details of civic government, the execution of which may make existence a blessing or a burden to him.

All this is ancient history, and government after government has pledged itself to the task of giving to London a satisfactory system of municipal government. But probably the one essential thing necessary to make this local government really successful is that it shall be complete, and that it shall no longer be necessary to face the enormous difficulties that are now entailed by having to get parliamentary sanction to almost every petty scheme of improvement. What London really wants is Home Rule; that is, the power to govern itself for purely local purposes, and it seems almost monstrous that such a want should need to be asserted at the latter part of the nineteenth century.

It is true that other cities, although enjoying to the full municipal privileges given by the Act of 1835, have yet to come to Parliament for sanction to schemes involving expenditure of money beyond a certain limit. It may be worth while considering what are the advantages or drawbacks to the attempt thus made by Parliament to interfere in the details of local government. Doubtless the piloting through Parliament of a local Bill has attractions to the civic mind of a provincial corporation. It gives, for instance, the opportunity of a holiday in town, and it has chances of excitement that are not without sporting interest to the average Englishman. But it has drawbacks. For instance, it has been alleged that the costs of a parliamentary campaign frequently exceed the sum to be expended in making the improvement that is authorized. These costs indeed are so great as to be incredible to a mind untrained in parliamentary practice. From the moment when the first notice is issued, begins a system of payment through the nose, which is probably without example in any other country for this or any other purpose. It is well known that directly the word "Parliamentary" is used, whether it be for inserting a notice in a newspaper, for printing any document, for retaining witnesses, or for employing counsel, ordinary fees and charges are ignored, and sums double, treble, or even more, are freely charged to the unfortunate municipality or other applicant for parliamentary powers. These almost ruinous costs are well known, and are amongst the most flagrant abuses which disgrace our public procedure at the present day. But beyond this is the element of chance, absolute chance, which is so great in parliamentary procedure as to render the whole thing almost a lottery. However meritorious may be the scheme which requires sanction, it must be brought forward as a private Bill; it is therefore open to be blocked by any one of the 670 members either from mere caprice, or for some purpose quite apart from the merits of the provisions it contains, and even if the Bill be lucky enough to reach committee, it is still exposed to any of the numberless chances of our parliamentary warfare.

"The following table, made up with much care and labour to insure accuracy, and from a mass of details, shows the expenses incurred by the Corporation (of Glasgow) and its several departments in promoting, opposing, or otherwise, in connection with Bills before Parliament since 1864:—

(1.) Corporation or common good	£39,385	9 10
(2.) Police	47,883	6 10
(3.) Water	23,790	18 5
(4.) Parks and galleries	3,848	5 2
(5.) Markets	6,951	5 7
(6.) Improvement trust	20,522	8 11
(7.) Gas	42,838	9 10
(8.) Tramways	43,513	16 6
(9.) Municipal buildings	2,237	3 11
(10.) Bridges	27,300	17 8
(11.) Court houses	5,274	9 7
(12.) Juvenile delinquency	3,267	19 7
(13.) Clyde embankments	1,378	4 3
(14.) Sundries	658	11 0
	£268,851	7 1

"This appears a large expenditure for one Corporation to make, and members of Council may have their minds exercised on the subject of private bill legislation, and as to whether local consideration of bills might be less expensive and equally satisfactory. Lord Salisbury dropped some weighty words in that direction when here in May."*

There must, of course, have been advantages of some kind, or supposed advantages, in making it necessary to obtain consent to improvements which appear to be matters of purely local concern. In the past there may have been the fear of jobbery on the part of corporations, or of expenditure too rashly incurred, or of improvements carried out, not so much from necessity, as from motives of interest. But in these days of publicity, where all local government is carried on in the fierce light cast by a vigilant and untiring press, such fears are no longer tenable. Indeed, the guarantee given by publicity is of infinitely greater value than any protection Parliament has been able to afford; for it is practically impossible for the opponents of local schemes to incur the vast expense and loss entailed by adequately representing their objections before a parliamentary committee. A local inquiry, publicly held in the town by an important government official, after all affords far better opportunity for ascertaining the real views of the ratepayers than any inquiry held in London by a committee composed of members of the Lower House.

There can be little question that the expense, delay, and uncertainty attached to obtaining the sanction of Parliament to local schemes of improvement has had a deterring and pernicious effect upon the development of provincial towns. Many deplore centralising tendencies, and would gladly welcome any means by which provincialism could be developed and strengthened. Not only so, but if the material improvement of our provincial towns had been free to progress in advance of their growth, and of modern requirements, it seems probable that larger scope would have been provided for provincial industries and energies. Wherever a city has shown great public spirit and has made itself an attractive and successful centre of trade (as, for instance, in the case of Birmingham), unquestionable advantage has resulted. Not only the prosperity of the town itself, but that of the whole district, has followed, and it therefore becomes a matter of great importance that no needless obstacles should be placed in the way of such developments. That the necessity for obtaining a Local Act for improvements is a serious obstacle cannot be doubted, and its removal would be a boon to many a provincial town.

Now that London has at last a fair prospect of obtaining a real municipal government, it becomes a matter of deep concern that that government should be

* 'Statistics of Glasgow,' 1885–1891, by James Nicol.

made completely efficient. This will certainly not be the case, if it is compelled to go to Parliament for sanction to every scheme of improvement. Certainly preserve imperial interests to the full, but subject to that, let London rule itself. By this means, and only by this means, will the best of its citizens be attracted to its governing body. When London has obtained a municipality with really adequate powers, the question of how those powers can best be utilized for regenerating the capital will have to be considered. It has been seen that in successful examples of the comprehensive improvements of other towns this has been done by adopting a complete scheme, and by gradually carrying that scheme into execution. Without adequate powers for compulsorily acquiring the necessary properties, such a scheme is of course unworkable, but with such power it becomes easily practicable, and its rate of execution would be regulated solely by the annual sum the municipality can set aside for the work.

The gradual formation and working out of the details of a plan for improving so large an area as London, is in itself of necessity a laborious and lengthy work. It may be of some assistance if I attempt to indicate the lines on which I venture to think this work might proceed.

 1. To speedily complete the re-survey of London as it now exists, and provide for recording future alterations.

The existing official map of London is from surveys made twenty years ago, consequently the streets formed and the improvements carried out since that time are not indicated. It is certainly an anomaly that the official map of London does not show the National Courts of Justice erected nearly twenty years ago.

 2. To lay down on a large-scale map of London the new thoroughfares essential to any general scheme for improving the more central districts, and where necessary, the widenings of existing streets.

In Chapter V. the principles on which new thoroughfares might be made have been set out, and I have embodied my own conceptions in the plan which accompanies this book.

 3. To also lay down any new main lines of thoroughfares for the proper development of the outer districts, leaving less important new roads to be added from time to time as the properties become ripe for development.

Any general plan for the London of the future should, of course, include good means of communication between the outer ring and the centre. Although in respect to such communications, we are probably better off than in most other respects, it will be found essential that some such additional connecting thoroughfares should be provided.

4. To determine the space that it is desirable to leave for recreation purposes in each district.

It is probable that some of the present open spaces, such as the filter beds, the grounds of Bethlehem Lunatic Asylum, and others, may become public property. Instead of leaving the whole of such spaces free from buildings, it might be desirable to sell portions for building purposes; thus providing the means for acquiring open spaces in more crowded districts. The present disproportionate allotment of large open spaces to some districts and none to others would thus gradually be adjusted.

5. To submit the draft map thus prepared, for the consideration of district councils, the Institutes of Architects, Engineers, and Surveyors, and those other bodies likely to take an interest in the scheme.

It seems desirable to obtain the opinion of representative bodies, especially as regards the portions of the plan affecting their own districts, and also to benefit by the technical knowledge and advice of professional experts through recognised channels. By this means not only will valuable suggestions be obtained, but great popular interest will be enlisted in the subject.

6. To consider suggestions with the aid of an expert committee which should advise on the preparation of the final plan.

The consideration of the suggestions on the draft plan, and the preparation of the final plan will unquestionably be matters of great importance and difficulty. For this work the Council may need professional advice. It may be worthy of consideration therefore, whether an expert committee formed of the representative engineers, architects, and surveyors of the day, should not give assistance to the Council at this stage. There will perhaps be a difficulty in obtaining sufficient competent professional advice, at any rate in connection with architecture. This arises from the want in that profession of any adequate training and recognised qualifications. In the medical, legal, and other professions, the excellence of the training and the sufficiency of the examinations are unquestioned, but unfortunately at present no qualifications are necessary for the practice of the profession of architecture. Any office boy, or clerk, who has picked up a little knowledge of draughtsmanship, can establish himself as an architect. The result of this is in evidence in every direction. As we all have an interest not only in the beauty and convenience, but in the health of our capital, it may be considered that the technical training of an architect is at any rate of equal importance to us as is the technical training of the artisan in the building trades, whose work must be carried into execution under the architect's supervision. It is to be hoped that our future municipality will not only undertake, through its technical schools and works department, adequate

· EXAMPLES · SHEWING · THE · DECENERACY · (

LAMP-POSTS OF TWENTY YEARS AGO ON THE EMBANI

ENT   LAMP-POSTS OF TO-DAY O

THE EMBANKMENT AND NEAR SHAFTESBURY AVENUE

architectural training, but will take means to prevent any but qualified men from practising that profession.

7. Adoption of the final plan which should have the force of law.

When the map of improved London has been finally settled and adopted by the Council, it should, as in the case of the official map of Paris, have the force of law.

I frankly admit, however, the impossibility of regenerating London while the existing system of compensation continues. At the present time it is not regarded as immoral, but almost praiseworthy, to make public authorities, or in other words the community, pay extravagant prices for all properties required for public purposes. There appears to be a conspiracy between our legislators, arbitrators, juries, and the large and costly army of professional experts to squeeze out of the public purse many times the real value of every property dealt with. What legal expenses and delays connected with improvements often amount to, is shown by the following evidence given before the Commission on the Housing of the Working Classes in 1884.

"By the Right Hon. G. J. Shaw Lefevre, M.P.

"12,635.—If this amount of loss cannot be very largely reduced it is idle, I suppose, to expect that further schemes would be passed in London?—I think, looking at the very great burden that it imposes upon the ratepayers, it is impossible to expect the Metropolitan Board of Works to embark very largely in any further schemes unless the cost can be greatly reduced.

"12,636.—How should you divide the causes of loss?—I consider that of the 1,250,000*l.*; about 400,000*l.* has been due to the obligation to reconstruct, and about 400,000*l.* I consider to be due to excessive compensation. That I have arrived at after a good deal of personal discussion with Mr. Goddard, the officer of the Metropolitan Board of Works, who has been engaged in compensation cases, and also with Sir Henry Hunt, and other persons with whom I have communicated upon the subject; I believe that the excessive cost may be fairly divided in these proportions under these two heads: firstly, the loss upon reconstruction, which has been 400,000*l.*; and secondly, the 400,000*l.* which I consider to be · the excessive compensation.

"12,641. (Sir Richard Cross.)—It would be very difficult to drive them out of the full compensation given under the Lands Clauses Act?—Yes, the general tendency of arbitrators in all these matters is to give very full compensation where property is taken for public purposes. I could give as an illustration a case which has come under my notice in the last few days. I have been very desirous to take a property with a view to a public improvement, and I was told that if I took this additional house it would involve a cost of about 40,000*l*. The rental of the house itself certainly cannot be more than 500*l*. a year; but on making inquiries I was told that there could be no doubt that the trade compensation to the owner of this house would in one way or another mount up to 40,000*l*. I pointed out that there were places on the other side of the street to which the owner of this property might go, but I was told that the same person had been in the fortunate condition of having occupied a house on the other side of the street from which he had been dispossessed for a public improvement, and had got enormous compensation, and had landed himself in his present place; and that if his shop was now taken again for a public improvement he would probably be equally fortunate in getting another enormous compensation for having to go once more to the other side. The kind of basis upon which it was represented to me that the claim would be made was this: it was believed that his profits amounted to 3000*l*. or 4000*l*. a year; he would probably get five or six years' purchase of those profits. He would then make a claim on the ground that the compulsory removal of his premises elsewhere would necessitate a forced sale of half his stock-in-trade, and an enormous compensation would have to be paid on that account, so that in one way or another it would, including the value of the premises, mount up to 40,000*l*., and I was consequently obliged to abandon the idea of taking the house. I merely mention that as an illustration of the excessive compensation which is given in the case of these improvements.

"12,645. The causes, generally speaking, of giving high compensation would, I presume, in your opinion, be in the first place the tendency that exists on the part of arbitrators and juries, to award very high compensation where they have the public purse or the rates to draw upon?—Yes, I consider that there are three main causes. The first, is the tendency of arbitrators and juries to award excessive compensation where the purse of the ratepayers is drawn upon. The second, is the very crowded state of the districts dealt with, the fact that there are many more houses upon the area than the area ought to bear, and that consequently the rent is driven up, and the compensation is necessarily high on that account. The third reason is, the multiplicity of the interests involved. It is very often found that besides the ground landlord there are two or three intervening persons between the ground landlord and the ultimate tenant, who have leases and sub-leases, each of whom has to be compensated; and although theoretically the compensation to all of them ought not to be more than the compensation to one person, assuming that the whole property were in the hands of one, yet practically it is very different, and each one of those separate interests has to be compensated, and each one involves a large amount of law costs, and so forth. I believe that to be a fruitful cause of the very high compensation that has to be paid."

By Sir C. M. Lampson, Bart.

Part of 11,648.—The Peabody Trustees had persuaded the Metropolitan Board of Works to clear two sites at Great Peter Street, Westminster, and Little Coram Street, Bloomsbury, under the Artisans' Dwellings Act. "The latter site has just been cleared, after having been in the hands of the arbitrator and solicitors for about four years. The superficial area of the freehold was 54,070 feet, or about an acre and a quarter. It cost 5400*l*. About half of the land was covered by these miserable old dwellings, the rental of which was about 778*l*. gross. Deducting from this amount the rates and taxes, and the ground rents, which were very heavy, it would show a net income of 300*l*. per annum. The value of this, being on a lease with 17½ years to run, would be about 4125*l*. For this interest there was paid to the lessees, partly by private settlement, 12,384*l*.; the weekly tenants received 470*l*. compensation; the solicitor's charges were 2206*l*.; the surveyor's charges were 288*l*.; the cost of the scheme was 360*l*., making a total of 15,705*l*. paid for the purchase of the leasehold, which was valued at 4125*l*., but which would have been dear at 3000*l*. In one case, for an old tenement, a broken-down house, 20*l*. was awarded, the solicitor's charges on which were 57*l*. 2*s*. 9*d*. That shows the working of that Act, and that is the experience which we have just had."

Similar evidence was given by Mr. Chamberlain (see Appendix I., questions 12,376 to 12,394, 12,405 to 12,415, 12,461 to 12,463, 12,470 to 12,500, 12,510 to 12,511).

The shortsighted policy with regard to compensation at present in force, makes any thorough scheme of improvements impossible in the immediate future on account of the great cost. Nor is this the only hindrance. It is well known that directly a property is likely to be wanted for any public purpose it is bought up by astute and unscrupulous persons who devise means for increasing the compensation to be paid. I say unscrupulous, not because the practice is immoral in the eyes of the law, but because a scrupulous man would never attempt to gain money by such unpatriotic means.

When we have reformed our system of assessing compensation, or municipalized the land, which is the alternative, the inducements to these unscrupulous speculators will cease, and we can then afford to be perfectly open in our procedure. The secrecy that is now adopted, amongst other evil effects, prevents that public interest in improvements, which, if present, would tend to create a municipal spirit amongst us.

It was seen in the last chapter that quite a contrary system is common in Paris. The French laws are such, that although the public are consulted in every possible way as regards improvements, and are even invited to criticise and interest themselves in the questions raised, the publicity given to the plans tends rather to decrease the possibility of unfair speculation and jobbery.

I have sketched the outlines of the main provisions which it appears desirable to enforce in connection with the formation of new streets, and the improvement of existing ones, and I venture to print them here for the consideration of future municipal councillors.

1. No building estate in any part of the county should be developed or remodelled without reference to the thoroughfares as laid down on the official plan of improvement.

2. Every new building, reconstruction, or addition which abuts on any public thoroughfare in the county, should be to the revised lines of frontage, as laid down on the official plan, and any land in advance of the line should become public property, reasonable compensation being paid. Where, after setting back to the line of frontage, the remaining site is insufficient in extent, the owner shall have the option of requiring the municipal authority to take the whole site.

3. Buildings which project over the new lines of frontage should never be allowed to be structurally renovated, and when at length it becomes necessary to pull them down, so much of their site as is beyond the new building line should be given up to the public, compensation being paid for the value of land only.

4. If, in the opinion of the Council, it is desirable to temporarily maintain the existing line of frontage in any street, either until the houses in the same street have been set back, or for any other reason, then the Council should have power to let to the occupier of the newly erected building, so much of the land fronting his premises as has been bought for the widening of the street. The rent not to exceed 4 per cent. on the cost of the land, and the term of years to be such as will eventually free all the spaces thus leased in the same street at the same date.

5. Whenever " municipal improvements " are carried out (as described in Chapter VI.), the following provisions should take effect :—

    (*a*) After public notice has been given, no further building or structural alterations should be allowed within the limit of the improvement.

    (*b*) When by reason of the formation of new, or the alteration of old roadways, existing buildings become at a distance behind the new line of frontage, the owner must either buy the land lying between his building and the new frontage, or sell his property to the authorities.

6. A new tribunal for arbitration should be created, consisting of an independent arbitrator, sitting with one or more assessors having knowledge of the locality. No appeal from this tribunal should be allowed.

7. The expenses of arbitration might be reduced by strictly limiting the costs allowed. This would tend to reduce the number of professional gentlemen retained on both sides, and the quantity of expert evidence.

8. Arbitrators should be required to base their awards upon either :—
   (a) The fair value which would be given as between a willing buyer and a willing seller in the open market if the improvement had not been contemplated, without any allowance for compulsory sale ; or
   (b) The estimated fair rents which could morally and properly have been received for the property during the precedent seven years, less the cost of necessary sanitary works and other repairs ; and without having regard to future circumstances which might affect the property, or allowance for compulsory sale.

9. Having arrived at the real value of the property to be acquired, it should be the duty of the arbitrator to assess the proportions of such value equitably due to freeholder, leaseholders, and occupiers, and the amount of compensation to be divided accordingly.

10. In assessing compensation for trade disturbance, the arbitrator should be required to take into account the opportunities for removing the displaced business to suitable sites in the neighbourhood afforded by other improvements.

11. In assessing compensation for any frontage land required for street widening, the arbitrator should be required to take into account the free space in the rear of the buildings ; for if garden land exists, the setting back is not a costly operation.

CHAPTER IV.

THE ADVANTAGES OF ADOPTING A GENERAL SCHEME IN MAKING IMPROVEMENTS.

Present difficulties have arisen from want of general scheme of improvement—Advantages of general scheme: 1. *For discovering causes of present inconveniences;* 2. *For producing best improvements:* (a) *complete utilization of every district for most valuable purpose;* (b) *creation of judiciously placed continuous arteries;* 3. *For producing improvements speedily;* 4. *For producing improvements cheaply;* 5. *For æsthetic reasons:* (a) *avoiding interference with ancient monuments;* (b) *raising municipal enthusiasm.*

In attempting to carry out extensive alterations in so conservative a capital as London, many great difficulties will have to be faced, most of which would not have existed if in the past there had been efficient municipal control and a general scheme of improvement, such as it is the purpose of this book to advocate. The want of a general plan showing future street alterations authoritatively settled, has also undoubtedly been the reason why many streets lately formed are not placed for general convenience, have not been financially successful, and have neither created enthusiasm amongst the public nor brought credit to the authorities.

Let us examine in detail, and under the following heads, the reasons for having a general scheme and plan, and as complete a plan as possible.

1. For discovering the causes of our present inconveniences.
2. For producing the best improvements that can be produced.
3. For forwarding them rapidly.
4. For making them economically.
5. For æsthetic reasons.

1. THE IMPORTANCE OF A GENERAL PLAN FOR DISCOVERING THE CAUSES OF OUR PRESENT INCONVENIENCES.

Immediately a general plan of London is examined by any one anxious to solve the many problems of our present inconvenient streets, to discover where slums are mostly to be found, and the reasons that have prevented improvement, he must be

INIQUITOUS OBSTRUCTIONS.

first struck by the fact that many slums exist in the very centre of our capital on sites which, in a well-arranged city, would be the most valuable.

The cause of this is soon apparent, and, as usual, the impediment to progress is the English law. Look at the shape and extent of the "Devil's own" estates,* which stretch for a distance of about three-quarters of a mile, from Theobald's Road on the north to the Thames embankment on the south, and which present a barrier against any attempt at opening up the most crowded districts of central London, of admitting to them more light and air, or of allowing any better means of communication between the City and the West End.

It seems incredible that an estate, three-quarters of a mile long, can still exist in such a position, pierced only by two public lines for vehicular traffic, namely, Holborn and the Strand. What words would be strong enough to describe the iniquity of an individual owner who interposed such barriers to all improvement; for undoubtedly the slums of Red Lion Street and Drury Lane on the west, and of Leather Lane and Fetter Lane on the east, would long since have been transformed if more main thoroughfares could have been constructed from east to west through those districts. No private owner could have mismanaged his estates as these have been mismanaged, and it has been left to the representatives of the English law to waste the most valuable area of London outside the City, by relegating its sole use to chambers, only to a small extent occupied by members of the legal profession. No one can pretend that these Inns are being used so as to afford the greatest benefit to the greatest number, to which use all land in the centre of a populous city should unquestionably be devoted, and I doubt if a better instance of the justification of a tax on ground values exists in any part of London. Here is a case where the public have been deprived of the use of land which is of vital importance to their health, their convenience, and to the beauty of their capital. So long as this continues, most undoubtedly such land should be taxed, not on what it now produces, but on the most it could be made to produce if it were used to its best advantage. In order that the people of London may fully enjoy the use of these Inns, I submit that the Benchers should offer the remainder of their heritage to the London County Council. If a sale takes place before ground values are taxed, so much the better for the Benchers, and so much the sooner would the public be enabled to enjoy these valuable breathing spaces.

Other impediments to free circulation will, unfortunately, be found.

South of the Thames, railway viaducts and embankments divide the metropolis into sections, and sever contiguous districts, when the trouble, danger, and nuisance thus caused would have been entirely avoided by making the lines in cuttings or

* These estates are coloured violet on the map of London which accompanies this book.

tunnels as on the north side of the river. Superb public parks and gardens are so enclosed and so difficult of access as to form most serious impediments to street improvement, and the full benefit of their presence is denied us, whilst their surrounding streets are filled to overflowing. A wide tidal river hems in, and is hemmed in by stifling purlieus that have become crowded and neglected for want of broad streets and bridges to lighten and brighten them.

These are a few of the difficulties that must be removed if London is to be made convenient and healthy. If it is also to be made beautiful, other difficulties have to be overcome, for we find many public and other important buildings so hidden away in tangled and crowded streets, as to be almost unapproachable, and entirely forgotten—so forgotten, indeed, that I must mention specimens, such as the Mint, the Record Office, Guildhall, Westminster Town Hall, and many of our county and other courts. While many hills in our home counties offer sites which are in every way suitable, we find here in central London asylums for lunatics, schools for the blind, homes for foundlings, occupying acres of unsuitable sites in crowded districts, impeding surrounding progress, and depriving hardworking people of healthy homes. Such unintelligible and wide-spread impediments as these, and many similar ones, will not easily be discovered if improvements are still to be considered in driblets, such as a street half a mile here and three-quarters of a mile there; whereas they become apparent immediately a general plan of improvement is taken in hand.

2. THE IMPORTANCE OF A GENERAL PLAN FOR PRODUCING THE BEST IMPROVEMENTS THAT CAN BE PRODUCED.

Probably the best plan of London improvements should embody—

(a) The complete utilisation of every district of London's enormous area for its most valuable purpose.

(b) The creation of continuous arteries, sufficiently wide for the future as well as for to-day, and judiciously placed so as to connect the most important centres of business and habitation, and the railway termini.

(a) *The complete utilization of every district for its most valuable purpose.*

For the health and convenience of the inhabitants of any crowded city, it is advisable that all land within its boundaries should be utilized for that purpose for which it is most valuable to the community. This consideration has up to the present time been entirely lost sight of whenever improvements have been considered, consequently, the rehousing of the displaced working population, a question inseparable from improvement schemes in London, has always been a most serious difficulty. As, for many reasons, it seems most probable that improvements will be carried out in the slums before elsewhere, this question still remains of the first importance. It may be necessary for the working classes to live within a moderate distance of their work, but surely it is not consistent with the general welfare, nor even reasonable, to give up the very central square mile of London to enable them to do so. Not consistent, because more comfortable and healthy dwellings can certainly be provided where land is much cheaper, and yet within half a mile of this central area. Not reasonable, because when once decent accommodation is provided in so eligible a position, close to the theatres, to the meeting halls of the learned societies, and to all that makes London attractive to the cultivated middle classes, such accommodation is bound to be eagerly competed for by tenants who can pay far higher rents than the working classes.

If a map of London be studied, acres upon acres of land, which could be made available for workmen's dwellings, and which are most likely always to remain the most valuable and suitable for this particular purpose, are at once discovered in Southwark, Lambeth, Clerkenwell, and Marylebone, all within a mile of the centre of the metropolis. Such sites are occupied by the Foundling Hospital, the military school and hospital at Chelsea, and many similar institutions; Bethlehem and St. Luke's Lunatic Asylums, many gas-works and water filtering beds, and other obstructions. Would it not be well to clear these sites for labourers' dwellings, removing their present occupants into the suburbs or the country? Some of us might regret the disturbance of old hospitals, but the majority would regret more sincerely what is apparently the only alternative—the removal of workmen to the suburbs, with the consequent loss of time and money in conveying them to and from their work.

The following extract from the *Times* of November 29, 1892, indicates that at any rate the inmates of Chelsea Hospital would gladly welcome the suggested change:—" In answer to an appeal from Chelsea pensioners in favour of abolishing the Royal Hospitals of Chelsea and Kilmainham, and appropriating the proceeds of the sales of the sites for the purpose of augmenting the out-pensions, a reply has been received in Portsmouth from the Secretary of State for War in which he states that the question has been examined more than once by specially appointed committees, and that it has been found that the general sentiment of the army and of the public was in favour of retaining these asylums for infirm and helpless old pensioners. In answer to a similar appeal the Duke of Cambridge points out that the only power vested in his Royal Highness with reference to Chelsea is that possessed by him as a commissioner."

I have calculated that fifteen sites coloured blue on the accompanying map of London, which I propose should be gradually devoted to this purpose, contain an area of 144 acres. After deducting one-fifth of this area for additional broad roadways, and assuming that the same density per acre will be as healthy on these sites as on the site of Peabody dwellings and playgrounds in Drury Lane, the extra number that can be accommodated within one mile of the centre of the metropolis is found to be 127,000 men, women, and children. If, in carrying out improvements, two areas be always dealt with together—a working-class area and a central area—the various districts would gradually become dedicated to their most valuable purposes, and the necessity for employers providing living rooms for their workmen either at or near their works (often a most costly process) or for the Council providing free train or tramway tickets to suburban dwellings, will be postponed. As each transformation is effected, the authorities would have the opportunity, under such a scheme as I suggest, of reserving as much ground for open spaces as they thought desirable, and the ground so reserved would be indicated on the comprehensive plan of improvement.

(*b*) *The creation of continuous arteries sufficiently wide for the future as well as for to-day, and judiciously placed, so as to connect the most important centres of business and habitation, and the railway termini.*

Immediately a comprehensive plan is studied, the small number of our main streets, and the shortness of our other streets, is at once manifest. As Mr. Albert Shaw remarks, " London, like all other old cities, is a vast, tangled network of streets that for the most part begin nowhere and end nowhere."

When we consider the principles on which London improvements should be determined, it will be found that the longer and the more uniform streets are made, the more valuable they become for many reasons. But length and uniformity can only be obtained by first planning streets to a small scale on a complete plan of the whole county. In many cases, too, only insignificant clearances at various points are required in order to render many of our side streets suitable for relieving to a very considerable extent the present overcrowded main streets. As, however, the various points at which these trifling obstructions occur are frequently at considerable distances apart, it is impossible to study them without first considering them on a general map. For instance, if Craven Hill, Lancaster Gate, were continued westward a distance of 300 yards to the Bayswater Road, and Praed Street at

Edgware Road joined to the Marylebone Road by a junction also about 300 yards long, we could obtain at a comparatively small cost a main artery as direct as Oxford Street from the Bayswater Road at Queen's Road, to the Angel at Islington. Again, if Grand Junction Road Edgware Road, were joined to Crawford Street a distance of 200 yards, and Marylebone Street joined to Devonshire Street, which could be accomplished by forming a quadrant, we should obtain direct communication from Lancaster Gate to Portland Place, Regent Street. If the Marlborough Road, Brompton, were continued southwards to the King's Road a distance of 60 yards, and northwards by a quadrant to Pelham Street, a direct route would be formed from Sloane Square to the Kensington Museums. Many similar examples will be found on my draft improvement plan.

Every surveyor knows what has been the cause of these small obstructions, and how they are still being created by the absurdities and difficulties that exist in connection with laying out building estates in London, especially in the suburbs. For instance, no matter how irregular may be the shape of an estate which is to be developed, the owner is allowed, in order to follow the contour of his boundaries and to cover with houses every corner of his property, to make his roads tortuous as snakes, so long as they at length lead from one existing road to another. He is not, however, allowed to form any road which stops at his own fence, no matter how essential such road may be for the development of the adjoining properties. Thus more and more unhealthy and badly ventilated districts are being daily created, whereas if a settled scheme were adopted, the development of each property would form an unsevered part of a complete whole, and the best improvements would thus be obtained. Of course there is an argument against allowing " culs-de-sac," but I submit that there are various kinds of " sacs." For instance, a permanent " cul-de-sac," where lofty houses are allowed to be erected facing the end of the street, is indefensible, whereas the formation at different periods of various sections of a lengthy thoroughfare, which has been laid down on a comprehensive plan, even although the various sections may be temporarily stopped at six-foot fences, is one of those minor evils which might well be tolerated for the benefit of the future.

3. THE IMPORTANCE OF A GENERAL SCHEME FOR FORWARDING IMPROVEMENTS SPEEDILY.

If a comprehensive scheme for improvement as proposed were authoritatively adopted in London, no single building in the whole county could be rebuilt without reference to the revised lines of frontage as laid down on the plan, or without

44   THE ADVANTAGES OF A GENERAL SCHEME.

becoming an integrant part of the grand city that it would be the ultimate object of the scheme to produce.

That such a system would be of importance for speedily effecting improvements, will probably be generally admitted. The annual average number of notices for new buildings and rebuildings issued to district surveyors during the last three years has been 21,932. As nearly all our streets admittedly want improving, as many central districts admittedly want entirely remodelling, and as all districts newly created in the suburbs are, at present, created without any reference whatever to the general convenience, we may fairly assume that a large proportion of these 21,932 annual notices refer to rebuildings which would each give an opportunity of advancing, under a comprehensive plan, the complete scheme for the improvement of London. The approximate number of houses that will be removed by the Council Broadway improvement is 1250, and what with legal and parliamentary delays, this improvement may take five years to complete, from the time it was first made public. From this it appears clear that the number of properties dealt with under the Council scheme would be infinitely less than the number which would be dealt with automatically during the same period under a general scheme. It follows therefore that progress in improvement would be much slower under the present system than under that which I advocate. Again, it must be remembered that in the one case, every opportunity would come without legal expenses or delay connected with compensation for disturbances; whereas, in the other, legal expenses and delays, and expensive compensations for disturbance, occur with each property taken, although in each case there should be the same compensation paid for any land given over to the public. If a comprehensive scheme be delayed, not only will hundreds of opportunities for improving London be lost every year, but the newly erected buildings will form impediments to be removed, each ten times as costly as the opportunities that are lost. It is true that Ludgate Hill has taken about thirty years to widen, and I know that this improvement is used as an argument against the so-called "automatic" principle. The case of Ludgate Hill, however, is an abnormal one. The greater cost of the properties more recently acquired there has been due to the fact that Ludgate Hill has been allowed to remain, practically, the only main line of communication through that part of London. All the enormously increased traffic is forced through that artery, with the result that its frontage sites have increased in value to an unnatural extent.

It is not suggested that we should rely entirely on the automatic plan. As will be fully explained in Chapter VI., the transformations should be simultaneously advanced by the Council carrying out "municipal improvements" wherever the urgency of the traffic or the health of the neighbourhood demand such a course.

4. THE IMPORTANCE OF A GENERAL SCHEME FOR MAKING IMPROVEMENTS CHEAPLY.

Not only do the foregoing arguments show the greater speed at which improvements might be made under a comprehensive scheme, but they also indicate how a great saving in " costs " might be effected.

Perhaps few of us realize what an important factor " costs " of various kinds are in all improvement schemes. In the preceding chapter I have endeavoured to bring this home in the minds of my readers by including some valuable and interesting evidence on the subject. It is necessary to mention another matter largely affecting the costs of improvements. Again and again when an improvement has been decided upon, speculators have bought up the property, have had drawings prepared for new buildings, have improved existing buildings, and put all possible legal impediments in the way for the sake of making the authorities pay largely augmented compensation. The economic importance of adopting a general scheme is here again apparent, for it would be impossible for any individual or even any syndicate to purchase all the land which will be affected by the whole scheme, consequently the Council would have so much choice that they could purchase small portions here and there whenever the owners wanted to sell or were willing to sell at a reasonable price. Mr. Chamberlain's experience on this point during the municipal improvements in Birmingham, as stated by him in his evidence before the Royal Commission on the Housing of the Working Classes, conclusively corroborates the correctness of this view.[*]

There are other economic reasons for a comprehensive scheme to be considered. For instance, when any isolated improvement is put in hand, it is necessary to calculate the approximate cost of the whole work, to borrow money to pay for it, to agree to complete it in a given time, and to refund, within a certain number of years, all that has been borrowed. In this way the cost of improvements is greatly augmented, for it not only includes the cost of the actual work, but a large annual amount for sinking fund, interest, and the accompanying expenses. If a comprehensive scheme ever be adopted, this running into debt will be totally unnecessary, for the Council would then be enabled to put just so much of the scheme in hand as the funds available for that purpose from the year's income would permit.

It is also absolutely essential that a settled plan should be adopted for another reason. As each new street is laid out, quadrants and *places* should be constructed with junctions left exactly where future new streets will eventually join them. A

---
[*] See Appendix I., Questions 12,371, 12,372.

46 THE ADVANTAGES OF A GENERAL SCHEME.

striking illustration of the want of this may be found in the case of the English Opera House recently erected in Cambridge Circus and Shaftesbury Avenue. This building has been placed exactly where a new street, which might become as important as Oxford Street or the Strand, should cross that Circus.

As already stated, large and most valuable sites are still occupied with slums of the poorest description. Under a settled scheme the whole of these sites would gradually be put to their proper uses, the recoupment that would arise from the sale of surplus lands would then go far towards the economic success of the improvement. A striking example of increased value has occurred at Chelsea, on the estate belonging to Earl Cadogan, who was advised on high authority to let a piece of ground at a ground rent of 85*l*. per annum. Because the whole neighbourhood has been developed in a statesmanlike manner, land has increased so much in value that the ground rent of this same piece of ground has been, within five years, improved by the leaseholder to 900*l*. a year. Not only so, but certain adjoining land which is held in trust for the public, has increased in value by the action of its noble neighbour to at least 300 per cent. That this is no solitary instance is proved by the following tables showing the increase of the rateable value of those parishes where statesmanlike developments have taken place, compared to others.

The first comparison is between St. George's and the adjoining parish of St. Marylebone where in both cases the total number of houses has remained nearly stationary.

St. George's, Hanover Square (containing portions of the Westminster estates) :—

Inhabited houses, increase during 20 years   7 per cent.
Rateable value   ,,   ,,   ,,   50 ,,

St. Marylebone :—

Inhabited houses, decrease during 20 years   ..   6 per cent.
Rateable value, increase   ,,   ,,   ..   28 ,,

The next comparison is between Chelsea and the whole of London, where, in both cases the total number of houses has greatly increased. Although the majority of new houses in the case of Chelsea involved the destruction of those already existing, and in the case of London generally the proportionate amount of clearances was infinitesimal, the better system adopted at Chelsea has raised the rateable value of that parish out of all proportion to that of London, thus—

Chelsea (containing portions of the Cadogan estates) :—

Inhabited houses, increase during 20 years   ..   46 per cent.
Rateable value   ,,   ,,   ,,   ..   110 ,,

London :—
Inhabited houses, increase during 20 years .. 54 per cent.
Rateable value ,, ,, ,, .. 79 ,,

If a comprehensive scheme of improvements were adopted, all the undeveloped land in the county would, as it became ripe for development, also be automatically, and thus economically, opened up in accordance with the scheme. Both the community and the landowner would benefit by this, the former by having its streets made in the most convenient position from a public point of view, and the latter by being guaranteed a greater number of important thoroughfares across his property.

5. THE IMPORTANCE OF A GENERAL PLAN FOR ÆSTHETIC REASONS.

The reasons I have already put forward are of a practical nature. I now give some æsthetic reasons.

(a) For providing sufficient improvements without interfering with our ancient architectural monuments.

"The works of those," said Sir Joshua Reynolds, "who have stood the test of ages, have a claim to that respect and veneration to which no modern can pretend." The knowledge that all improvements will now be carried out at a time when ancient architectural monuments are as jealously guarded as ancient sculptures and paintings, is a consoling thought when we remember the delays that have occurred in our street improvements.

Is it possible that any scheme can produce sufficient improvements in an ever-increasing metropolis, like London, without of necessity doing away with well-known architectural landmarks, which, be they ever so faulty, have naturally become endeared by familiarity? Undoubtedly, and at once, I say, Yes. For I know with what intense relief this will be received by the antiquaries of a conservative nation, whose taste for comprehensive improvements has never been roused. What Londoner is there who would not regret any interference with St. Mary-le-Strand, with those awe-inspiring columns which denote the entrance to Exeter Hall, with the narrowness of Bond-street, or with those solid English walls which encircle the precincts of Marlborough House, Devonshire House, and the modern æsthetic Lowther Lodge? Such sights are to us as precious as a Lord Mayor's show, and do not let it be thought that I consider this anything but a compliment to the "sticks and stones." By studying a comprehensive plan it is soon discovered that sufficient lengthy arteries connecting the most important centres of business and habitation can be provided in such a way as would not only obviate the interference with our present main streets, or with such heirlooms and landmarks as I have mentioned, but would make these monuments more conspicuous by isolating them. For this reason alone, such a scheme should commend itself to many of us.

(*b*) *For raising municipal enthusiasm.*

What has been up to now the despair of all reformers of London municipal life? Has it not been the huge size of the city and the supposed impossibility of uniting for one common object the inhabitants of its distant parts? Can anything be more calculated to raise the pride and enthusiasm of all Londoners, and weld them together for one common object than a really great scheme of improvement, such a scheme too, as we can show was made by our patriotic neighbours a short forty years ago, and has already produced such startling results? As each rebuilding in each district progressed, every Londoner would see a further development of that grand city all would have agreed to produce. Can one imagine the enthusiasm and pride that would be roused—some few years ahead—as the last block of houses in each new thoroughfare gradually came down, and for the first time an uninterrupted view of the new street with its palatial architecture was obtained? Each Londoner might even welcome the opportunity of setting back his own premises if only he was sure that the authorities would give him, without the annoyances and delays of our present system, the fair value for his land, for it would be to the common interest of the inhabitants to obtain the completion of the improvement in their own street. Pressure of public opinion would in most cases be sufficient to overcome the hesitation of less enterprising, or even less scrupulous owners, who might be standing out for better terms, especially when they had become convinced that under no circumstance would the municipality pay more than the fair value of the land given up. This has proved to be the case both in Paris and in Birmingham. Mr. Chamberlain, in his evidence before the Commission on the Housing of the Working Classes, bore striking testimony of this, when speaking of the transformation of Birmingham.*

* See Appendix I., Question 12,370.

CHAPTER V.

SUGGESTIONS TOWARDS THE FORMATION OF A GENERAL PLAN FOR IMPROVING LONDON.

Six general principles—1. *Open out parks*—2. *Open up crowded districts*—3. *Create more main arteries* (*a*) *sufficiently wide* (*b*) *straight and uniform in width* (*c*) *without steep gradients* (*d*) *each an integrant part of whole scheme* (*e*) *with convenient and safe street junctions*—4. *Provide additional bridges*—5. *Facilitate approaches to railway termini*—6. *Open out public buildings.*

THE following are six general principles by which a comprehensive plan for the improvement of the London street system may conveniently be studied :—

1. To open up our town parks and other open spaces.
2. To open up the most crowded districts and admit more light and air.
3. To create many more great arteries, connecting the most important centres of business and habitation.
4. To provide additional bridges over the Thames.
5. To facilitate the approaches to the several railway termini.
6. To open out, as much as possible, our public and ancient buildings, and to provide sites for new.

1. TO OPEN UP OUR TOWN PARKS AND OTHER OPEN SPACES.

Undoubtedly London possesses in its very centre some of the grandest town parks and commons in the world, and no one can be a more intense admirer of them than I am. I cannot believe, however, that the parks are being used to their best advantage, considering that they are town parks, and am convinced that without destroying their beauty in any way, they might be made much more a part of the life of the people, to the great benefit of health, and to the immense relief of the present streets.

Let us examine how our neighbours use their parks and open spaces.

No one can fail to admire the open spaces in the centre of Paris. The Champs-

Élysées, the Embankments, the gardens of the royal palaces of the Louvre, &c., how well we all know them, and why ? because they are intersected by public roads over which the general traffic passes at all hours. Most of us must remember how pleasant it is to walk through the Champs Élysées Park at any time in the day, and to watch the quick traffic of all sorts. Omnibuses, victorias, and horsemen continuously pass along the spacious Avenue, and, with pedestrians, form part of a busy throng going to or coming from their daily work. On either side, lawns with their pink and white chestnuts, their cherry-trees, their lilacs, hawthorns, and rhododendrons, give brilliancy to the scene.

Compare this charming and useful space with our locked and barred St. James' Park. Both parks are about the same size, both are situated in practically the centre of their respective cities, and both are adjoining the Royal Palaces and Parliament Houses. Here, however, the similarity ends. Our park is practically shut off from any part of the everyday life of the people, whilst theirs is one of the gayest, brightest centres of a gay and bright city, a result which has been attained, without sacrificing the essential uses and charms of the place, by simply running through its centre a roadway of ample width. With skilful management every charming spot that now exists in our own park could be made bright and gay to the same extent. The beautiful vistas, the flowers, the water, and all that gives the park its charm could be opened out and vastly improved upon, and whilst every taste could be consulted I submit the result would be that for one person who is now able to obtain from it real pleasure there would be a dozen, as a reference to the accompanying sketch will to some extent indicate. In addition to this, it must not be forgotten that St. James' Park, and indeed all our parks, have stood sadly in the way of street improvements for many years. The opening up of these parks to the people would not only add to the general enjoyment, but would at the same time be of enormous advantage to all, by relieving our congested streets. Not only so, but if this were done we should speedily make clear to all classes of Londoners that, at least in one respect, they are more fortunate than Parisians.

In first considering St. James' Park I have not dealt with the strongest, but the weakest illustration in favour of opening up the London parks, St. James' Park being already infinitely more opened up and used than any other park; the adjoining Green Park, for instance, not even having a road all round its edges, let alone one through its centre, whilst Hyde Park, although intersected by some roads, contains scores of acres unused by, and almost unknown to the great majority of Londoners.

Probably the main reason why our town parks have not yet been opened up, so as to form an essential part of our daily lives, is a sentiment entirely false and

|·THE·NATION·ENCOVRAGES·FREEDOM·AND·DISTRIBVTES·HONOVRS·IN·|

ST. JAMES' PARK, LOOK

)ER·THAT·SOCIETY·SHALL·BE·FOVNDED·ON·PRINCIPLES·OF·GENERAL·V1

ARTHVR CAWSTON, A.R.

G EAST FROM EXISTING LAKE

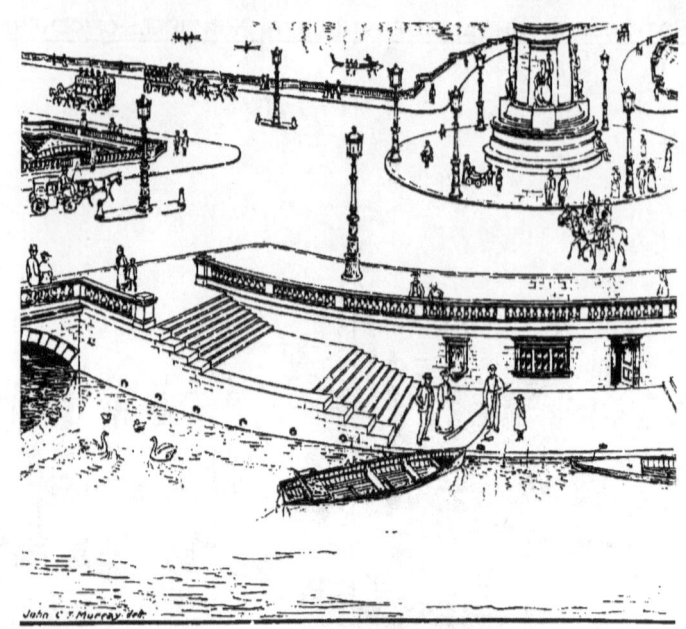

ST. JAMES' PARK, LOOK

G EAST FROM EXISTING LAKE

visionary, which dominates a large section of our countrymen. Just as it has been our pride to say that "an Englishman's house is his castle," so it has been equally our pride to boast that nothing should invade the sanctity of our parks. It may appear at first sight Quixotic to attack this sentiment, but I am encouraged by the fact, that almost every competent critic who has at first met the proposals with this sentiment on his tongue, has, when the germ has had time to fructify in his mind, become completely converted.

At the cost only of the labour employed, we might transform parts of our parks into sloping lawns, rockeries, and flower-beds, such as exist at present in one little corner of Hyde Park. Instead of this one beautiful spot, we could, in Hyde Park alone, have a dozen, and this park is so wide-spread that these could be as entirely foreign to the present drive, as the cloisters of Westminster Abbey are to the members of St. Stephen's, or the delightful Temple Gardens to the editors of Fleet Street. Besides such alterations, I submit that our parks should be opened up by roads, somewhat as shown on the accompanying plan. At the sides of these highways should be formed footpaths of sufficient width for kiosks, band-stands, and for thousands of seats. These paths, whilst being shaded from the sun by trees, could be illuminated by night; at their outer edges should be found lawns gay with flowers, and again a few feet further back should be placed the light unclimbable railings such as are now to be found in St. James' Park.

Surely such roads would conduce to the beauty of London, and to the health and convenience of its people. Properly placed they would not hinder the enjoyment of any, even during London's three-months' season. They could be made more beautiful than the present roads, and thus add to the general charms of the surroundings. Far from curtailing the space now devoted to riding and driving, my plan, while retaining the privacy of this portion, actually trebles the length of both Rotten Row and the Drive, and thus provides infinitely more variety and convenience. No doubt the existing roads were sufficient for the private coaches of the early part of this century, but all admit that more space is essential for the greatly increased numbers who already use these select roads.

Again, if five such convenient wide thoroughfares met on an island in the centre of the lake in St. James' Park (see sketch), the roomy Horse Guards Parade, opened up as it would be by the busiest of arteries, would at once become the popular meeting place in this central district, thus removing a difficulty experienced by successive Governments in connection with Trafalgar Square. For the same reason, if Hyde Park and Regent's Park were opened up, certain spots in these parks would doubtless become the popular meeting places of their respective localities.

Let us endeavour to consider all the objections that can be raised to such roads across our parks. It may be thought that the parks would thus be cut up too much and that all their quietude would be sacrificed. But surely Russell Square is large enough for any one who wants quietude, and, as shown, the sizes of the portions of Hyde Park still left free from roads, would nearly all of them be at least five times the size of that square. No doubt the public roads that I propose would bring more traffic into the parks, but as long as this traffic does not interfere with the present park traffic it would be neither a nuisance nor unsightly. Is the traffic of Piccadilly ugly or disagreeable to watch? Certainly not! Piccadilly is one of the most interesting and popular streets in London; and this is largely due to the variety of its traffic. Possibly such thoroughfares would interfere with the enjoyment of the quietude of the parks to a few, to just a few, who, after all, only use the grass for a few weeks in the year, and who certainly would still have plenty of room elsewhere. I mean the vagabonds and tramps who at present migrate to sleep on the grass as soon as the weather permits their dispensing with the accommodation provided for them elsewhere. This, however, would probably not be considered an unwelcome interference by the majority of Londoners.

I would be the last person in the world to underrate the universal importance and charms of the parks as they exist at present. Indeed, it is only those careful students of London life who have watched them at all times in the year, and almost at all times of day and night, as I have done, who can adequately judge of their unique beauties, or gauge their full value to the health of Londoners. Artists, poets, not only of our own country but of the rest of the world, unite in praising both the glories of their natural beauties, and the varieties of their inimitable atmospheric effects, nor will I ever advocate the disturbance of these charms. All I propose would rather increase than destroy them, and would certainly render them more valuable by enabling the many to share in their enjoyment.

There are still other reasons, with which we are unfortunately too familiar, why the parks should be dealt with somewhat in the way I propose. At frequent intervals our newspapers are burdened with complaints of the dangers of the parks at night, and of their uses for purposes which, as they exist at present, are perhaps unavoidable. Is this not entirely due to the darkness and solitude of these places after nightfall, when it is dangerous for men, and impossible for women to traverse them? Without a doubt this is so, and the simple remedy is to be found in forming avenues, which, by being brilliantly lit after dark, will render them safe for all. It may be said that even then dark and solitary spaces must remain, but for this a remedy is easily found. At the extreme edges of these avenues should be placed the light unclimbable railings already mentioned. By this means the public could be entirely prevented from straying far from the well-beaten tracks, whilst these would become as

> AH! WHEN SHALL ALL MEN'S GOOD
> BE EACH MAN'S RVLE, AND VNIVERSAL PEACE
> LIE LIKE A SHAFT OF LIGHT ACROSS THE LAND
> AND LIKE A LANE OF BEAMS ATHWART THE SEA.
> *The Golden Year.*

HYDE PARK LOOKING TOWARDS

ARTHVR CAWSTON, A.R.I.B.A. ARCHT

KENSINGTON

bright and busy by night as by day, and pleasant for health and recreation for those who, on account of their industry, cannot use them at other times. I know of no valid argument against this course. As there is room for all, and to spare, surely our true policy is to so open out these town parks as to make them benefit the masses as they now do the classes, and I venture to think that when that most powerful of objections —novelty—has disappeared, other present objections will disappear also. In that happy time, where will the Londoner be found who will advocate the present restricted policy ? a policy by which the immense majority of our fellow-citizens are practically debarred from any real share of what, properly used, might become a glorious heritage for all.

Fortunately the development and management of the commons and open spaces which embellish the suburbs of London have been so uniformly good as to leave little room for adverse criticism. In their recent developments, the London County Council have been particularly successful, as all can testify who know intimately the excellent work done to the commons under their control. In one respect, however, doubtless all of us would like to see a different principle adopted, and this can be easily attained under a comprehensive scheme as proposed in this book. Where land about to be developed abuts on a common or other public open space the authorities should require a road to be made on its edge, even if this involves converting a portion of the grass of the open space into roadway. The houses would then have their frontages towards the public land ; when this is not done, the open spaces are fringed with yards, the ugly backs of houses, and their frequently offensive outbuildings. Instances of the two methods may be seen almost side by side on Wandsworth, Clapham, and Tooting commons, and no one who compares them can fail to see the immense advantage of the one over the other. There is another reason and a far greater one, in favour of skirting open spaces with roads ; when this is done the space is freely opened up to the surrounding neighbourhoods, because all the roads leading in its direction are carried right through to its edge. By the other plan the spaces are closely hemmed in by continuous houses which effectually shut it off from the other roads in the neighbourhood. Like the heart in the human frame, an open space should be in complete communication by means of arteries with the whole district surrounding it. In this way, and in this way only, can its regenerative influence be freely felt.

Besides its parks and commons London has numerous smaller gardens and open spaces which are gradually being thrown open to the public. Many of these, and especially those in the more central districts such as the gardens of the Inns of Court, Lincoln's Inn Fields, and others, could with great advantage be opened up. I have endeavoured in some of the accompanying sketches to show what would be attained by doing this. Most of us are convinced that the conditions affecting these places have so altered as to make the suggested change desirable in these cases, but of course there are many gardens in West End squares which still amply fulfil the purposes for which they were intended. With these therefore no alteration appears to be either necessary or desirable.

2. TO OPEN UP THE MOST CROWDED DISTRICTS AND ADMIT MORE LIGHT AND AIR.

In opening up these most crowded districts it will be absolutely essential to bear in mind, both for economy and also for the comfort of the working classes, that at present many of the most valuable parts of London are occupied with slums; such as the neighbourhoods of the Houses of Parliament, Regent Street, the Law Courts, and elsewhere. As has been shown in Chapter IV., it is neither consistent with the general welfare, or even reasonable, to give up these most valuable districts for workmen's dwellings. I therefore consider that all that central portion of London bounded by Oxford Street and Holborn on the north; Piccadilly, the Strand, and Fleet Street on the south; Farringdon Road on the east; and Hyde Park on the west, is quite unsuited for the purpose of workmen's dwellings, and if it was used to its best advantage it could be made the most valuable in London; the western portion being devoted to squares and mansions as at present; the central portion to a series of grand avenues containing shops, theatres, markets, colleges, public offices, and official residences; and the eastern portion covered with similar grand avenues lined with warehouses, factories, and other private business premises, as it partly is at present.

Mr. Frederick Harrison in his article on "London Improvements" in the *New Review* for October 1892, says: "The working masses of London have perhaps a deeper and more healthy love for their great city, more pride in it, more interest in its management, than any other class whatever. The governing classes and professional classes are wont to look on (central) London as the field of severe labour, occasional resort, or especial excitement. Their ideas of rest, comfort, and happiness imply the " getting away " from it, or ultimate retirement to a very different region. The trading classes, large or small, view London with a rather local and parochial spirit, from the point of view of market, exchange, warehouse, and shop. They will work in it like miners in a pit; but they run out of it at every opportunity, and hope to end their days in a distant suburb."

Although it is not very complimentary to London or to its " loving inhabitants " (comme dit Sir Charles Dilke)* to say that every one who *can*, " gets out " of it as

* Essay on London in 'Les Capitales du Monde,' 1892.

LINCOLN'S INN AND FIELDS

"from a pit" as quickly as possible, yet the statement is to a large extent true. If, however, the slums are swept away from the central portions, there is no reason whatever why the "rich, well-to-do persons" should not again make it their permanent abode. Indeed, something of the sort has already taken place on the Westminster and Cadogan estates, where stately mansions and flats have lately replaced squalid and dismal rookeries.

3. TO CREATE MANY MORE GREAT ARTERIES CONNECTING THE MOST IMPORTANT CENTRES OF BUSINESS AND HABITATION.

I know of no streets formed in London during our time that have been quite successful both financially and architecturally, and this has probably arisen from the absence of any settled principles in planning them. The following principles appear essential if new streets are to add to our health and convenience, to beautify our town, and at the same time to be financially successful.

(a) They must be sufficiently wide for ventilating their districts; for accommodating both quick and slow traffic, and for the wants of the future as well as those of to-day.

(b) They should be as straight as possible and of uniform width from end to end.

(c) No street should contain a steep gradient, although slight undulations are desirable.

(d) Each street must form an integrant part of the general plan.

(e) Street junctions should be designed both with regard to danger and convenience.

(a) *The width of future London streets.*

(a) When Sir Christopher Wren made his plan for rebuilding that central portion of London which was destroyed by the great fire, he especially stated that he proposed making the thoroughfares sufficiently wide to do away with the necessity of forming parks or gardens; his reason being that parks and gardens can only confer a benefit all the year round to the health of those people who live in their immediate neighbourhood, whereas the same space devoted to wide streets would perpetually be bringing fresh air and sunlight to every window (see plan, p. 56).

If lofty blocks of dwellings are surrounded by wide roads they can no doubt be made healthy, but the present custom of pulling down cottages which face narrow streets and replacing them with lofty blocks of dwellings, without widening the streets is no doubt a retrograde step as far as health is concerned. It is therefore essential for hygienic reasons alone, that as the height of modern buildings increases so must our streets be made wider. What should be the future width of streets to fulfil this purpose, and at the same time to provide for that increased traffic when eventually London is a city of wide streets and lofty buildings? Our experience of wide streets is insufficient to enable us to answer this question with accuracy. We must turn to the experience of Paris.

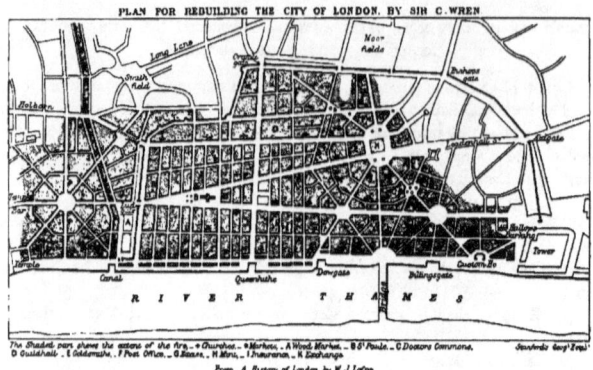

PLAN FOR REBUILDING THE CITY OF LONDON, BY SIR C. WREN

From, A History of London by W J Loftie

The width of some of the principal Parisian streets will astonish my readers when compared with our own. The inner and outer Boulevards which encircle Paris and together measure about 20 miles, average in width 140 feet throughout. In two districts for a distance of about two miles in each case the width is 240 feet. The Avenue des Champs Elysées is 275 feet wide, and continues that width in a straight line for a distance of over four miles. The Avenue de l'Opéra, lately formed through the most expensive part of Paris, is 120 feet wide, and nearly three-quarters of a mile long. The old Rue de Rivoli, also constructed in what *was* the most expensive part of Paris, is 100 feet wide and nearly two miles long.

These are but samples of what exist throughout Paris, in fact that city, with very little heavy slow traffic, is now composed of wide streets running close to one another and crossing in all directions. To such an extent is this the case that of the

PONT DE LA CONCORDE, PARIS

PRESENT WIDTH OF LONDON THOROUGHFARES.

30 square miles on which Paris stands, exactly one-third, or 10 square miles, is occupied by its roadways and open spaces. Some of the widths mentioned may seem extravagant, but these cases partly arise from the fact that the fortifications round Paris have been three times extended. Thus, the ground they stood upon was freed, and has enabled the municipality to form these wide avenues without the excessive cost of clearing the land of buildings :—

As a contrast to these widths, the following widths of the principal streets in London are given:—

Holborn, Oxford Street, and the Bayswater Road } average 70 ft. wide for a distance of about 4 miles.

Street	Width	Distance
Regent Street	80 „	1 mile.
Clerkenwell Road and continuation	60 „	2 „
Queen Victoria Street	75 „	$\frac{3}{8}$ „
Tottenham Court Road	70 „	$\frac{3}{4}$ „
Charing Cross Road	75 „	$\frac{1}{2}$ „
Edgware Road and continuation	65 „	3 „

In comparing these widths people are apt to think that land must be of less value there than here. That, however, is not so, for although some frontage sites in London sell for a higher price than any Parisian land, yet the average cost is greater in Paris than in London (the City excepted), and this is due to the lofty blocks of dwellings that Paris consists of. The general width of London streets is far less than the examples cited—which are absolutely the widest main thoroughfares we possess—such important main thoroughfares as Knightsbridge, Borough High Street, and Fleet Street being less than 50 feet in their narrowest part, which must always be taken as the effective width of a street. Nor is there any guarantee that these widths will not continue to be made, as new streets can anywhere be formed of the admittedly inadequate width of 40 feet.

Even for the suburbs of an important town 40 feet is too narrow. Bearing in mind the absence of all squares and other open spaces in modern developments, and the convenience of broad footpaths, a width of 75 feet is probably not too much for suburban main streets, and 50 feet for suburban side-streets, the footpaths in each case being 12 feet wide. As to the width of the streets in inner London, the following considerations should not be overlooked :—

I. The rapidly increasing traffic which already exceeds the capacity of our streets, including even newly widened main thoroughfares, such as the Clerkenwell Road.

II. The large proportion of heavy slow traffic, and the impediment caused by its loading and unloading.

III. The constantly increasing height of modern buildings, and the consequent necessity for increased means of giving light and ventilation.

Having regard to these considerations, probably the minimum width that it is prudent to give to reconstructed main thoroughfares in central London is 100 feet, and 75 feet for less important thoroughfares. If this be done, and wherever practicable, the streets beautified by trees and relieved by ample open spaces at important street junctions, the modern tendency to again make central London a residential quarter will be encouraged.

(b) Streets should be as straight as possible and of uniform width from end to end.

I know that some few contemporary English architects differ as to whether streets should be straight like our neighbours' or gracefully curved like Regent Street. The convenience of planning the frontage houses, however, demands straight lines ; for police purposes, too, straight lines are the more convenient. Some architects and artists may deplore the loss of the picturesque corners and surprises that exist in London and many ancient towns ; but elegance, dignity, and regularity are the true qualities to be aimed at in a well ordered city such as one day we hope ours may become. Quaintness, picturesqueness, and irregularity may be all charming qualities in the country—their proper place—but there is neither rhyme nor reason for their encouragement anywhere on a map near those big black circles which signify a closely packed population of so many thousands.*

No impediment or local obstruction should therefore prevent the streets from being the same width throughout. Not that all our London streets should be made as straight as the Camberwell New Road, for a compromise will enable us to obtain the charming variety due to curves with all the advantages of straight streets. There should be formed at the junctions of all important streets, open spaces somewhat larger than Oxford Circus, and the streets should proceed from junction to junction in straight lines. It will be found that nowhere need the same line be unduly prolonged, for at every junction a slightly new direction can be taken.

* The President of the Royal Institute of British Architects for this year (J. Macvicar Anderson, Esq) echoed these sentiments in the last words of his annual address, thus : " I gladly record my conviction that the architecture of to-day, although falling short of what we long to see, although exhibiting an exaggerated enthusiasm for the element of quaint picturesqueness which I hope at no distant date to see leavened by the spirit of classic purity and simplicity, is yet not altogether unworthy of the enlightenment of these latter days, nor altogether out of harmony with this age of progress."

(c) *No street should contain a steep gradient, although slight undulations are desirable.*

I especially mention this because it is to be hoped that when our water supply is owned by our Council, we shall see in London the frequent running of water in our gutters. This, it will be remembered, is universal abroad during an hour in the mornings and the afternoons. A uniform inclination in the roadways for considerable distances, easily arranged when the streets are being laid out, but difficult to provide for when once they are formed, is essential for this purpose.

A treatise on street designing would be incomplete unless reference was made to the objectionable English custom of creating unnecessary breaks in the levels of public footpaths. Although instances are not so frequent in inner London, yet all must remember scores of cases in the suburbs; here breaks often occur at every few yards, where carriage approaches to private houses cross the public footpath. These approaches are frequently sunk several inches below the path and thus form disagreeable and dangerous impediments to foot traffic. The object of sinking these approaches is difficult to determine, for it is far simpler to put one steep slope from the gutter to the pavement, thus leaving the causeway practically level. The victims who suffer most severely from these unnecessary impediments are, undoubtedly, old people, ladies and children at all times, and all people in the dark. It is a curious fact that steps across public footpaths, and at entrances to shops, are peculiar to England, as they cannot be found elsewhere. Dickens gave as a reason for the frequency of steps in old country inns, that both architect and builder had so many opportunities in these places of forgetting their levels. I can find no better reason for the existence of steps in modern streets. If, for instance, one retail tradesman in fifty, or one lady in five hundred could be found who approves of a step to a shop, there would be some excuse, but a step in such a position is universally condemned by them. The thoughtful amongst shopmen even say that a step to a shop frequented by ladies keeps away 20 per cent. of chance customers. Remembering, too, the frequent accidents that happen during the winter from these steps, it seems desirable that in this matter the example set by the Paris authorities should be followed: they forbid any step being placed either along the foot pavements, or between the pavements and premises open to the public.

(d) *Each street must form an integrant part of the general plan.*

Few really important street improvement schemes have been carried out in London during the past forty years, and even these have not all proved entirely successful either in relieving traffic or financially. By financially I mean that the recoupment by the sale of the surplus land in the improved frontages has frequently fallen short of what was expected; not only so, but even when the land has gone off and the buildings been erected, they have, in the case of many improvements, been anything but remunerative. The reason for this want of success is not far to seek. Few schemes for improving London have contained new streets of adequate length and directness for them to become integrant parts of the general system.

Streets that end at another street which crosses at right angles, an arrangement almost as ineffectual as a cul-de-sac, must inevitably be comparative failures, whereas streets designed so as to form parts of continuous thoroughfares, invite all the through traffic from the adjoining districts, and thus become important arteries of the general system. We have examples all over London: Gray's Inn Road abruptly terminates at Holborn; Garrick Street, which although opening up Covent Garden and answering its purpose in early mornings, is comparatively deserted for the rest of the day; Portland Place, which should be continued through Regent's Park to the great northern roads; Vauxhall Bridge Road, which should be continued to Buckingham Gate and from thence across the park to St. James' Street, another comparatively empty street; Pall Mall, which should unquestionably be carried through the Green Park to Hyde Park corner, and we shall have yet another example if Council Broadway is carried out as at present proposed. These faults could hardly have been possible had the streets been constructed as part of a settled plan, which would have ensured each one of them being continuous right through the metropolis.

(*e*) *Street junctions must be designed with equal regard to danger as to convenience.*

The rounding-off of corners to a *convex* curve, either at the ends of streets or along the line, should be absolutely forbidden. I do not mean by this that " places " should not be formed where important streets meet one another, but I wish to draw attention to the fact that of necessity the danger of crossing such places must be greater than the danger of crossing roads elsewhere; and that it becomes intensified if the corners are rounded off to a large *convex* curve as is now generally the custom in London. The reason is simple; a large convex curve encourages drivers to drive round without checking their speed, and makes them cross the causeways whilst describing the circle. Convex curves also make the buildings on the adjoining sites most inconvenient and inartistic; in fact these disadvantages have proved so serious in Paris, that the rounding-off of the corners of building sites to a large radius is forbidden. Of course each junction must be considered on its own merits; with reference

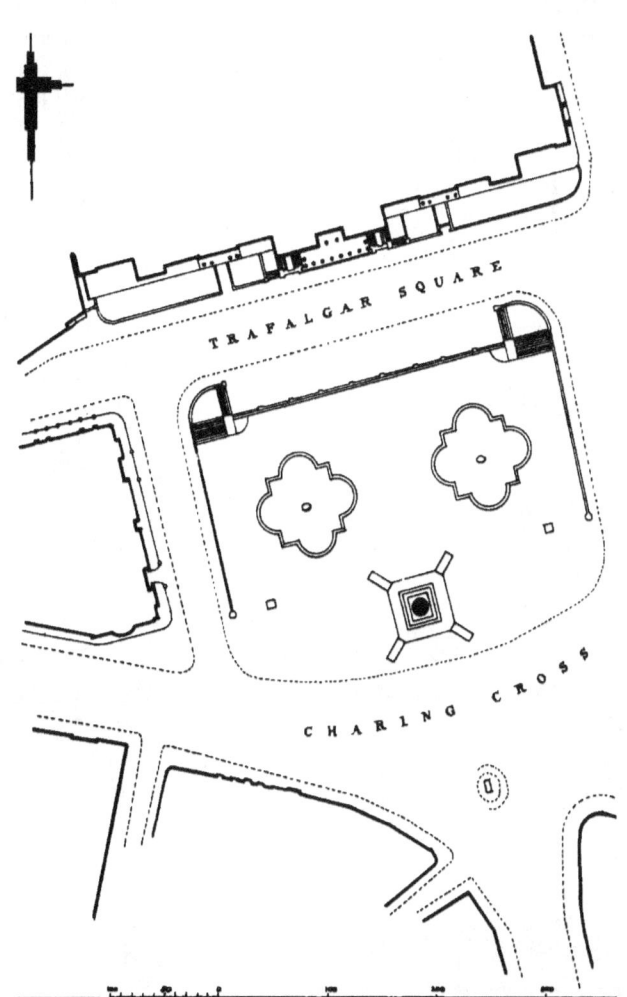

TRAFALGAR SQUARE AS LATELY ALTERED.

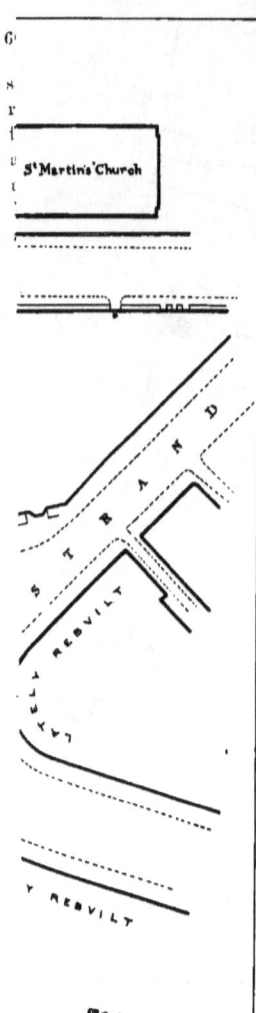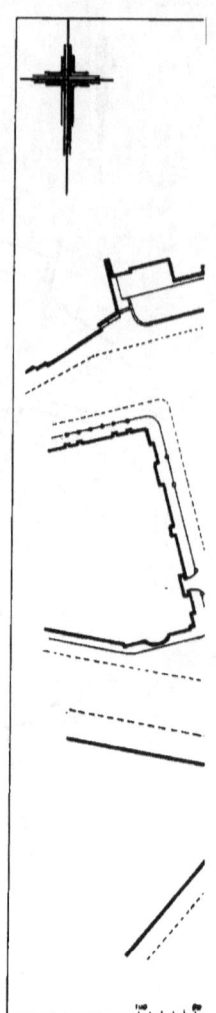

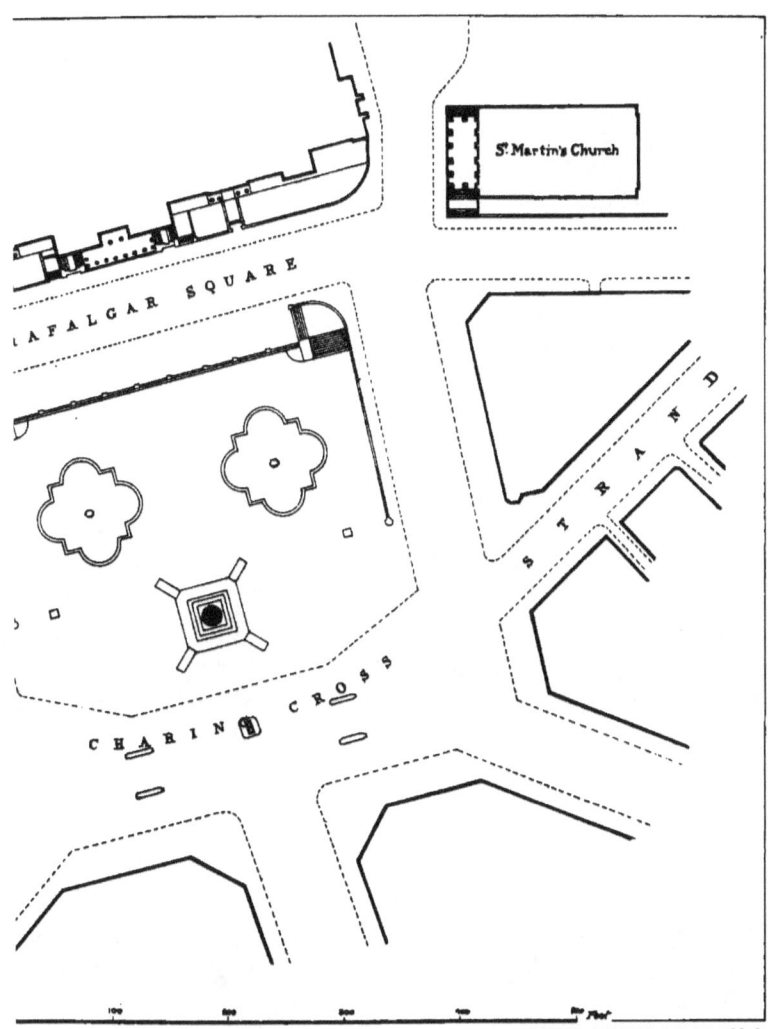

TRAFALGAR SQUARE AS IT MIGHT HAVE BEEN IMPROVED.

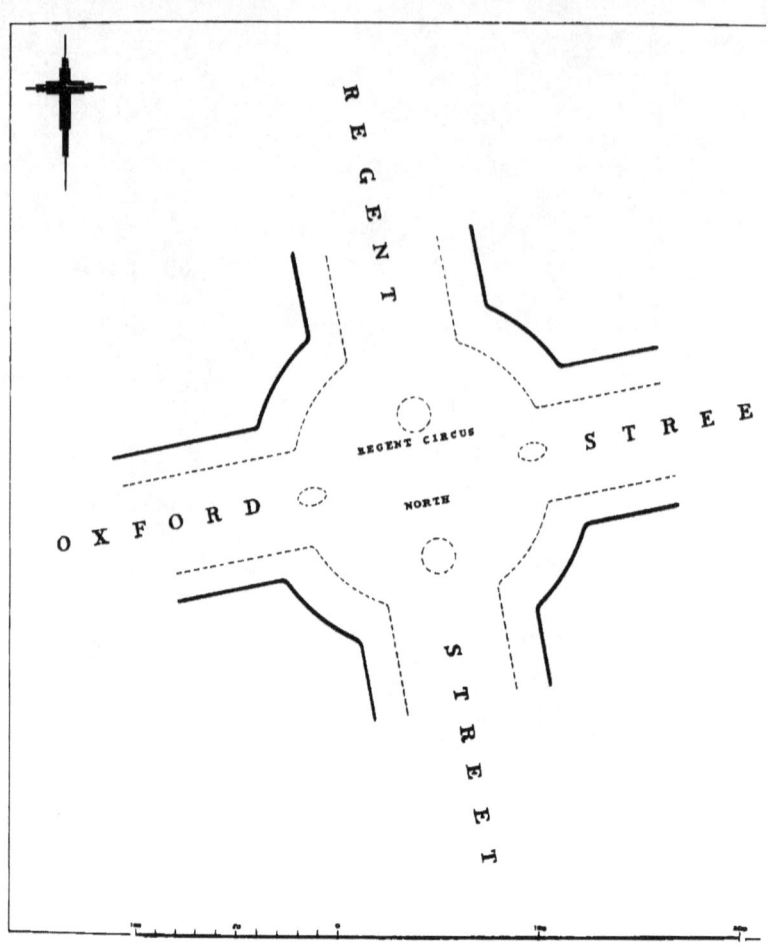

REGENT CIRCUS AS DESIGNED BY JOHN NASH. AN EXCELLENT EXAMPLE.

STREET JUNCTIONS.

to size, the number of roads that converge, their widths, and other considerations, but in order to lessen the danger common to all such places the three following conditions are essential:—

I. They should be laid out as hexagons, octagons, polygons, or if circles, with concave sides, not convex. In this way the curbs create obtuse angles, at which drivers would naturally check their speed.

II. The footpaths should be considerably widened round such places. This would lessen the length of the crossings for pedestrians, and would enable the drivers to see right and left, long before they arrive at the actual corner of the curb.

III. The buildings facing such places should have straight or concave frontages, never convex, and their frontages should, for æsthetic reasons, be as nearly equal in length as possible.

Oxford Circus is a very good example of the concave method of treating street junctions, but that excellent little model has evidently been entirely forgotten of late years. I have dwelt at some length on this fifth essential condition of street planning, because the unsafe, inconvenient, and inartistic system of rounding off corners to a large convex curve without widening the footpaths has become so usual in London of late years, and is consequently being frequently copied by our provincial towns. I regret to add, too, that many of our recent opportunities for improving the architectural appearance of the capital have been comparatively spoilt owing to this vicious fault of street planning. Compare for instance the buildings round Oxford Circus or St. Stephen's Club, Westminster (a charming corner design with three *straight* sides), to such swollen-looking excrescences as the Grand Hotel, or the St. Martin's parochial offices, Charing Cross; or to many similarly placed modern buildings which have neither architectural dignity nor repose.

4. TO PROVIDE ADDITIONAL BRIDGES OVER THE THAMES.

At present we have only fifteen bridges along the whole nine-and-a-half miles of river frontage, whilst Paris has twenty-one bridges in seven miles of frontage. It is so unreasonable as to be almost incredible, that from Vauxhall and Westminster Bridges, both situated between parishes which might be as wealthy as any in London, the adjoining vehicular bridges on one side, in each case, are so far away as to be almost invisible. How much more convenient and valuable the parishes of Battersea and Pimlico, Vauxhall and Westminster, Blackfriars and Southwark, might all become if they were more frequently connected by new bridges and pierced by the busy approaches which would of necessity be created to such bridges! How much more healthy, too, these parishes would be made when these same broad approaches, going right through their centres, connected them to that powerful and ever-moving body of air and water!

Such additional bridges and their necessary approaches are not only wanted to improve the health, convenience, and value of the various parishes; but they are also wanted for the convenience of the whole of the southern portions of the metropolis. For if the direction of the approaches to the proposed bridges as shown on my draft plan be examined, it will be seen how many more direct routes from the south and south-west to the business centres can advantageously be provided. These approaches would not only form most valuable business streets, but they would all help to relieve the present congested routes.

5. TO FACILITATE THE APPROACHES TO THE SEVERAL RAILWAY TERMINI.

The public importance of this principle as well as its importance to the railway companies is undeniable as soon as one attempts to analyse an ordinary day's traffic. Undoubtedly an immense proportion of the whole traffic in the streets is in connection with the railways. First, the foot passengers from the underground stations, and from the main termini; then the omnibuses that start from stations, those that stop at stations, and those that purposely pass stations; then the cabs that delight to wait near stations, as well as the station cabs. All the foregoing traffic is for passengers only; besides these, there are the railway vans, and parcels delivery vans of every sort, journeying to and from the goods termini, and the post carts of all descriptions. It would clearly be for the general convenience to specially consider this large traffic in connection with all important street improvement schemes, and it is, of course, an important and essential factor in any general scheme for the improvement of London.

Probably, too, the railway companies have been allowed admittance to central districts on terms easy to themselves but not advantageous to the convenience of the public. Combined with any scheme for the extension of a line into the heart of London, and the creation of a large terminal station, there should have been some reasonable street improvements to distribute the traffic from that station. There might also have been some conditions as to the retention of an adequately sized open space outside the station itself. Something of this sort is clearly essential, both in the interests of the railway companies and of the public, otherwise the companies would not have voluntarily provided them, as they have done with such beneficial results at Norwich, Bristol, Newcastle, and York.

GRIFFIN STREET WATERLOO

ARTHVR CAWSTON, A.R.I.B.A. ARCH?

)VLD BE

PALAIS DE JUSTICE, BRUSSELS

6. To OPEN OUT AS MUCH AS POSSIBLE OUR PUBLIC AND HISTORIC BUILDINGS AND TO PROVIDE SITES FOR NEW.

A remark a French workman once made to me at Amiens forcibly brought out how far we in England have failed in our duty towards our historic buildings. I was standing on a fine open space, which had been cleared round the new Hôtel de Ville, admiring the wisdom of providing so fine a setting to a public building right in the centre of that town. I made some remark about this; at once the good fellow replied, "One must indeed clear spaces round our monumental buildings, or what good would they be, one could not see them!" Here, at an out-of-the-way French provincial town, even the workmen are imbued with an artistic feeling and boldness of conception which, although not really extravagant, would make a prime minister in England quake for fear of the expense. Throughout continental towns the same good sense is invariably found, for every public building is now surrounded by space and roads.

At first this principle may seem extravagant to Londoners, for London possesses so many historic and other grand buildings. These, however, are often so hidden as to be comparatively unknown, and no means would beautify the metropolis more effectively and cheaply than opening out these historical monuments. All such buildings as Government offices, theatres, churches, and museums, require opening out for convenience as well as for the effect they would produce. Their prominence would also make the adjoining neighbourhoods easier of recognition, an important consideration in so vast and cosmopolitan a city; would render the buildings easier of approach; and lessen their danger from fire. Where is our English common sense in spending vast sums in making our public offices and museums fireproof, and at the same time leaving them hemmed in by stables, public-houses or barracks, such as we now see round New Scotland Yard, the National Gallery, the South Kensington Museum, and, of all places, the Record Office!

In many cases, the opening out of public buildings would render them more useful to the public. For instance, Columbia Market is practically useless because it has been built one or two hundred yards away from the main lines of traffic. If, in improving this portion of London, main thoroughfares could be arranged to converge upon this building, as shown on my draft plan, I have no doubt whatever that this costly white elephant would be made to fulfil most usefully the purpose for which it was built.

As to providing sites for new buildings, I have mentioned in Chapter I. some of the many public buildings at present urgently required in London, but which cannot be built until sites are found for them. In preparing a comprehensive plan of improvements, it would of course be necessary, and a matter of comparative ease, to consider the most suitable positions for these different buildings. For instance, I presume that King's College would not again be assigned a position so close to the alluring temptations of the Gaiety Theatre, and other music halls. At the present time the students of both spheres of life mix together as they pass backwards and forwards to their rehearsals and work, with a freedom that could only exist in this moral and too free metropolis. The National Gallery, with its priceless treasures, would hardly again be allowed to be divided only by a thin party wall from soldiers' barracks. Again, the hardworking and necessary coster cannot much longer be so cruelly neglected, left on damp pavements, without shelter for himself or his goods ; and thus driven from gutter to drink and an early grave. One important detail in a comprehensive scheme should be the provision of handsome retail markets such as are illustrated in Chapter I., and which should be situated adjoining the busiest streets of every thickly populated district. Such buildings would serve not only for markets and for covered promenades, where the municipal bands should play during the winter's evenings, and where volunteers could be drilled, but they would also supply the admitted want of public meeting-places.

Besides the sites which are so urgently required for public buildings such as these, others are wanted equally pressingly for private purposes. We all know how London tradesmen have constantly complained that they have no freedom of contract with regard to trade premises, because of the comparatively few good business streets that exist. If, in preparing a comprehensive plan, streets are laid down in such judicious positions as will provide many more valuable business sites than exist at present, such complaints will entirely disappear. It must not, however, be supposed that when London is traversed in all directions by broad arteries, which are so essential to health as buildings become higher and higher, all these roads will become good business streets, as experience proves the contrary. Doubtless many acres of London slums can be transformed and the land used for more valuable purposes than at present ; doubtless, too, many more good business streets can be formed ; but to imagine that because a road is sufficiently wide to bring sunlight and air between two lofty blocks of buildings, it is therefore bound to be a good business street is to imagine a fallacy;

CHAPTER VI.

THE APPLICATION OF THE SUGGESTIONS, AND THE SEQUENCE IN CARRYING OUT IMPROVEMENTS.

Formation of draft improvement plan—Details of some proposed new streets and some difficulties—Description of Ordnance sheet—Criticism of Council Broadway—Description of map of Paris—Two methods of advancing improvements—By increasing width of present thoroughfares—By avoiding interference with existing thoroughfares until others are formed—Reasons in favour of each method.

MY DRAFT IMPROVEMENT PLAN.

In order to illustrate how the principles which have been advocated in the last chapter can be applied, I have prepared a suggestive draft of a comprehensive plan for improving London. The formation of such a plan is a work, the magnitude and difficulty of which I, perhaps more than most others, can now fully appreciate, for it is only when any one has made a serious attempt to accomplish it that the difficulties are brought home. It was essential to the purpose of this book that some illustration of the principles advocated should be prepared, and I have therefore ventured on the task, although with much hesitation and diffidence.

In placing the result before my readers I desire emphatically to disclaim that this particular plan of improvements is just what I advocate. My purpose mainly is to win over my fellow-Londoners to the belief that it is impossible to really regenerate London without working to a settled plan. What the plan ultimately settled upon will really include is a matter of comparatively minor importance, so long as a plan is prepared and systematically adhered to. The task of settling the details and of perfecting the plan will necessarily fall upon the responsible government of London, and if my draft proves useful in this work, it will have served its purpose.

Doubtless the first sight of this plan with its many new streets will produce on my readers a feeling of dismay at the magnitude of the work proposed to be accomplished. If, however, I had also submitted a plan showing all the improvements that have been completed in London during the present century, I doubt if

K

my plan would appear the more startling of the two. To be of any practical value the scheme must contain all the main improvements which are likely to be required during the next few generations. Some of the improvements may not be fully carried out for fifty years or more, but directly a plan has been finally adopted and has the force of law, it will almost at once automatically begin the work by the result of fires and other unexpected opportunities for clearing away any buildings which stand in the way. Should my readers consider that in some cases the proposed new streets shown on my plan are unnecessarily close to each other, or to existing streets, I would urge that we must not only provide for the present, but for the future needs of London. A glance, too, at the map of Paris which accompanies this book, or at Sir Christopher Wren's plan (see p. 56), will show broad thoroughfares still closer together; and in order to prevent deterioration in the health of London, as it becomes a city of lofty buildings and residential flats, it is absolutely essential to increase the width of all roadways and the proportion of spaces to the adjoining building areas. I say "adjoining" advisedly, as a park or other open space some hundreds of yards distant, will have little effect on the health of the inhabitants compared with the benefit from air and light given by wide streets at their very doors and windows.

I will now describe the formation of my plan. After the physical features such as the Thames and the levels of the ground have been considered, the next most striking fact in connection with London of to-day, as has already been mentioned elsewhere, is undoubtedly the large areas covered by narrow streets and courts in its very centre; and looking at the enormous commercial value of the land, one cannot but wonder at the cause of this want of development. On either side of the various Inns of Court which stretch almost uninterruptedly from the Theobald's Road on the north to the Thames Embankment on the south (see areas coloured violet on plan), these tangled streets and dilapidated, unwholesome properties abound. Not only so, but except where pierced by Holborn and the Strand, these Inns have hitherto proved an effectual barrier against intercommunication between the City and the west.

Wherever barriers to free circulation exist, whether in a river, a human frame, or a city, there will be formed an unhealthy aggregation of scum, disease, or of slums. This is just what has happened in central London, and hence the slums. The first urgent need for improvement, therefore, as will be perceived by every earnest student of the map of London, is the opening up of these districts by broad thoroughfares, which must, of course, pierce the sanctuaries of the law. That this can be done without real injury to the Inns will be seen by a study of the sketches showing how Lincoln's Inn Fields and the Temple would be affected if the suggested alterations were carried out. That it can also be done without interfering with the

:·THAT· DOES·NOT·IMPEDE· OVR· NEIGHBOVR • THE

" LE QVARTIER LATIN "
OR
TEMPLE

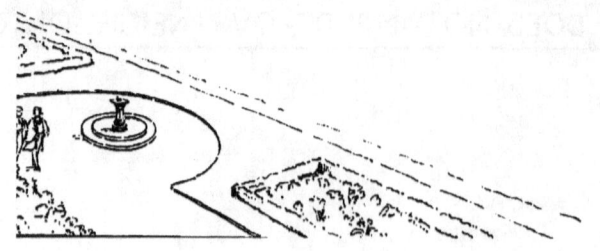

work of their inhabitants is at once apparent when we think of the many instances already existing in London where a few yards from one of our busiest of thoroughfares absolute quietude and seclusion are obtained. One sees this in the case of Gray's Inn, immediately adjoining Holborn; the north side of the Temple just behind the houses in Fleet Street; in the inner quadrangle of the Bank of England, surrounded on every side by the most intense business life; and in numerous other places both in and out of the City. Can it then be seriously urged that these thoroughfares, so essential for London's convenience, will materially distract from the study of the law? Moreover, are these Inns solely inhabited by lawyers? A glance at the Directory for 1893 tells us this is not so. In New Inn are sixty-seven solicitors, no barristers, and seventeen persons apparently not connected with the law; whilst in Staple Inn are thirteen solicitors, no barristers, and thirty-three others.

"Barristers are now so much in excess of litigants that many of them are unable to live on their briefs. They therefore let lodgings in the Inns of Court to which they are attached, and do it to such an extent that a legal contemporary declares the practice to be a scandal and a disgrace. The impecunious barrister, it appears, takes residential chambers in his Inn, which he at once proceeds to let at an exorbitant rent to one or more outsiders, who, not having been 'called,' are unable to hire them themselves. Then he gets a set, ostensibly for business purposes, which he deals with in the same way. He may then get another set taken in the name of a legal friend, seldom in town, but who wishes to preserve his name on the door, and these rooms are at once furnished and let out in the same manner. And so on. In this way the industrious gentleman is able to live out of the law, but not on it; and in due time may 'let' himself into a competency and the honour of a Queen's Counsel, springing entirely from chamber practice. These scandalous proceedings, says the authority, ought to be put down with a high hand. If they were, rents in the Temple would be more reasonable than they are."*

On attempting a really careful examination of the plan of the metropolis for the position of new main thoroughfares, it soon became apparent that either the parks and these Inns must be pierced, or that London's streets must remain the shapeless, meaningless tangle that has been our reproach for so long. Frankly admitting then this necessity, my plan has been gradually evolved on this first, and on the other principles which have already been fully explained in Chapter V., the headings of which are again repeated.

2. To open up the most crowded districts and admit more light and air.

3. To create many more great arteries for the convenience of traffic, connecting the most important centres of business and habitation.

* *The Daily Telegraph*, Feb. 13, 1893.

4. To provide additional bridges over the Thames.
5. To facilitate the approaches to the several railway termini.
6. To open out as much as possible our public and historic buildings, and to provide sites for more.

On these lines my plan has been gradually evolved, and as it is only put forward as a draft, there is no necessity to describe it in detail; I will, however, direct attention to the reasons for one or two of the more important thoroughfares that it suggests. All admit the inadequacy of Knightsbridge and Piccadilly. Is this surprising, considering that the east and west traffic is certainly the largest and heaviest in the metropolis, and that a great share of it falls to this one poor little artery. Many niggling alterations have been carried out for the purpose of relieving these streets, but without success, and undoubtedly some comprehensive alterations must soon be put in hand. It will be noticed that the parks have up to the present formed an obstacle to any parallel relief thoroughfares being provided between Oxford Street on the north, and Victoria Street, Westminster, and the Pimlico Road on the south. My plan shows the three following relief streets running east and west.

I. Mount Street, Grosvenor Square, continued direct eastwards to St. Paul's Cathedral, and westwards to High Street, Kensington.

II. The Cromwell Road continued direct eastwards (*a*) to Charing Cross; (*b*) to the Houses of Parliament; (*c*) to Camberwell and the Tower Bridge viâ Victoria Station and Lambeth Bridge; westwards, the same road is continued direct to Fulham and Hammersmith. A weighty reason for these extensions of the Cromwell Road is that they would make the national treasures and the central Schools of Art at Kensington more accessible from all quarters.

III. A new street from the Fulham Road eastwards direct to the Tower, viâ Sloane Square Station, Lambeth Bridge, the Fire Brigade Headquarters, and Southwark or London Bridge.

In addition to these three new thoroughfares to relieve the enormous traffic from the western centres of habitation to the eastern centres of business, Piccadilly and Knightsbridge are shown to be further relieved from the inconvenience of the cross traffic to and from the park by the addition of three new entrances to the park from those roads, connected by additional streets running in a northerly direction from the Cadogan estate. One of these additional streets would open out the east side of the Museum and Oratory, and all would pierce that tangled network of streets which at present is so largely responsible for the continual block at Albert Gate. It will be noticed that whilst this triangle of streets which is bounded by Kensington Road and Knightsbridge on the north, Brompton Road on the south-east, and Prince's Gate on the west, remains unpenetrated, the whole of

SVGGESTED TREATMENT FOR SOVTHERN EMBANKMENT

the park traffic from the recently developed wealthy districts west of Sloane Street is forced to the Albert Gate.

Another well-known instance of an inadequate thoroughfare is the Westminster Bridge Road, the main approach to the west from the south of London and from Waterloo Station. This road is shown to be relieved on the east by new roads starting at the end of the Kennington Park Road, and proceeding northwards past Waterloo Station to Islington, viâ Gray's Inn Road ; and to St. Paul's, viâ Blackfriars Bridge ; with a spur street to Charing Cross, viâ a new bridge. By continuing this spur to St. James' Park the traffic from the whole of the west to Waterloo Station would be largely diverted from the Westminster Bridge Road.

As the beautiful Opera House in Paris is made a central feature in that city, so our more solid looking British Museum is made a central feature in my plan. This result was not obtained by following æsthetic principles only. It has been shown in a previous chapter that a large proportion of an ordinary day's traffic goes to and from the railway stations, and it was in providing new routes for this traffic, that the British Museum proved to be a natural centre to which many of these streets must converge. Although hemmed in, and comparatively unknown, this building is one of the finest London possesses, and its main front is a grand specimen of classic architecture. From every point of view therefore, it appears desirable to make this museum one of the important centres of a new street system, and in doing so to provide for its necessary enlargement and isolation. From the centre of its southern front is shown what would probably be the finest street in central London, and which would lead direct to the unrivalled Waterloo Bridge. This street has long been advocated by many leading architects. In addition to forming a most important link in the new street system, it would open out on the one side, the classic church of St. Peter's, Bloomsbury, Drury Lane Theatre, and the western front of Somerset House ; whilst on the other side, it would open out the Opera House, Bow Street Police Station, and Covent Garden Market. If it be urged that Waterloo Bridge is too narrow for any additional traffic, it can be answered that this beautiful bridge and its approaches can readily be widened on the western side.

It will be noticed that the completion of the Thames Embankments in the manner which it has always been contemplated to complete them is shown in dotted lines. On account of the winding of the river, these Embankments do not form an essential link of any street system, and in my opinion they should not be undertaken until many more urgent improvements are completed. When the work is carried out, it may be found undesirable to devote the whole space which will be obtained from the river to traffic and pleasure grounds as is the case on the northern side. Instead of this, I suggest the formation in front of the existing warehouses of an embankment which shall be part quay and roadway and part fish market and roadway, as is usually adopted in other commercial cities. Such quays might be made quite as ornate as our present Embankments, and they would probably be far more interesting to the majority of Londoners; whilst their construction would be more economical, because of the lesser disturbance to the trade and the labour market of the metropolis.

Many architectural and engineering difficulties will doubtless be met with in the formation of streets as shown on this plan, but I do not believe that any are insurmountable. This is not the place to enter upon a detailed description of such problems, but I will refer to one of them. We all know the unfortunate effect produced by the London, Chatham, and Dover Railway bridge across Ludgate Hill. The continuation of this line, carried as it is to Holborn Viaduct terminus, and to the junction with the Underground at Snow Hill, at present forms an effectual barrier against any new street from the West End to the City. The recent developments of cheap tunnelling now render it possible to overcome the engineering difficulty. Admitting the necessity for the continuance of this link between the railway systems of the north and south of England, I suggest that the Metropolitan line should be continued from Snow Hill *under* the Thames; a spacious underground station being also provided in place of the present inadequate Ludgate Hill station. As regards the portion of the main Chatham line at present running through St. Paul's station to Ludgate Hill station and Holborn Viaduct terminus, there appears to be no reason why the line should not stop at St. Paul's station, which could be enlarged to form the terminus. Thus could easily be removed the barrier which has frightened many from suggesting an adequate relief to Fleet Street and Ludgate Hill, for the cost of the alterations would be largely covered by the sale of the land now occupied by the two stations, their yards, and the railway itself.

As has already been stated in Chapter III., the areas coloured blue on the plan indicate some of the many sites near central London which might well be occupied by workmen's dwellings.

THE COLOURED ORDNANCE SHEET OF CENTRAL LONDON.

This is a reproduction of the Ordnance survey, which, however, was made over twenty years ago, so that it has been necessary to correct it as regards the more important street alterations since made. The objects of including an enlarged and coloured plan of this thickly populated and very valuable part of London are as follows:—

I. To show the ground still uncovered which is available for the improvements

· VARIETY'S · THE · VE

AN AMERICAN'S FIRST IMPRESSION OF LONDON
VIA WATERLOO STATION AND A NEW BRIDGE.

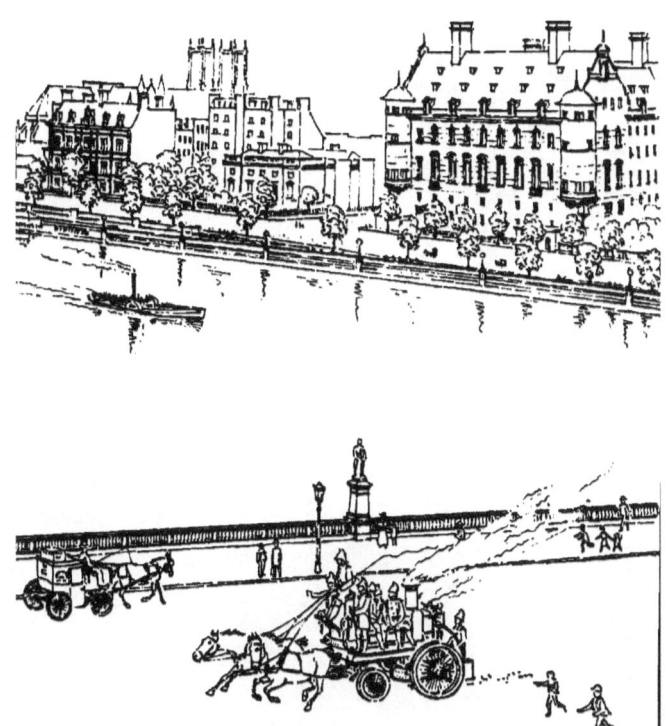

as proposed in the draft plan. Attention is directed to the extent of this space (coloured pink) and to the fact that it must enormously reduce the cost of making the suggested improvements. Light-blue colour on this map shows the existing buildings which occupy the space required for the proposed roads. It is necessary to point out that much more property than is coloured will be required if we are to obtain the recoupment which the improved frontages will produce.

II. To show those buildings which have all been rebuilt during the last four or five years on the sites of the proposed roads. These are coloured dark blue, and they have all been ascertained by actual survey. If a comprehensive plan and the frontage laws had been adopted so short a time ago as four years, all these rebuildings in this central portion of London would have formed opportunities of forwarding the general scheme without any legal delays or costs connected with compensation for disturbances, whereas they now form expensive obstructions to be overcome.

III. To indicate the principal public buildings that will be opened out or otherwise affected by the alterations. These are coloured dark red.

IV. To show the proposed position of "Council Broadway," the centre of which is indicated by a thick dotted blue line.

I venture to think that this plan shows how much a settled scheme would have accomplished almost automatically towards improving central London in the past few years, and how supremely important it is that the adoption of such a scheme should not be unduly delayed. The plan also serves to show what an unimportant part the proposed Council Broadway must play in any really effectual general plan of improvements. Apart from a general scheme this roadway has been boldly conceived, but alas, it only proves that the best isolated street improvements must be doomed to failure unless they form an integrant part of the whole street system. Let us apply to the present proposed position of this street the six essential principles for the general rearrangement of the London streets which I have ventured to lay down, in order to ascertain how far this street will possess the vital requirements of an important thoroughfare through this district.

1. So far from opening out the only open space in its immediate neighbourhood—the comparatively large area known as Lincoln's Inn Fields—the high buildings that are sure to be erected on both sides of the new street will form a yet more formidable barrier to the free circulation of air from that space. Treated as I suggest this portion of London should be treated, this large area would be so opened out that it would become one of the most attractive spots in central London, even rivalling in its usefulness and beauty so famous a centre as the Place de la Concorde.

2. As regards opening up the poorest, unhealthiest, and most crowded districts in London, the proposed position of the street is excellent.

3. As to the width of the street. A hundred feet as proposed will probably be sufficient both for present and future needs, especially as, from its position, it can never become an important thoroughfare, or an integrant part of any complete system.

If the street is formed, as shown, it will be impossible to continue it further towards the south, and I venture to prophesy that the southern portion will not be financially successful, but will remain wide and empty, like Gray's Inn Road, Conduit Street, Garrick Street, Vauxhall Bridge Road, and Portland Place. It may well be asked what proportion of travellers from the north want to be landed at King's College, with no means of going further south, and only the narrow Fleet Street or Strand to conduct them either to the east or to the west?

4. No future bridge could be connected with the street where proposed, for it would be against all ideas, both of architectural beauty and economy, to erect a second bridge and its accompanying approaches so close to Waterloo Bridge, in the first place because this would completely hem in the river front of Somerset House; and secondly, because Waterloo Bridge itself and its approaches can be economically doubled in width.

5. For the same reason the position is not the best for facilitating the approach to the northern railway termini, for which purpose the street has been to a great extent advocated.

6. As to the advantage of the proposed site for opening out our public buildings, I venture to think it could not be worse. Our Law Courts, our Bankruptcy Buildings, and King's College Hospital are all three much frequented public buildings, at present placed in most crowded and inconvenient positions. One cannot conceive a more splendid opportunity than is here possible of opening out these three important buildings. Properly planned, a new street of less than a quarter of a mile in length would make all three buildings easy of approach from the whole of the north and north-west of London, and would bring out their architecture in bold relief. Instead of this the plan proposed merely brings out the flank view of a church, intended by its architect only to be viewed, as at present, on its charming western front; while the main street will not open out any important public building at all.

As regards the provision of sites for new buildings, doubtless the proposed plan will be adequate.

The Chairman of the Improvements Committee of the London County Council, in an article on London Improvements,* admits the unsoundness and inadequacy of the present fragmentary system—" The scheme for a new street from Holborn to the Strand as adopted by the Council in July last, did not include any dealing with the northern approaches to Waterloo Bridge, apparently for the reason that this bridge

* 'New Review,' October 1892.

ROND POINT. CHAMPS-ÉLYSÉES, PARIS

must be soon improved, or a new bridge built, and that it will be better to deal with the approaches in a single distinct scheme. . . . . Nothing, however, has yet been decided as to the architectural character of the new avenue, the main purpose of which is to be a central thoroughfare rather than an artistic adornment."

THE MAP OF PARIS.

With this book is included a map of Paris to the same scale as the London map. The Paris map is included not only because convenience and beauty have always gone hand in hand in the transformation of that city, but also because the map affords an illustration of a successful application of the comprehensive method I am advocating.

A glance at this map explains the statement that Paris has one acre of open space to every thirty-seven of her inhabitants, for it is at once seen that the Parisian Boulevards are sufficiently wide to be called continuous parks rather than roads; and the roads, properly so called, are also wide, and run in very close proximity. To such an extent is this the case, that of the thirty square miles on which the city stands, ten square miles are taken up with roads and other open spaces. The splendid width of these roads, and the inadequacy of our own, can be forcibly realized by comparing the two maps, which, as stated above, are drawn practically to the same scale.

The map of Paris also shows how completely the important buildings, such as churches, palaces, and museums, are isolated, and are thus made the features of this magnificent city; how well the town-parks, such as the Parc Monceaux, Parc des Buttes Chaumont, and others, are opened out by roads running through their most beautiful portions, and how frequently the Seine is spanned by bridges. In this way the people are enabled to live in the midst of, and receive the full benefit from, the beautiful natural features which adorn the city.

On a careful examination of this map it will be found that all the street projects which still remain to be carried out are shown in dotted lines. It will be seen that there are also many improvements which are only partially completed. Thus, circuses or open spaces for street junctions have been formed, and the ends of avenues that will eventually run into them have been made, although it may be years before these avenues are completed throughout their entire length to the full width they are ultimately intended to be. For it must be remembered that the completion of the widening proceeds only as opportunities occur for the removal of the buildings, either by the expiration of tenancies, by the dilapidation of the properties, or from other causes.

74 THE SEQUENCE IN CARRYING OUT IMPROVEMENTS.

As already stated, the official map of Paris is corrected and reprinted every year, so this one, which is dated 1890, would be considered by Parisians to be "passée."

Let us now consider the order of carrying out improvements in London, if a general scheme be adopted. Where the scheme simply involves the widening of existing streets, it will probably be forwarded sufficiently quickly, especially in the suburbs, by taking advantage of the opportunities afforded by that rebuilding of premises which is so continuous. No doubt this system, which for convenience I call the "automatic system," would forward the complete transformation more persistently and economically than any other method, but I do not for one moment suggest that we should rely exclusively on this. The transformation should be advanced simultaneously by the Council spending a certain fixed sum per annum in carrying out complete schemes of widening streets, or forming entirely new ones, wherever they consider the urgency of the traffic, or the health of the neighbourhood demand such a course. For convenience, I call these forced improvement schemes, "municipal improvements."

With regard to the order of carrying out these municipal improvements there are two distinct principles on which they can be forwarded.

1. By increasing the width of existing main thoroughfares.
2. By avoiding interference with existing main thoroughfares, until others are formed.

1. *By increasing the width of existing main thoroughfares.*

The weighty reason in favour of this first method is as follows:—

Those roads which have naturally become the main lines of traffic have generally retained their popularity, however many new wide and convenient roads may have been made for the express purpose of relieving them; and it has therefore been argued that no new roads can relieve them. If, however, the direction of the main lines of traffic in London be examined, it will be found that many of these ancient roads have kept their popularity, simply because of the absence of more direct routes. But if, for instance, the northern side of St. Paul's Cathedral were widened and thrown open to vehicular traffic, it is not likely that the present detour round the south and east sides would remain the route for all the vehicular traffic from Ludgate Hill to the Post Office. Again, if the northern end of Gower Street were thrown open, in front of the east side of University Hospital, it is not possible that the traffic would still go all round the other three sides of that building, as at present.

Similarly, but on a larger scale, if a direct route led from Victoria Station to Charing Cross or Piccadilly Circus, the omnibuses would certainly not continue to make the present circuitous route either round the south and east of St. James's Park, by Victoria Street and Parliament Street; or round the west and north of Buckingham Palace and the Green Park by Grosvenor Place and Piccadilly.

2. *By avoiding interference with existing thoroughfares, until others are formed.*

The following are the reasons that may be urged in favour of this second method of carrying out municipal improvements.

(*a*) As shown above, many of our main lines of communication in London are not sufficiently direct, and it seems reasonable to expect that routes which are more direct, if judiciously placed, will be popular, and will therefore be the means of relieving the present congested streets.

(*b*) With few exceptions our present main thoroughfares, if doubled in width, would hardly be too wide for the traffic that passes through them to-day, and in planning our street improvements, it is essential to provide accommodation for the estimated traffic of at least fifty years ahead.

(*c*) That more good business streets are urgently wanted is shown by the fact that the best of the existing thoroughfares hold a practical monopoly of retail trade, resulting in rents so excessive as to form a severe tax on both seller and buyer.

(*d*) If three or four times as many good business streets were provided, connecting the important centres of business, habitation, and railways, it is possible that the present main thoroughfares (which naturally will be the most expensive to improve) will not then want such extensive alterations.

(*e*) The formation of judiciously placed thoroughfares would provide additional valuable sites for retail trade, to which tenants of the present main thoroughfares could remove, when ultimately those thoroughfares are widened.

(*f*) It has been proved again and again, that the more good business streets that are formed, the more retail trading is encouraged. At the present day it seems almost incredible that the retail merchants of Cheapside were adverse to the formation of Queen Victoria Street, because they were certain that there was not sufficient trade for both streets, and that consequently they expected to lose their means of livelihood.

(*g*) Health demands that the first money spent, should be spent in remodelling the most unhealthy districts, and this is naturally more radically effected by creating new thoroughfares through the slums than by increasing the width and convenience of our present comparatively healthy main streets.

(h) Financial considerations demand the same order of procedure, first because the remodelling of the slums is undoubtedly the less expensive work to carry out; second, because their improvement will effect the greater increase in the rateable value of the county.

(i) In a country so thoroughly conservative as England, and also for æsthetic reasons, it will doubtless be politic not to interfere with our existing familiar main streets and landmarks, excepting where absolutely necessary. If it be found possible to provide sufficient accommodation for our increasing traffic by the creation of new arteries, rather than by increasing the width of those existing, much of that sentimental opposition, which generally arises against improvements, and which is so troublesome to defeat, will be avoided.

In whatever order these municipal improvements are executed, I submit that they should be continuous year by year, and that they should always be carried out in at least two areas at the same time—a working-class area and a central area. In this way each district would be gradually occupied by those buildings for which purpose it is most suited, and the minimum inconvenience to the displaced population would be caused. For instance it might be possible to form the road connecting the British Museum with Waterloo Bridge, and to widen that bridge, after having erected on the site of Bethlehem Lunatic Asylum more than sufficient tenement accommodation for the population that would be displaced by the improvement. The Museum Street could be formed partly automatically, and partly by municipal or forced improvements. The municipal improvements would economically convert slums into healthy valuable properties without interfering with any historic landmarks; whilst the utilization of Bethlehem's thirteen acres for wide roads, artisan dwellings, and playgrounds, would provide much of that accommodation where it is so urgently needed.

CHAPTER VII.

THE COST, AND HOW TO MEET IT.

Cost the final test—Extravagance of borrowing—Unjustifiable for street improvements—Various sources apart from rates from which money might be raised, gas, water, trams, docks, municipalization of land—Impossibility of poorer ratepayers contributing—Suggested rates (1) graduated death duty on land (2) on buildings (3) Graduated improvement rate on occupiers—Minor sources, from nation, from omnibus and cab companies, from railway, gas, and water companies.

THE regeneration of London must, like many another grand scheme, be finally settled on the question of cost. Ugly as London may be, even sordid and squalid, its rehabilitation can only be seriously attempted when some means can be devised for paying the cost, other than by fresh taxes upon the poorer occupier, who is already overburdened. The scheme advocated in this book must, therefore, like all other schemes of improvement, be submitted to, and largely decided by, the final test of cost. Hitherto the impossibility of adding to the burdens of the poorer of the London ratepayers has stopped the way to adequate improvement, for both the Metropolitan Board of Works and the London County Council have felt very strongly that it would be impossible, after the abolition of the coal and wine dues, to carry out further work of improvement without provision of a new fund for the purpose.

Many schemes for raising money have been suggested, but as yet the acceptable and practical plan has evidently not appeared. In one important particular I suggest an entire departure from previous practice; future improvements should, I submit, only be carried on out of the funds annually raised, and not, as in the past, by means of borrowed money. By this plan the ratepayer will keep a real control of the expenditure, and will not burden himself, as at present, with a vast debt and the payment of interest. This, at the present time, already amounts to one million per annum.

As is well known, the system of carrying out metropolitan improvements adopted both by the Board and by the Council has been by creating consolidated stock, and extending the repayment of principal and interest over a period of sixty years. The Metropolitan Board of Works, during thirty-one years of its existence, spent on improvements of a permanent character—such as the main drainage of London, the Thames bridges and embankments, and street improvements—the sum of about twenty millions.* Assuming that all this sum of twenty millions was raised in the way described above, the total amount that will have been paid by the London ratepayer at the end of the period, for capital and interest, will be 43,362,500*l*., which means an annual tax of 722,708*l*. for the whole term. If it had been possible to have spread the execution of these works over the sixty years, the annual cost to London would have been 333,333*l*. instead of 722,708*l*., and in the end the ratepayer would have saved no less a sum than 23,362,500*l*. It was not possible, however, to carry out such gigantic works as the main drainage and the embankments of the river by annual instalments, for it is obvious that works of such a character must, when once begun, be completed as speedily as possible, and it was merely equitable that posterity should bear its fair share of the cost as well as sharing in the benefit. It is quite otherwise with street improvements. For such a purpose, there appears to be no justification whatever for incurring the enormous additional expense involved in the payment of interest on borrowed money, as the carrying on of such works beyond our present means is neither required by necessity nor justified by morality. It is, indeed, an offence against the principles of political economy to burden posterity with debts for our street improvements, and so prevent them carrying out other improvements that may be necessary in their own day. It is true that the present system offers the temptation given by the speedy completion of the particular improvement undertaken—a more speedy completion than would, perhaps, be possible if it had to wait for funds arising from current income; but the delay would, after all, be small, and the enormous additional cost of the borrowing system altogether outweighs the small advantages given. The present system is so obviously an extravagant and unsound one, that it is unnecessary to dwell upon it further; its application to street improvements cannot be justified, and can only be explained by the fact that, having been necessarily applied to main drainage works and embankments, it was applied almost as a matter of course to other improvements. Another reason may possibly be found in the manner in which the coal and wine dues were dealt with; Parliament allocated these for a series of years to certain specific works, and the dues were accordingly mortgaged for the purpose of raising the necessary funds. Justifiable under such conditions as arose in the past, the spendthrift policy of mortgaging our future income so that only half of it becomes really productive, is, to say the least, a policy which may be described as un-English.

Apart from rates, the special sources of income that appear to be legitimately open to a municipality include the profits from water, gas, tramways, markets, and

* London Statistics, 1891–92, p. 266.

docks, all of which are undertakings of a municipal character, and in the profits of which the community should share. Whether or not London can profitably take over these undertakings depends entirely upon the price she will be required to pay for them. On equitable terms they could all be made growing sources of income which might in the end almost extinguish local taxation. It is needless to say that the money required to purchase these undertakings must be raised by the issue of stock, and the principal and interest repaid by a sinking fund extending over a long period. That this can be done and yet a surplus remain for the reduction of rates has been proved by many of our leading municipalities, a good example of which is that of Glasgow, where the figures are as follows:—

REVENUE AND EXPENDITURE OF SOME OF THE TRUSTS OF THE CORPORATION OF GLASGOW FOR THE YEAR 1890-1891.

	Revenue.	Expenditure.	Amount put aside for Interest, Sinking Fund, &c.
	£	£	£
Markets Commissioners—including the business of all markets, abattoirs, the veterinary inspection of animals, dairies, &c.	19,803	10,163	7,121
The Clyde Navigation—including dredging account and all expenses	354,581	151,066	173,126
Gas Trust—including the supply of all public lamps, and of private lights at 2s. 6d. per thousand feet	483,576	435,358	50,769
Water Trust—including the domestic rate at 6d. in the £, and for an unlimited constant supply for both public and private purposes..	168,408	125,055	40,719
Corporation Tramways.—Income from rents only, the tramways not yet being worked by the Corporation* ..	29,703	189	about 20,000

* PARTICULARS OF TRAMWAY COMPANY'S AFFAIRS.

Half-year ending.	Miles run daily, average.	Gross receipts by cars, omnibuses, hiring, carriage of mails, cabs, and general receipts.	Average per mile by cars and omnibuses.	Total expenditure per mile, including corporation charges.	Net available balance.	Amount of dividend paid.	Rate per cent. per annum on capital called up.
		£	s. d.	s. d.	£	£	
Dec. 31, 1890.	14,656	133,642	1 1·122	1 0·025	19,037	13,125	8⅓

THE COST, AND HOW TO MEET IT.

There is, however, a possible source of income far more important than any of these, which many economists consider should be in the hands of every municipality. The immense growth of public feeling in favour of the principle of the municipalization of town lands is striking. No less than 80 to 100 of the candidates for the present House of Commons were pledged to the principle, and it is therefore one which must be carefully considered, and in the near future, frankly dealt with. No one can approach the subject without being met at every turn with the difficulties created by the leasehold system so largely peculiar to the metropolis, and one ends with the conviction that the simplest way of overcoming these difficulties may be found in the municipalization of the land. Convenient though it is in some ways, the leasehold system has unquestionably been the cause of many of the evils that it will now cost London so much to remove. Inadequate streets and badly built houses have resulted from it, caused probably by the fact that lessees having only a temporary interest in the property, deal with it solely with the view of their own immediate profit, and not at all with a view to the future, or to the general interests of the neighbourhood.

Most of us have also doubtless met with instances of cruelty and hardship caused by the system, such as widows and children suddenly deprived of all income by the running out of leases, or through unexpected falls in values in particular neighbourhoods; for not only do properties under this system at times cease to produce a revenue, but actually become a serious burden. I mention one instance, which probably every reader will be able to supplement from his own experience. The land on which No. — New Bond Street is built, belongs to the Corporation of London, who have let it on a perpetual lease, with a ground rent of about 50*l.* a year, subject to the payment of a small fine every fourteenth year. A few years ago property in this neighbourhood was more valuable than now, and the lessee was able to grant a sub-lease for 80 years conditionally on the erection of a building costing 7000*l.*, and the payment of a ground rent of 1100*l.* a year. Values have since fallen, and in order to make up the ground rent due to his landlord the sub-lessee has now to pay, even when the building is fully let, not only all the rack rent he receives from the property but 100*l.* in addition. Nor can he escape from this obligation, although he has offered to surrender his lease and give up possession of his buildings. This property, now in trust, must in a few years be divided amongst ten children, any one of whom will unfortunately become liable to this monstrous contract.

Serious as the objections to the system are, the difficulties of uprooting it appear almost insuperable, and perhaps the only way of putting an end to it would be by in some way municipalizing the land. That this could be done without real injury to ground landlords and yet with great advantage to the community I thoroughly believe, and there can scarcely be a question that in this way, and in this way alone, the land can be made to bear its just proportion of our civic burdens with the minimum of hardship and inconvenience. There are, of course, well-known practical difficulties in connection with the subject, but probably some system by which the land could be held under perpetual leases granted by the municipality on a ground rent or ground tax readjusted quinquennially, would afford a satisfactory solution. I do not, of course, propose any system under which existing vested interests would be confiscated, but if these interests could be acquired at a reasonable price, there is scarcely any doubt that in the end the community would immensely benefit. Even a liberal price, calculated exactly on present values, might be given, because the future natural increment, to which the community and not the private owner is undoubtedly entitled, would in time enable the municipality, not only to extinguish the capital debt, but largely to reduce taxation and at the same time improve and beautify the metropolis.

Neither the municipalization of the land nor the purchase of the great monopolies are, however, within measurable distance, and it therefore becomes necessary to consider in what way the immediate improvement of the London streets can be proceeded with, without putting fresh burdens on the poorer occupiers, for we all admit that they can bear no further burden. With a rate for municipal purposes averaging throughout London more than 5s. in the pound, and reaching, in some of the poorest districts, nearly 7s., the main question is the relief of the poorer occupier rather than the extraction from him of further sums. That this relief cannot come in the shape of the reduction of expenditure is, I think, clear. Indeed, it appears probable that if our local administration is to be made as thorough and efficient as we all desire that it should be, some addition to the cost will be essential. Some relief will doubtless be brought to the poorer ratepayer by the equalization of rates, to the principle of which not only the Government, but both sides of the House of Commons are practically pledged. In addition to this, there will probably be some readjustment of the incidence of taxation for local purposes, which will shift a portion of the burden of existing local taxation from occupiers to owners. Even when this relief is given, it will be impossible to ask the poorer occupier to make any adequate contribution towards the cost of improvements.

Bearing this in mind, and carefully weighing the various propositions which have in recent years been put forward, I venture to think that money required for metropolitan improvements should be raised in the following ways :—

1. A graduated death duty on freehold land in London, assessed on its municipal value.

2. A graduated death duty on buildings.
3. A graduated improvement rate on occupiers.

1. *A graduated death duty on freehold land in London, assessed on its municipal value.*

This is not the place, nor do I propose, to discuss at any length the various problems of the incidence of local taxation, especially as that has been gone into by so many thoroughly capable authorities. There appears, however, to have been a considerable growth of opinion in recent years in favour of the death duties as the readiest means of taxing ground values, and a careful consideration of the problems affecting this complex subject induces an agreement with this view. To any other method of taxing the land, there is the fatal objection that the tax can, by readjusted rents, be readily shifted on the occupier. Death duties will moreover produce a far larger revenue than a direct annual tax on land of moderate amount; they would also be much less felt, and therefore be less unpopular than an annual tax. One difficulty in connection with the death duties is, a probable disinclination of any government to surrender them for local purposes, but there appears to be good ground for the view that so far as land and buildings are concerned the tax is one equitably applicable to local purposes, and which ought not to be claimed by the Imperial exchequer. It is at any rate clear that both land and buildings are inseparably connected with their surroundings, and that their value largely depends upon local government and municipal enterprise.

On the question of the valuation of the land for these duties a distinct valuation of land must undoubtedly be made. This, as my readers are probably aware, is quite practicable, and if such valuation were made quinquennially, it would facilitate the assessment of the duties at the municipal value of the land, independently of the value it now produces in the shape of rent. There are, of course, some thorny questions in this method of assessment which it is necessary to mention, both in connection with vacant land more or less ripe for development, and with other land which is far less productive than it could be made; but that these questions can be equitably dealt with, will I think, readily be seen from the following illustrations.

(*a*) Two adjoining plots in Belgrave Square, similar in size and surroundings, with similar houses erected on them, would doubtless be valued at the same amount, although one might be producing a ground rent of only 10*l.* a year, and the other a ground rent of 100*l.* a year. At first sight there appears as if there might be difficulty in imposing a death duty on one of these properties whilst the present lease lasts, but in reality there is nothing of the kind. The municipal value of the

PLACE DE LA BASTILLE, PARIS

two sites is exactly the same, but in one case the whole value belongs to the freeholder, and in the other case it is divided between freeholder and lessee. If it be argued that there would be the double trouble of registering the freehold value and the leasehold value, and of collecting part of the duty on the death of the freeholder and the remainder on the death of the lessee, I submit that that is an argument for abolishing the leasehold system, rather than for not imposing the death duty on the municipal value of land.

(*b*) The vacant lands within the railings of such squares as Belgrave and Grosvenor Squares are now being used for that purpose for which they are most suited. They increase the value of the houses which face them, they form no obstruction to the general traffic, and they help to beautify London. The municipal value of lands such as these, for taxing purposes, is nil, for it can be shown that whatever value they possess is transferred to the adjoining houses, which are increased in municipal value by their proximity to the open spaces.

(*c*) As an example of land not used for that purpose to which it was most suited, I will cite a case well known to all, and where the facts are indisputable. Before the Metropolitan Board of Works bought Northumberland House and its grounds, that estate formed an obstruction in the heart of the metropolis, and when at length it was opened up for one of our most successful of recent street improvements—Northumberland Avenue—its municipal value proved to be about 800,000*l*. I submit that no Englishman who could afford such an establishment, and particularly wished the luxury of such extensive pleasure-grounds in the centre of London, could reasonably object to being rated on the municipal value of the property.

Some incidental advantages would probably arise from the land being taxed at its municipal value. It would gradually be the means of inducing owners to put the land to its most suitable use, and not to allow it to continue practically unproductive, because unburdened with its just share of local taxation. A proper quinquennial valuation of land would also probably tend to discourage the present London leasehold system. This may be illustrated by the case of the freeholder who, granting a lease of an estate to a speculator at a ground rent of a thousand pounds a year, receives, as the estate is developed, the total ground rent from plots forming, say, two-thirds of the estate. It follows that the remaining plots are held by the speculator at a peppercorn, and that his profit consists of the amount realized by their sale. If in future the ground landlord has to pay a tax on the municipal value of each plot, whether held on a peppercorn or not, he will probably hesitate to dispose of his land in this manner. But possibly the greatest advantage of taxing land at its municipal value, would be that it would gradually lead up to the municipalization of the land.

The next question to be determined will be the proportion of taxation for improvement which the land should bear. In his draft report, dated 1892, Mr. Munro Ferguson, a member of the Town Holdings Committee, points out that :—" The growth of towns has added an exceptional value to the land on which those towns are built, so that it commonly possesses a value many times as great as the original agricultural value. This increase of value has ordinarily been treated as a case of unearned increment passing to the owners of the land. But the increment in this case is due, to a very large extent, to the continued municipal expenditure on streets and roads, lighting, sewers, &c., and is only maintained by such expenditure, the cessation of which would at once render it impossible to obtain the returns which town lands yield. It is therefore equitable that a large portion of this expenditure should be borne by those who reap the fruits of it in the enhanced value of these town lands.

" There is also a great difference in the extent to which land and buildings are benefited by municipal expenditure. Houses fall into decay and must from time to time be rebuilt. They become obsolete in form and have to be removed to make way for others of a newer type. The progress and prosperity of a town hastens this operation, but speaking generally the value of the land increases with everything that conduces to the advance of the town. All permanent improvements more especially, directly increase the value of the land affected, although they by no means necessarily increase that of the houses upon the land. The improvements that have been affected in most of our large towns in late years have very largely augmented the value of the land therein, both directly in the way indicated above, and indirectly by decreasing the amount of land available for building.

" Finally, the imposition of a uniform rate upon the total annual value of the land and buildings is unfair, because the annual value of the land is of the nature of a net return from an improving property, while that from the buildings (even after allowances have been made in the assessments) represents a gross return from a wasting property."

As regards the graduation between richer and poorer landowners, it has already been stated that the poorer ratepayer has, in the past, not only paid his share of municipal burdens but has borne a portion of the just share of his richer brethren, and although a readjustment of incidence will remove the grosser part of this injustice, it will not, as it should, place the heavier burdens on the richer inhabitant. This can only be accomplished by a system of graduated taxation, and the feeling in favour of some sort of graduation appears to be steadily growing. The Chancellor of the Exchequer in his Budget speech (1893) mentioned that he was unable to deal with the readjustment of the death duties during the year, owing to the many questions of practical difficulty that arose, some of which were in connection with the necessity for a graduated tax. Assuming that the principle of graduation be accepted, the nature of the graduation remains to be determined. By way of illustration I submit a scheme for a graduated death duty on land, the scale of payment being determined on the total value of the estate of the deceased person :—

When the affidavit of value
for probate exceeds—   Death duty to be—
£1,000, and is under £10,000   ..   £2 per cent. on value of all land forming part of the estate.
10,000   „   50,000   ..   3   „   „   „   „
50,000   „   100,000   ..   4   „   „   „   „
100,000 and above   ..   6   „   „   „   „

Sir Thomas Farrer, in his evidence before the Town Holdings Committee, stated that the capital value of the assessment of London was 750,000,000*l*. Assuming that one-fifth of this represents the value of the land, we get 150,000,000*l*. as being the capital value of London land. This would change hands by death every 25 years, and would give 6,000,000*l*. as falling to be taxed by death duties every year. Five per cent. on this would produce 300,000*l*. ; but of course under a graduated system it would be impossible to predict what the yield would be.

2. *A graduated death duty on buildings.*

For the reasons already stated it appears desirable to require buildings to contribute to permanent improvements on a lower scale than land. I suggest that the following would be an equitable scale :—

When the affidavit of value for probate exceeds—   Death duty to be—
£1,000, and is under £10,000   ..   £1 per cent. on value of any building.
10,000   „   50,000   ..   2   „   „
50,000   „   100,000   ..   3   „   „
100,000 and above   ..   4   „   „

As already stated, it has been calculated that property changes hands, on the average, every 25 years. In the case of property held in trust or by companies or corporations, it will be necessary to provide an equivalent to the death duty, and probably the most convenient way will be by an annual tax equal to one twenty-fifth of the duty on the higher scale, leaving the onus of proof for any rebate upon the body taxed. A provision that all properties may be liable to pay this duty at least once in every 33 years would probably counteract any deed of gift during lifetime or false sale for the purpose of avoiding the duty.

3. *A graduated improvement rate on occupiers.*

Although the taxes already advocated will produce a large annual sum, this may still be found insufficient to carry out improvements on a scale necessary to meet London's requirements in the near future, and in that case the more wealthy amongst the occupiers might be called upon to contribute some portion of the cost of improvement, in the benefits of which they will share. I say the more wealthy amongst the occupiers as there appears to be a general consensus of opinion that the poorer occupier should bear no further burden. As already stated, it was acknowledged by both parties in the House of Commons during the recent debate on the equalization of metropolitan rates that it is the poorer inhabitants of London who are heavily taxed. The simple statement of the hardships now endured by them, and the comparative immunity of the rich, was sufficient to make both sides of the House agree " That provision ought to be made for further equalizing the rates throughout the metropolis." It was shown in the debate that " the nearer to the workhouse are the ratepayers, the more stringently are the rates exacted from them. High rates mean high rents, high rents mean crowded tenements, and crowded tenements mean disorder, poverty, disease, immorality, and crime. High rates mean labour handicapped, hopes blighted, enterprise crushed." The rate in Bromley for sanitary purposes, local lighting, sewers, and interest on local debts, is at present 3s. 7d. in the pound. In Poplar and Mile End the rate for the same purposes is at present 3s. 8d., while in St. James', Westminster, it is only 1s. 0¼d., and in St. George's, Hanover Square, it is only 1s. 3d., that is to say, it is three times as heavy in the poorer districts as in the richer. Not only so, but there are at present gross inequalities in the method of assessing property for rating purposes. In all the poorer neighbourhoods, the assessors are always under the obligation of making the valuation as high as possible, because the rates are so high. For the converse reason, the wealthy districts of London do not need to raise their assessment value, otherwise their rates in the pound would be so small as all the more to attract public attention to the contrast between the way they are taxed and the way the poorer districts are taxed. The varying figures of this local sanitary and lighting rate, together with the common charge of 3s. 3d. in the pound which is at present levied throughout London for the purposes of Police, School Board, County Council, Asylums Board, and Poor Fund, show that at the present time the total rates in poorer parishes, such as Bow, Bromley, and Poplar, is 6s. 10d. and 6s. 11d. in the pound, whilst in the richer parishes of the West the total rates amount to 4s. 3d. to 4s. 6d. in the pound only.

Although the equalization of rates which will now probably be given will

GRADUATION OF IMPROVEMENT RATE.

redress a hardship, and give some measure of relief to the poorer occupier, it would even then be impossible to raise from a *uniform* rate such as the poorer occupier can afford, anything like an adequate sum for improvements. Although not free from difficulties or anomalies, a graduated improvement rate, somewhat on the following basis, will possibly be found amongst the most satisfactory means for supplementing the revenue required for improvements in London.

Number of houses affected.	Rated at.			Improvement Tax.			Average amount raised per House.			Total amount per class of House.
	£		£	*s.*	*d.*	£	*s.*	*d.*	£
68,240	20 and under 25			—						
54,831	25	„	„ 30	0	1		0	2	3	6,791
92,585	30	„	„ 40	0	2		0	5	10	30,862
55,498	40	„	„ 50	0	4		0	15	0	41,623
32,574	50	„	„ 60	0	6		1	7	0	48,861
38,131	60	„	„ 80	0	8		2	6	0	95,327
16,345	80	„	„ 100	0	9		3	7	0	52,035
21,522	100	„	„ 150	0	10		5	5	0	107,610
8,637	150	„	„ 200	1	0		8	15	0	77,733
8,022	200	„	„ 300	1	6		18	15	0	160,440
6,279	300	„	„ 600	2	0		45	0	0	250,395
2,084			above 600	2	0		85	0	0	191,860
							Total	..		£1,063,537

The objection may, of course, be urged that such a graduated tax will be unfair to the wealthier occupiers, because they already give freely and voluntarily to the charities expressly maintained for their poorer neighbours. This is unquestionably true of a large number, but it may be that a portion of the immense sums given in charity could, with advantage, be diverted from their present direction to a purpose of admittedly permanent advantage to the community. The work of transforming London would be of such great benefit to the poor and to the working class generally, that while in course of execution the large amount now wanted for charitable purposes would be very much reduced. The provision of so much work would lessen the number needing charity, and tend to stop the excessive waste which is now so frequent in connection with its dispensation. The Bishop of Bedford, whose diocese includes East London, has stated * that four times the amount of charity money is sent to the East End as would suffice if the money were not wasted, and all other clergymen speak in the same strain. Mr. John Burns, M.P., writes: †—" For the weak, the sick, the physically unfit, food and sustenance must be found; but this

* *Times*, Dec. 28, 1892. † 'Nineteenth Century,' Dec. 1892.

should be undertaken by the proper authorities and existing paid officials in such a way as to confer no obligation. . . . That these authorities have not done their work well, are unsympathetic, is a reason for alteration, but is no justification for all the quack remedies that neurotic Christians and fanatical faddists, combining universal brotherhood with incompetence and good salaries, try to impose upon us. I go further, and as a trade unionist, a member of a friendly society, and a labour representative, knowing the life, the needs, and requirements of the working people, particularly the unskilled labourers and the unemployed, say that the time has arrived when the common sense of all sections of the community, represented by Parliament, should prevent utopian philanthropists like General Booth and Mr. Arnold White, and all such unscientific amateurs and spasmodic manipulators of other people's charity, from making London, as they are, the happy hunting ground of charitable debauchees, and the centre to which loafers and tramps are drawn from all parts of the country, to the confusion of the proper authorities and the detriment of the London poor."

The amount given in charity is almost fabulous. In London alone there are 763 institutions, of which 546 together boast of an annual income of 6,246,136*l.** Of this sum Mr. Loch, of the Charity Organization Society, calculated in 1888 that *for relief only*, not including educational or ecclesiastical charities, nearly two and a half millions was voluntarily given; an amount slightly more than the total of London's poor rate.

Although the munificence of these voluntary gifts compels our admiration, it is dimmed by the knowledge that so large a proportion is absolutely wasted, and by the unpleasant fact that the munificence of some, relieves the ungenerous and indifferent from their just share of what should be a common burden. How much better for the community would it be that the greater part of this sum should be spent in payment for honest work in carrying out improvements from which all would benefit, rather than that it should be spent in indiscriminate charity with its admittedly pauperizing effects.

MINOR SOURCES OF REVENUE FOR IMPROVEMENTS.

In addition to the main sources from which revenues for carrying out all except mere local improvements must necessarily be obtained, there may be mentioned some minor sources of revenue, which elsewhere have been made to contribute towards permanent improvements. It appears to be a sound principle that where an improvement brings with it a distinct benefit, the service, the company, or the person

* 'Directory of Metropolitan Charities,' 1892.

benefited should in some way especially contribute to the cost. For instance, the more important metropolitan improvements are distinctly national gains, and it is not unreasonable that a contribution should be made towards them out of Imperial revenue. In addition to those general national advantages which are bound up with the capital, there may be mentioned certain special advantages to various departments of the government by improvements in our street system. Important national buildings such as the Houses of Parliament, the Government Offices, the British and other museums, and the post offices, will clearly gain by isolation, and the services will also gain by facilities of communication. Buildings and services are maintained out of the national Exchequer, and from the same source might be contributed some portion of the cost of those improvements which may fairly be termed national in character.

Another minor source of municipal revenue is found in Paris by a tax on vehicles plying publicly for hire; there, each omnibus pays about 80*l*., and every cab about 50*l*. a year to the municipality. Doubtless the equity of this especial tax lies in the fact that the revenues of both omnibuses and cabs are entirely earned by the use of the public streets, and that it is only reasonable for them to especially contribute towards the pavements they so largely wear out, and to those improvements, the benefit of which they will especially feel. It is not suggested that tramway companies should be taxed, for two reasons; first, because they already contribute by the construction and repair of a portion of the roadway; and second, because their lines will revert to the municipal authority in a given time. The relative extent to which tramways, omnibuses, and cabs use the streets is shown by the following estimated numbers of metropolitan travellers for the year 1891, which were stated to have been carefully compiled from a variety of sources :*—

1. By railway 327,000,000
2. ,, tram 200,000,000
3. ,, omnibus 200,000,000
4. ,, cab and steamboat .. 30,000,000

It may be a question whether the great railway companies and the gas and water companies should not also contribute towards the cost of such improvements as it can be shown will afford especial facilities, or bring increased business to them. An instance in point would be the construction, as shown on my draft plan, of a direct route from the Horse Guards to Waterloo Station, which would of course, necessitate the construction of a new bridge over the Thames. The advan-

* 'The Quarterly Review,' Oct. 1892.

tage of such an improvement to the South-Western Railway Company would be so great that that company might reasonably be called upon to bear some part of the cost.

Public attention has lately been directed to the application to local improvements of the law of betterment. In France this is part of the law of the 16th of September, 1807, which provides that in every case where public works cause an important addition to the value of individual properties, their owners can be called upon to contribute to the cost of the works to the extent of one-half of the additional value so received. This is no doubt an excellent principle when applied to undeveloped estates, but the impracticability of applying it to individual houses was soon experienced in Paris, where the proof of the addition to value according to the forms required by law was found to be surrounded by so many difficulties and complications, legal expenses and delays, that advantage was rarely taken of the provision.

The sources of revenue mentioned in this chapter, if all utilized, would produce a total annual income for the purpose of improvement, of from two to two-and-a-half millions; and if London is to be brought up to the level of the best examples of modern cities during the ensuing century, this sum at least will be required for the work. However, the particular rate at which improvements are to be carried out appears to be of less importance than that they should be continuously and steadily advanced to a comprehensive plan, and that this comprehensive plan should be considered with the least possible delay. For it must be remembered that during every year that passes, not only are numberless opportunities for improvement lost through the reconstruction of premises on sites where improvements should be made, but that the purchase and removal of these new buildings will add enormously to the cost when ultimately the improvements are made.

A Royal Commission for the unification of the Government of London is now sitting, and if this Commission submits, and Parliament adopts, a scheme which will give as complete self-government as is possessed by almost every other city in the world, then, and then only, will the regeneration of London, as advocated in this book, become possible. Experience proves that a municipality finds popular sympathy and support in carrying out such schemes of improvement. By such means we shall also, for the first time, be able to combine for a purpose in which we are all deeply interested, and which is sure to create amongst us that municipal spirit hitherto so lacking in London.

VIEW OF THE COURTYARD OF THE PRIVY COUNCIL OFFICES OF T
AS SEEN FROM, AND COMPARATIVELY CLOSE TO, SOME OF THE PRINCIPA

E UNITED KINGDOM OF GREAT BRITAIN AND IRELAND

WINDOWS OF THE PRIME MINISTER'S OFFICIAL RESIDENCE.

ions, being nearly twelve feet cube. It is the receptacle for the vegetable refuse
windows surround it. Dustbins in London are generally emptied at least once a

APPENDIX I.

EVIDENCE of the RIGHT HON. *JOSEPH CHAMBERLAIN, M.P., given before the* ROYAL COMMISSION ON THE HOUSING OF THE WORKING CLASSES.

No. 8 Richmond Terrace, Whitehall.
Tuesday, 17th June 1884.

TWENTY-SECOND DAY.

PRESENT:

HIS ROYAL HIGHNESS THE PRINCE OF WALES, K.G.

THE MOST HON. THE MARQUESS OF SALISBURY, K.G.
THE RT. HON. THE EARL BROWNLOW.
THE RT. HON. THE LORD CARRINGTON.
THE RT. HON. GEORGE JOACHIM GOSCHEN, M.P.
THE RT. HON. SIR RICHARD ASSHETON CROSS, G.C.B., M.P.
THE RT. HON. SIR CHARLES WENTWORTH DILKE, BART., M.P.

THE RT. REV. THE BISHOP SUFFRAGAN OF BEDFORD.
THE HON. EDWARD LYULPH STANLEY, M.P.
MR. W. T. McCULLAGH TORRENS, M.P.
MR. HENRY BROADHURST, M.P.
MR. JESSE COLLINGS, M.P.
MR. GEORGE GODWIN, F.R.S.
MR. SAMUEL MORLEY, M.P.
MR. JOHN EDWARD COURTENAY BODLEY, *Secretary.*

THE RT. HON. SIR CHARLES WENTWORTH DILKE, BART., M.P., IN THE CHAIR.

THE RT. HON. JOSEPH CHAMBERLAIN, M.P., President of the Board of Trade, examined.

12,354. (*The Chairman.*) You are, as we know, member for Birmingham and President of the Board of Trade?—Yes.

12,355. We have asked you to come here to-day partly in reference to Birmingham, and partly also in reference to your present office; but in the first place I would ask leave to examine you as member for Birmingham; you were a member of the town council from 1869 to 1880, and mayor of Birmingham in the years 1874, 1875, and 1876; and, as I understand, your personal experience in this matter is rather as concerns Birmingham and the large provincial towns than of the metropolis?—Yes, I have no personal knowledge of the circumstances of London.

12,356. It would be your opinion, would it not, that the problem in the provinces differs materially from that in the metropolis?—Yes; I think that the problem in the provinces is a very simple one; it really consists almost entirely in making provision for the destruction of unhealthy and overcrowded dwellings, and the re-construction and re-housing of the poor may be safely left to private enterprise. In the case of London it is no doubt absolutely necessary, if the question is to be satisfactorily solved, that provision should be made of a character adequate, both in kind and in amount, to the provision which is destroyed; and that adds enormously to the cost of any scheme which may be proposed; it becomes necessary to do this in London because the distances are so tremendous; it is impossible for the working classes to live in the suburbs, it being too far away from their work.

12,357. And there would also be special difficulty in London with regard to the re-construction which would be necessary in London, on account of the great cost of land in the centre of the metropolis?—Yes.

N 2

The Rt.
Hon. J.
Chamberlain,
M.P.

17 June 1884.

12,358. With regard to Birmingham, its circumstances are somewhat special, are they not?—Yes. In the first place, the town is really a new town; the increase of the population of Birmingham has been something very remarkable, almost equivalent to that of an American city. At the beginning of the century in 1801 the population of Birmingham was 73,670; it rose in 1841 to 182,922; and in the next 40 years it has risen again until it is now 408,004.

12,359. (*Sir Richard Cross.*) Is that all within the Corporation?—It is all within the limits of the municipal borough. Then the town extends over a large area; the borough comprising in the whole 8,400 acres. The population is 49·4 to the acre; a great deal less than in some of the large provincial cities. The population in Liverpool is 108 to the acre; in Glasgow it is 85 to the acre; and in Manchester it is 79 to the acre; although it is more in Birmingham than in some of the other towns such as Sheffield and Leeds, which also extend over a very large space. The result of this condition of things is that some of the difficulties that have arisen in London, Liverpool, Glasgow, and Manchester have never been apparent in Birmingham. For instance, there has never been any serious overcrowding within the limits of the borough. The habits of the people are to have separate houses; they do not to any very considerable extent take lodgers, but each workman has a separate tenement. These tenements are generally built round small courts of back houses with an entrance into the principal street.

12,360. (*The Chairman.*) Are there no flats?—No, we have no flats and no cellars.

12,361. There has been a recent inquiry, I believe, at Birmingham?—Yes; arising out of the public attention which has been recently called to this subject, a committee of the town council was appointed, under the presidency of the mayor, to consider the whole question so far as Birmingham was concerned, and to inquire specially as to whether the accommodation for the working classes in Birmingham was adequate and of a sanitary description. The committee took a great deal of evidence and the members of the committee personally visited all the worst quarters of the town.

12,362. What was the nature of the report of that committee?—They reported generally that they found the accommodation sufficient and in a fairly sanitary condition, while there was very little overcrowding. They obtained, in reference to the last point, from the officers of the school board, an account of the number of persons in each of the tenements inhabited by the working classes, and it appears from this return that overcrowding at present in Birmingham only affects something like 2,082 persons out of a total population of over 400,000.

12,363. Do you know what that return cost the school board?—I do not think it cost anything; it was carried out in connection with the ordinary visiting of the school board officers. The particulars of this overcrowding were as follows: They found 12 families, comprising altogether 44 persons, housed in 11 single rooms; 40 families, comprising 184 persons, were housed in 25 habitations of two rooms each; 325 families, comprising 1,129 persons, in 159 tenements of three rooms each; and 150 families, comprising 725 persons, in tenements of more than three rooms apiece. So that it is evident from that that overcrowding does not exist to any appreciable extent in the town of Birmingham.

12,364. There are some quarters of the town, are there not, which you would think come within the preamble of the Artizans and Labourers Dwellings Improvement Act?—Yes, certainly; there are still three or four districts in the town to which, in my opinion, the provisions of the Act will properly apply, because these courts, especially the older courts, were built without any sufficient provision for ventilation of the courts or proper light and air, or even with anything like proper attention to sanitary precautions, and I do not believe that they could possibly be put into proper order except by something in the nature of general reconstruction of a considerable part of the area.

12,365. With regard to those districts, were they dealt with by the Birmingham Improvement Scheme of 1876?—Yes.

12,366. Will you please state the circumstances under which that scheme was promoted?—In 1874, I think it was, particular attention was devoted to the subject. At that time the general sanitary state of Birmingham was very unsatisfactory, the death-rate was continually and rapidly increasing. In the five years previous the average had been 23·8 per 1,000 and it rose to 26·8 per 1,000, and showed no sign whatever of diminution. This was due to various causes. In the first place the sewage of the town was in a very bad state, it was not completed; there were a great number of dwelling-houses which were only accommodated by middens, open in many cases to the air, and they were a source of the greatest inconvenience and even of danger to health. The water supply was inadequate and was very largely provided by surface wells, which were found to be upon chemical analysis largely polluted with organic sewage matter. Then there was no proper supervision at that time exercised over the erection of new buildings; the byelaws were altogether inadequate to the purpose, and consequently the new houses which were being built, especially in the outskirts of the town, were being built after what is called the fashion of jerry building, that is to say, with insufficient materials and without any proper attention to sanitary appliances.

12,367. It was in 1875 that the corporation first took action, was it not?—Yes, the attention of the corporation was then seriously directed to the whole of these circumstances, and as a result, in the first place, it acquired the waterworks from a private company who had up to that time supplied the town; since then the supply has been enormously increased at a large expenditure of money; in fact, the water supply has been greatly improved in quality, and at the same time it has been increased in quantity. The surface wells have to a large extent been closed by order of the local authorities and the waterworks water has been supplied in its place. At the same time the undertaking has been so successfully conducted that there has been what would have been a large profit, but which is a balance which has been applied to a reduction in the cost of the water and specially in the case of the smaller houses, inasmuch as the charge for water to the smaller houses has now been very materially reduced. At the same time the sewerage of the town has been completed; the old system of middens has been almost entirely abolished, and very large works have been carried out for the removal and disposal of the sewage. Then again, in 1876 a new code of building byelaws was prepared and adopted. This code, although not exactly the same, is almost the same as what is known as the model code of the Local Government Board; and since that time there has been very careful supervision of every new building; that is to say, no house can be built in the borough without undergoing five separate inspections by the surveyor of the local authority. These byelaws are not only advantageous in securing that proper materials should be used, and that the sanitary arrangements in each house should be sufficient, but they are also of immense advantage in preventing the buildings from being placed in too close proximity and without sufficient provision for ventilation. I observe in the evidence taken before the mayor's committee a curious illustration of that. They quote one case in which there were 20 small houses built before the new byelaws on a piece of land which, under the new byelaws, would only have been allowed to accommodate nine houses.

12,368. The Artizans Dwellings Act was passed in 1875, at the time at which you were mayor of Birmingham, was it not?—Yes.

12,369. And you recommended its adoption in Birmingham, did you not?—Yes. I brought the Act before the Council and recommended the adoption of a very large scheme, which has since been carried into effect. I think it is by far the largest scheme that has been carried into effect under the Artizans Dwellings Act. Speaking for myself, I should like to say that I have always held that the Artizans Dwellings Act is the most important contribution that has been made to the settlement of this question.

12,370. The scheme was one of 43 acres, as originally contemplated, was it not? The scheme affected a district of 93 acres, from which total the town council had authority to select 43¼ acres for purchase. The total cost of the scheme was calculated to be 1,344,000l., of which it was estimated that the ultimate charge that would come upon the rates (that is to say, the deficiency) would be 550,000l. I have got here a plan of the borough and of the scheme, which will show the particular nature of it. That is a plan of the borough (*producing the same*), and I may point out here that that coloured land takes the whole of the district; the small piece marked blue is what is known as the improvement part of the scheme; the piece marked red is known as the unhealthy area, the fact being that one of the great peculiarities of this scheme (which I venture to think is of very great importance in reference to any further operations under the Act) is that we combined what is commonly known as a town's improvement with the reconstruction of the unhealthy area. The best part of the town is here, where the land is coloured blue; that is the centre of the town, close to the great station of the London and North-Western Railway Company. We propose, and have in effect carried a great street from this centre of the town, which is the best part of the town, right through the unhealthy area, and for that purpose we treated the blue land, in the best part of the town, as an approach under the terms of the Artizans Dwellings Act to the unhealthy area (*describing the same*

The Rt. Hon. J. Chamberlain, M.P.

17 June 1884.

The Rt.
Hon. J.
Chamberlain,
M.P.

17 June 1884.

on the plan to the committee). This is a map on a larger scale of the scheme as it has been carried out (*producing the same*); that shows the part of the land which has been actually acquired; the other plan showing the whole of the district that was included from which that land has been selected; and this map also shows the new street. But I attach, as I say, very great importance to this combination of the two portions of the scheme, for this reason : in the first place, there was in our case a distinct sanitary advantage. The object was to carry a wide street through the insanitary district, and thereby to ventilate the whole district, because nothing appears to be more absolutely true than that wide streets contribute to the health of great cities; they are, in fact, the lungs of the place, and in order to get anything like a thorough ventilation it was necessary that this street should be continued into the centre of the town, otherwise it would have come out and been blocked, as it were, by rows of lofty buildings. But in addition to that the combination also had the effect of cheapening what I may call the insanitary part of the scheme, because by bringing this poor district into communication with the centre of the town, additional value was given to all the property after the improvement was made. If we had carried out the insanitary portion of the scheme alone, it would have cost much more in proportion than it is now likely to do. Then there is a third reason, which is not unimportant, and that is that by the combination of these two things the scheme was greatly popularised with the ratepayers. The great cost of these schemes is, of course, the great difficulty that local authorities have to face; but by the combination of the two things, that is to say, by providing what is a necessity for every growing towns, a great town's improvement at the same time, we were able to carry our proposals, I may say, practically with unanimity in the town; there was no opposition whatever made to the proposals which were laid before the town or to the cost which it was understood would be entailed upon the rates.

12,371. There was another peculiarity in the power of selection, was there not ?—Yes. I also attach great importance to that power of selection. It will be seen at once that one advantage of it was that it enabled us to buy land more cheaply. Our object was to buy land by voluntary agreement wherever we could without bringing into operation the compulsory clauses. We were encouraged by what had taken place in Glasgow to believe that that could be done to a considerable extent; and having a right of selection we were able, if people made extortionate demands upon us, to put them aside and to say that we would not buy their property. We had the power of selecting about half of the whole area, and we could say to the owners, "If you ask so high a figure we will pass you by and go to your neighbour," and I have no doubt that that enabled us to buy upon much better terms. The condition of things in the case of the Metropolitan Board of Works, and of other local authorities, has been, I think, that where they have made a scheme embracing a particular area, they have laid themselves under an absolute obligation to purchase the whole of the area, and have by so doing put themselves in the hands of the sellers who have been able to make unreasonable demands with the chance, at all events, that they would get the arbitrators and juries to support them. In our case we again and again told people who came to us with offers of land, "We are willing to purchase on such and such terms, if you object to that we shall put you aside altogether."

12,372. In some cases the owners improved their property without your acquiring it, I believe ?—Yes; that is a further advantage of this power of selection, namely, that we were enabled in a good number of cases to make arrangements with the private owners by which they undertook the improvement of their property, and we agreed that we would leave them in full possession of it. Generally, I may say, the effect has been that for the cost of a scheme to deal with 43 acres we have really improved a district of 93 acres. The streets and all those arrangements have been carried out for the whole district of 93 acres, and the whole of the 93 acres may be said to have been improved and almost reconstructed, although the Corporation only had the charge of purchasing the 43 acres.

12,373. With regard to the land that has been purchased, the Corporation decided, I think, to retain the freehold in their own hands ; is not that so ?—Yes, I observe that in almost all the other schemes, certainly in the London schemes, the local authorities have proposed immediately to resell the property, either for the purpose of workmen's dwellings or such purposes as were permitted under the scheme; they have never held it in their own hands; but we determined from the first that we would become and remain the freeholders of the land, and hold it for the community. That has, I think, a double advantage. In the first place, it renders it unnecessary for us to make anything in the nature of a forced sale. We have not had to throw upon the market an immense quantity of land that must be almost immediately disposed of, and therefore we were enabled to keep up the price of the land; and, secondly, we reserved to ourselves all the improvements, the unearned increment, as it is called, which we anticipate will attach to this land in consequence of the gradual increase and improvement in the town of Birmingham.

12,374. Can you state the general results of the purchase of the property?—The whole of the property has now been purchased in the improvement area; that is to say, on the part coloured blue on our plan. We have bought 22,791 square yards at a cost of 660,000*l*. In the unhealthy area, the part coloured red, we have bought 166,429 yards at a cost of 854,000*l*. Altogether we have spent in the purchase of freehold property over a million and a half of money. Of the total area 39,280 square yards, or more than one-fifth of the whole, will ultimately be devoted to new streets or the widening of old ones.

12,375. Can you compare the estimated cost with the actual cost of the scheme?—No, I cannot make an absolute or exact comparison; I do not know yet exactly what the net cost will be.

12,376. The cost has been greater that it was expected to be, has it not?—Yes, I have no doubt that it has been considerably greater than was originally estimated.

12,377. Can you state the reasons for that increase of cost?—It was owing chiefly to two circumstances. In the first place, the Local Government Board refused to allow us to purchase the land coloured blue, in what is called the improvement part of this scheme, under the terms of the Artizans Dwellings Act; we were obliged to purchase it under the terms of the Lands Clauses Act. I believe that that decision of the Local Government Board is a correct interpretation of the Artizans Dwellings Act; but as to whether it ought to be the law I am very doubtful.

12,378. You are aware that the opposite principle has been recognised in the introduction of the obstructive houses provision?—Undoubtedly; but that applies only to small properties, although the principle is the same; but I would carry it so far as to say that in all purchase of land by a local authority for what are recognised by the Legislature to be great public purposes, they ought to be entitled to purchase upon terms that will secure the fair value and no more to the owners of the property. The Lands Clauses Act secures in every case an excessive value. Then another cause, to which I take a much greater exception, was the decision of the arbitrator, Sir Henry Hunt, when he came to be called in, that all interests in each property to be taken compulsorily must be purchased and dealt with at the same time. I may make that clearer in this way. We intended to purchase the freeholds only and to leave the temporary interests, the remains of leases and short tenancies, to run out unless we could deal with the owners of them on very reasonable terms; but we were forced by Sir Henry Hunt to purchase all these temporary interests, which involved the necessity for giving compensation for the businesses established in connection with these temporary interests. That enabled the owners to make very large demands upon us, which we thought in many cases quite unreasonable, and which certainly added greatly to the cost of the property we had to purchase, after his decision was made known, that is to say, it increased the prices paid under agreement as well.

12,379. (*Mr. Lyulph Stanley.*) Was the Corporation of Birmingham required to serve notices at once for all the land that they took under the Lands Clauses Acts as well as under the Artizans Dwellings Act?—Yes, no doubt.

12,380. (*The Chairman.*) Are you aware that Sir Henry Hunt in his purchases for the Government in this neighbourhood has acted on the opposite principle; that he advised the Government not to take these interests?—I am not aware of that; I am totally unable to understand on what principle he proceeded in our case. I thought it fell hardly upon us, and that it was injurious to the proper execution of the scheme. I would just point out, to enforce that for a moment, that after all one of the most difficult interests to purchase is the interest in a business; it is a speculative thing; the moment a man has to value his business he puts upon it the most extraordinary valuation; he makes all sorts of sanguine calculations as to what he anticipates that he will do, and generally appears to be convinced that he cannot do the same thing even though he moves only a few yards further off. The result is that when the case goes before a jury or an arbitrator, although he may not get what he asks, he always gets a vast deal more than the property is really worth. If we were allowed to say to him, "You have only got a 10 years' interest in this place, it is not necessary to purchase before

The Rt. Hon. J. Chamberlain, M.P.

17 June 1884.

96   APPENDIX I.

The Rt.
Hon. J.
Chamberlain,
M.P.

17 June 1881.

the end of 10 years, and therefore we will wait until they have run out when you will have to find another location," I am quite sure that we should have very much more moderate returns.

12,381. (*Lord Carrington.*) There is nothing in the Act of Parliament to compel that, is there ?—No.

12,382. (*Mr. Lyulph Stanley.*) How could the arbitrator compel you to serve notices to treat ?—Under the Act you are bound to serve notices to everybody; that is a statutory obligation.

12,383. That is so under the Artizans Dwellings Act ?—Yes.

12,384. But I am asking you under the other Act, the Lands Clauses Act ?—It is just the same; we dealt with it under the Artizans Dwellings Act, although not on the terms for valuation under the Artizans Dwellings Act; we bought the blue land as an approach to the unsanitary area.

12,385. (*The Chairman.*) Can you estimate what was the amount of the additional charge that was thrown upon you by the adoption of that principle by the arbitrator; what was the additional charge thrown upon you by this decision ?—I cannot say how much these decisions cost us; I can only give a rough estimate, which I would not wish to rely upon absolutely, as to what I consider to be the excess of the cost of the whole scheme. I measure the excess of the cost by this: I think it is an excessive cost when we pay more than would have been paid for the property if it had been bought as an ordinary purchase in the open market, assuming that there were willing purchasers as well as willing sellers. Upon that footing I consider that we have paid under the Artizans Dwellings Act, even with all the advantage of it, some 300,000*l.* or 400,000*l.* more than the property would have fetched if it had been disposed of as private property.

12,386. (*Mr. Goschen.*) Did they produce their income tax returns in the case of those businesses you had to deal with ?—I do not recollect whether that has been done; but, as you know, that has never been found to be a check either to an extravagant demand or an extravagant award. Again and again where property has been taken by local authorities, if they have been able to show that the income tax has been exceedingly small, that has not been allowed to preclude the owner from obtaining upon a very different scale of calculation when he came to be compensated.

12,387. (*The Chairman.*) Have you seen the report by Mr. Harrison to the Local Government Board upon the subject of the various provincial schemes, including that of Birmingham ?—Yes, I have, and I observe one paragraph in the report which I do not understand; but if I correctly apprehend it, Mr. Harrison seems to be of opinion that in spite of the prices we have had to pay, the scheme will not ultimately involve any cost to the ratepayers of Birmingham. If that is his meaning, I differ from him entirely; I do not think that we have any reason to doubt that the original estimate will not at all events be materially departed from, and that the ultimate cost will be probably half a million at least. I should say that up to the present time the deficiency, in the few years since we commenced the scheme, has already been 187,553*l.*, of which the rates have provided 121,607*l.*; and the annual deficit shown by the last annual statement of accounts was 38,000*l.* That of course is excessive; because we have cleared a great quantity of land, and it is not all at present re-let. As the re-letting goes on this annual deficit will be very considerably decreased, and will in time entirely disappear; but still, as I say, I imagine that the net result of the whole transaction will be a loss of something like 500,000*l.* and the annual charge upon the rates will be something between 3*d.* and 4*d.* in the £. That would bring up the total rates of Birmingham to 6*s.* 9*d.* in the £.

12,388. At the end of 60 years the whole freehold will be part of the town, will it not ?—Yes, because we have to provide a sinking fund that will pay the whole sum off in 60 years, and the freehold therefore will belong to us then, and the absolute property will come to the Corporation in about 20 years later, because the land is now being let on long leases of 75 years.

12,389. At the end of 80 years the district will be the Corporation's property ?—The Corporation will be the absolute owners of the freehold of 43 acres in the heart of the town.

12,390. Have you any possible means of contrasting the sums which have been actually paid under agreement, and the prices awarded under arbitration ?—I cannot make a perfectly trustworthy estimate. I should of course point out that from the moment it became known what kind of valuation Sir Henry Hunt would make all our agreements were controlled by that knowledge, and prices went up after his first arbitration, until even where we made a voluntary agreement we had to pay on a higher scale than we had been paying before. I have had some cases taken out, to see if

I could make out some calculation, of the property purchased under the arbitrator, and of similar property in almost the same neighbourhood bought by agreement, and so far as I can judge there is a difference always in favour of agreement which ranges from 10 to 50 per cent., and in one instance is as much as 100 per cent.; but I do not wish to press that very much. I am convinced that the prices paid under arbitration are higher, but I cannot really say how much.

12,391. What number of cases were taken before a jury?—Only nine cases.

12,392. Were they taken by the Corporation or by the owners?—Two cases were taken by the Corporation, and in both cases there was a very considerable reduction, and seven cases were taken by the owners, in all of which there was some increase obtained; the net result of all the appeals was an increase of 3,723*l*. in the valuation; it is no considerable difference.

12,393. What were the general sanitary results of the scheme, besides the opening of the new streets?—Altogether 1,368 artizans' dwellings were acquired in the whole area, and they accommodated at the time the scheme was projected a population of about 9,000, the total artizan population in the whole 93 acres, that is, the whole district, being about 13,500. Of the 1,368 dwellings which the Corporation acquired, we have already removed for new streets 150. We have destroyed as unfit for habitation 418; we have closed as unfit for habitation 53, and these houses will be ultimately pulled down or completely repaired; 28 have been removed for the ventilation of courts, as being obstructive buildings within the meaning of Torrens' Act, and the whole of the remainder, all the houses still occupied, have been thoroughly repaired, and improved; the courts have been paved, and in many cases lighted with gas at the expense of the Corporation; and water has been supplied and the sewage arrangements perfected. Altogether, in the four or five years during which we have been in possession of the property we have spent 30,000*l*. upon repairs alone. That I would point out is of course a great deal more than could have been spent by any private owner holding this property with the intention of making a fair interest upon his investment. He could not by any possibility have laid out so large a sum of money as the Corporation felt themselves justified in doing.

12,394. What has been the effect on the death-rate?—The effect on the death-rate has been very remarkable indeed. The eight most insanitary streets in the area before the scheme averaged for the three years before the proposals were in operation 53·2 per thousand; since then, in the last three years, the same streets have averaged 21·3 per thousand, and the scheme in part, with the other causes to which I have referred, throughout the borough of Birmingham have led to a general reduction of the death-rate throughout the borough, from 26 in the thousand for the three years 1873, 1874, and 1875 to 20 in the thousand for the three years 1880, 1881, and 1882.

12,395. You would probably think that this latter reduction, that is to say, this general reduction of the death-rate in the borough, is largely owing to other causes?—Yes, certainly. The scheme of course applied to the district in which the death-rate was highest, and has affected the general average.

12,396. You are aware of the fact that there has been a general reduction of the death-rate in nearly all provincial towns during those years?—Yes, but not so much. As I say, the death-rate of Birmingham had been rising considerably at the time these measures were taken, consequently the improvement has been more marked there than I think in any other town.

12,397. What has been done as regards reconstruction?—Practically nothing. I should say that the scheme included the purchase of a small piece of land, marked on the plan, which is some distance from the scheme, but in close enough proximity to it, and which has been much cheaper than the rest of the land. The Corporation bought it with a special view to securing the provision of the artizans' dwellings upon it, but after they cleared the land they found it almost impossible to get any offers for it for that purpose, and ultimately a considerable portion was sold to the School Board for the erection of a board school, with a playground attached to it; but a portion, amounting altogether to 4120 square yards, has been now let for the erection of artizans' dwellings, and that is really all that has been done in the way of reconstruction.

12,398. Do you consider, for the reasons which you have previously given, that that is not a matter of great importance in Birmingham?—I think it is a matter of no importance at all. We found, although we could hardly have assumed it beforehand, but experience has shown us that we may safely rely upon private enterprise to provide all the dwellings necessary and adequate, both in quality as well as quantity. I have got these

The Rt. Hon. J. Chamberlain, M.P.

17 June 1884.

o

The Rt. Hon. J. Chamberlain, M.P.

17 June 1884.

particulars with regard to it. I find that where the houses were destroyed in the unhealthy area, in most cases the inhabitants provided for themselves elsewhere long before the houses were pulled down; in only 137 cases were the tenants actually displaced by the improvement; they were all offered accommodation in close proximity, but only 34 accepted the offer. I think that is due to the fact, probably, that the result of an improvement of this kind is very greatly to change the whole character of the district; that whereas it was necessary for the working classes to be housed in close proximity to the factories and other similar buildings which were upon the area, now that these factories have given place to warehouses or shops and public buildings, the workpeople have followed the factories to other parts; at all events, only 34 accepted the offer for provision upon the spot. Then I find, speaking generally for the whole borough, that the erection of new houses for the artizan class has for a long time past exceeded the demand; that in seven years, from 1876 to 1882, additional accommodation of artizans' dwellings has been provided for 45,000 people, while the total increase in population of all classes, not artizans alone, was only 36,000 during the same time.

12,399. Then the mayor's inquiry shows a good many houses empty?—Apparently 5,273 houses were void at the time of the mayor's inquiry, a few months ago, of the class inhabited by artizans rated at 10l. and under.

12,400. So far as Birmingham and similar towns are concerned, are you of opinion that the whole of the greatest evil which exists can be satisfactorily dealt with under the plan pursued?—Yes, I think so. I consider that if schemes of this kind can be carried out at a moderate cost, and if they were in all cases accompanied by proper byelaws, that would prevent the re-creation of the evils which they were intended to prevent, the question, so far as provincial towns are concerned, might be considered as finally solved.

12,401. (Sir Richard Cross.) Under the Act of 1875, do you mean?—Yes.

12,402. (The Chairman.) Then so far as regards the growing up of such evils in future, you consider that laws, and byelaws which can be made under the existing law should be sufficient to prevent that?—Yes, I think so.

12,403. You think that good building byelaws would prevent the growth of these evils?—I think so; the only thing that stands in the way (and it is a most serious obstacle which for the last few years has absolutely prevented anything being done under the Act) is the excessive cost. We indulged in Birmingham in this tremendous luxury of an improvement scheme to reconstruct a single district of the town at the cost of half a million of money; but we have exhausted all our capacities in that respect; we cannot undertake to burden the ratepayers any more for that purpose; and unless any means can be found by which similar schemes can be carried out at much less cost, we have done all that this generation at any rate will be able to do, I should say.

12,404. Have you considered the various proposals made for reducing the excessive cost?—Yes.

12,405. (The Prince of Wales.) May I ask why these schemes have been so very expensive; are the buildings very expensive, or is it owing to the builders?—I think, Sir, it is because in all cases in which public authorities are called upon to acquire private property they have been called upon to pay an excessive price.

12,406. (The Chairman.) With regard to reducing the excessive cost in future, have you considered the proposals for granting State money in the way of loans?—Yes, I should like to say upon that, you are aware, no doubt, that in 1879 an Act was passed for the amendment of the Public Works Loans Act, which Act imposed very much more stringent conditions than were originally contemplated by the Artizans' Dwellings Act of 1875. I recollect predicting in my place in the House of Commons, when that Act was under consideration, that if it passed in its present form no scheme would be proposed by any corporation; and my prediction proved to be true. The Act was passed with some slight modifications and the result is that the terms were so onerous that no corporation would be likely to avail itself of it. That has not had, however, all the effect I anticipated, and it does not entirely account for the fact that no schemes have been proposed. Since then a great advance has been made in enabling corporations of large towns to issue consolidated loans, and the result is that great towns like Birmingham, Manchester, Liverpool, and London can borrow almost as cheaply as the State can lend to them. We can borrow in Birmingham at $3\frac{1}{2}$ per cent. and the Metropolitan Board of Works borrows at 3 per cent.; the State could not lend at less than 3 per cent., and the difference therefore is so slight, that so far as we are concerned, I do not think any alteration of the Public Works

APPENDIX I.

Loans Act would be now of advantage. But I have no doubt whatever that as regards the smaller corporations who can only borrow, owing to the smallness of their demands, having no market for their stocks, at 4½ and 5 per cent., in their case no doubt the Public Works Loans Act of 1879 has killed the Artizans' Dwellings Act, and that until it is altered back again, until they are allowed to borrow at something like 3½ per cent., they will not undertake any scheme.

12,407. Sir Reginald Welby in his evidence with regard to this branch of the subject appeared to throw out a suggestion which I believe has been made before a committee which is at present considering the question of harbours, to the effect that money might be lent at a cheaper rate where there was a double security. I suppose he referred to the security of the rates and of the land and buildings upon which money could be advanced; have you formed any opinion with regard to that suggestion?—I should approve of that.

12,408. As regards other suggestions, you have already alluded to the provisions of the Artizans' Dwellings Act for the valuation of the property, and you have already spoken of what you consider the mistake made by the arbitrators in their mode of acting upon its provisions; have you any further remark that you would wish to make upon that head or can you suggest any amendment of the law in that respect?—I will just remind you of the terms of the Artizans' Dwellings Act of 1875; that is the original Act. It provided that the estimated value of the lands within the unhealthy area shall be based upon the fair market value as estimated at the time of the valuation being made, due regard being had to the nature and the condition of the property, to the probable duration of the buildings, and the state of repairs thereof, and of all circumstances affecting such value without any additional allowance for compulsory purchase. If I had had myself to draw the Act, I do not think I could have improved upon the terms of it; because, so far as the intention of the Act goes, it appears manifest that the object of the authors and the object of Parliament was that the owners of this property should only obtain its fair value and nothing more; but, as a matter of fact, and in practice, they have succeeded in spite of the Act in obtaining a vast deal more.

12,409. (*Sir Richard Cross.*) That is the fault of the arbitrators, and not of the Act, is it not?—I do not think it is the fault of the Act. If I had had to deal with the thing, without the experience of the Act, I do not think I could have devised words which should better carry out the fair consideration in these cases. At all events we are now face to face with the fact that whatever the intention of the Act, and however it is worded, these excessive prices have been given under the Act; and I consider that we ought to go on altering the formula until we have found one which arbitrators will interpret in the evident sense of the intention of the promoters of this legislation; and the formula I would supply I will tell you. I should, perhaps, say before coming to my proposal that I am aware that there has been an amendment Act passed in the year 1882, the chief result of which was to strike out the words having regard to all the circumstances affecting such value. I should myself have supposed that those words were very properly introduced in the original Act, and that to leave them out might have even had the effect of increasing the valuation; but I suppose the amendment was due to evidence given by the arbitrators that they had been influenced by those words to increase their valuation. We have yet to see what the effect of the omission of those words will be, because I am not aware that any scheme has been carried out since the amendment Act was passed.

12,410. Those words were introduced at the suggestion of Mr. Cawley, and with regard to the evidence of arbitrators, they seemed to have taken into consideration, under those words, the prospective increase in value which the property would have, owing to the rest of the bad neighbourhood being taken away, so that the owner of a particular spot was practically receiving benefit from what was done by the Corporation by improving the district in which the spot was placed. That was the origin of those words, and that was the object of doing away with them in 1882?—I am afraid the arbitrators never excluded from their minds the improvement to the property that would be due to the scheme, and have given a prospective value to the unhealthy property which made the scheme necessary in consequence of their impression that it would be increased in value when the improvement was effected.

12,411. You have not mentioned the alteration in the Act of 1879, which was considerable?—At the moment I have forgotten what it was.

12,412. Here is a copy of the Act, if you will read the third section?—"On the occasion of assessing the compensation payable under any

The Rt. Hon. J Chamberlain, M.P.

17 June 1884.

o 2

The Rt.
Hon. J.
Chamberlain,
M.P.

17 June 1881.

improvement scheme in respect of any house or premises situate within an unhealthy area, evidence shall be receivable by the arbitrator to prove that at the date of the confirming Act authorizing such schemes, or at some previous date not earlier than the date of the official representation in which the scheme originated, such house or premises was, by reason of its unhealthy state or by reason of overcrowding or otherwise, in such a condition as to be a nuisance within the meaning of the Acts relating to nuisances; and if the arbitrator is satisfied that, from either of such causes as aforesaid, such house or premises was at such dates as aforesaid, or either of them, a nuisance as aforesaid, he shall then determine what would have been the value of such house or premises, supposing the nuisance to have been abated, and what would have been the expense of abating the nuisance, and the amount of compensation payable in respect of such house or premises shall be an amount equal to the estimated value of the house or premises after the nuisance was abated and after deducting the estimated expense of abating the nuisance." I must say I am afraid that would not help us very materially. The ordinary case is this: you have a house which at the present moment is a nuisance, insanitary, and dangerous to health. Under that provision there would have to be deducted from the value of the house the cost of putting it into sanitary repair; but then the arbitrator will not be content to give the value of the house as it stood, and for the purposes for which it was then used; he will take into account the probability that that house, or the land upon which it stands, may subsequently be used for other purposes, such as factories, warehouses, new streets, or something of that kind; and the value given, therefore, is something altogether different and out of proportion to the value if the property be regarded in connexion with all its existing incidents.

12,413. (*The Chairman.*) Your desire in short is that the arbitrator should be required to give only such value as willing sellers would obtain in the market supposing there were willing purchasers? —Yes; I desire in every case that the man should not be allowed to obtain a larger price from the community than he would from a willing private purchaser, in all cases in which the community, as I say, have sufficient public reasons for claiming his property for expropriating it.

12,414. What is your view with regard to the power of appeal in these cases?—I should abolish the right of appeal. I doubt whether these appeals are of great advantage to anybody; they increase the uncertainty enormously; they increase the cost of professional services, and I should be inclined, having established a satisfactory tribunal in the first place, to make its decisions in all cases final. I should like also (and I consider this of great importance) to establish a fixed scale of professional charges in connexion with the working of the Artizans' Dwellings Act. Similar provisions to those have been made in connexion with the Bankruptcy Act, for instance, and I do not see why they should not be inserted in the statute in connexion with these improvements.

12,415. Could you suggest to us who could give evidence upon that point of the scale of professional charges from your experience in the working of the Bankruptcy Act provisions?—Yes, I think I could easily procure evidence on that point.

12,416. Then it is also an opinion which you have expressed elsewhere, I believe, that all lands benefited by the improvement should be specially taxed and contribute towards it?—Yes; I think if you would consider the scheme I have been describing as it appears on the map, you will see that this expenditure of half a million of money upon that district must have an immense effect in improving and increasing the value of land immediately around it. I think that the persons who are so benefited, even if they are benefited without their consent, should be called upon to pay a special contribution to the costs of the scheme.

12,417. That was the plan described, I think, by Mr. Shaw-Lefevre in his speech of 1875 on Sir Richard Cross's Bill; he spoke of a plan that existed in America which is described there as "betterment"? —Yes; it exists in several of the American States, and in New York especially, and we have also a precedent for it in English legislation on the same subject. In Torrens' Act I think there is a provision that where an obstructive building is removed under the Act, and where its removal benefits property belonging to the same owner, the estimated value of the improvement to the remaining property shall be deducted or deductable from the compensation payable for the obstructive building.

12,418. (*Mr. Lyulph Stanley.*) That is under the Artizans' Dwellings Act, 1882?—Yes; that really is under the Artizans' and Labourers' Dwellings Act, 1882.

12,419. (*The Chairman.*) Would that be, in your opinion, a scale to be provided for by local inquiry by some officer, or how would you arrive at it?—I should proceed as we do now, only widening the scope of the inquiry. The inspector of the Local Government Board, in considering the scheme to be made, would take also into view the proposal by the local authority to levy a special tax either within a certain radius or upon certain properties which they allege would be greatly benefited by the improvement; he would hear the persons interested and would decide according to the merits of the case. I take it for granted that such a tax would never be more than a proportion of the total improvement, but I would levy the rate in higher measure upon the persons who derive a distinct and direct advantage from the improvement than I would upon the community generally who only have the advantage of the general improvement in the health of the town.

12,420. There are, of course, examples of proportional rates over a portion of the area of the levying authority at the present time?—Yes, there are frequently cases of that kind. For instance, in Leeds, I think that most of their local improvements have been charged to special districts.

12,421. In the case of a clause of this kind in the amending Act of 1882, the clause applies only to the improvement of property belonging to the same owner?—So I understand, and that seems to me to be illogical. If it is fair to charge it upon the same owner I cannot conceive why it is not fair to charge it, when the benefit is equal, to another owner.

12,422. (*Mr. Goschen.*) Have you considered whether that should be charged upon the owner or the occupier?—The cost of the improvement would be fairly chargeable upon the owner and occupier; of course, assuming that the occupier has a real tangible interest; if he were merely a casual tenant I should not consider the benefit of the improvement, but if the occupier were occupying on a long lease it would be just as fair as to charge it upon him as upon the ground landlord. That brings me to another point which is the only other recommendation I have to make. With regard to all these improvement rates I cannot understand why the ground landlord should escape from his share of the contribution; at present it is charged upon the occupier. It appears to me that the ground landlord is benefited immensely by the general improvement to the place to which the improvement contributes, and I do not see why he should escape scot free.

12,423. (*The Chairman.*) To pass to certain other matters, you are not yourself practically acquainted, I think, with the working of the byelaws in Birmingham under the 90th section of the Public Health Act?—With regard to lodging houses, do you mean?

12,424. Yes, not common lodging houses?—My impression is that much more is being done under those byelaws than was done at the time when I was connected with the town council.

12,425. Perhaps you have heard that there are 210 houses on the register at the present time under the byelaws in Birmingham, and that the byelaws are now under revision?—So I understand.

12,426. To pass to another question to which I referred at the beginning of your evidence, I wish to ask you a few questions with regard to the provision of railway accommodation for the working classes in connexion with this matter which the Commission has to inquire into. There has been some evidence given here by the secretary of the railway department of the Board of Trade, Mr. Calcraft, on the subject of the Act of last session, relating to workmen's trains, a matter which has, of course, great importance in London owing to considerations which you yourself stated of the great distance between the centre of the town and the places where many of the workmen have to live; can you state the general principles upon which the Board of Trade proceeds in reference to this matter?—Yes. My attention has been called to Mr. Calcraft's evidence and to the questions asked him; he, of course, is much better acquainted than I am with the details of our work, but the general principles have come before me. I should say in the first place that I do not understand that the Act of last session was in the nature of a bargain between the State and the railway companies, the railway companies undertaking to give as consideration for the repeal of the passenger duty additional accommodation in workmen's trains, because the repeal of the passenger duty can be justified on public grounds quite independently of any question of the provision of workmen's trains; but at the same time the opportunity was taken to give greater powers to the Board of Trade with the expectation no doubt that they would from time to time apply a pressure to the railway companies to increase this accommodation. The question of the principle upon which we are to proceed is of extreme importance. We might proceed upon one of two principles. We might undertake in every case the initiative, and we might examine for ourselves into the provision made. We might determine what we thought to be adequate

The Rt. Hon. J. Chamberlain, M.P.

17 June 1884.

102   APPENDIX I.

The Rt.
Hon. J.
Chamberlain,
M.P.

17 June 1881.

provision, and we might enforce it upon the railway companies. We have tremendous penalties in our power if we choose to enforce them. That, I think, would be a most imprudent step for the Board of Trade or a Government department to take; it would practically mean our undertaking the administration of railways, and in that case we should have to proceed upon hypotheses in every case, upon hypotheses with which we have much less practical acquaintance than the railway companies themselves. We should have to proceed upon the assumption of their being unwilling to afford this accommodation; it would be necessary for us to enforce a minimum which in every case would tend to become the maximum, and I believe the result would be that less accommodation would be provided than if we leave a great deal to the initiative of the companies. Then we should have to settle what constitutes a workmen's train; the only definition I can give is that it is a train that is run for their convenience at certain early hours in the day, in the early morning, and at certain moderate and reasonable prices, and under the Act we have to settle what are reasonable prices. To do that we must examine the accounts of the company to make ourselves acquainted with the costs of these trains, to ascertain whether the proposed rate of fare would or would not be reasonable. Then there is a still greater difficulty, namely, that if we were to enforce those trains we must interpose them into the regular traffic of the company, and we might upset the whole of their traffic arrangements. We should at once have to do what is the most difficult part of the work of a traffic manager of a railway (who has the most difficult administration, I venture to think, of any subject of the Queen) if we were to take that work from his shoulders and put it upon ours. Nothing but the most tremendous necessity would, in my opinion, justify anything like that sort of interference on the part of the Board of Trade, and I should strongly oppose on behalf of the Board of Trade undertaking any work of the kind. I do not think that any necessity does exist for it; I think the evidence we have shows that we may safely rely upon the voluntary action of the railway companies, stimulated as it will be from time to time by a certain amount of judicious pressure. What the railway companies have done is very remarkable. I am not quite certain whether Mr. Calcraft brought the figures to the notice of the Commission, but I find for instance, an enormous increase in the third-class traffic. At one time Parliament thought it necessary to impose a statutory obligation upon the company to make ample provision for third-class traffic; the voluntary work of the companies has long ago passed far beyond anything which Parliament imposed.

12,427. Does not that rather answer your own observation that the minimum would become the maximum; in that particular case it struck me while you were giving that answer that you had a case where Parliament had laid down an instruction which had been vastly exceeded?—The interests of the companies in the case of third-class traffic is so clearly manifest that their voluntary efforts have passed altogether beyond any minimum which the State could possibly have imposed. I find, for instance, that since the year 1852, that is to say, within about 30 years, while the first and second-class traffic has increased less than three-fold, and is now a diminishing quantity, the third-class traffic has increased 15 times, and continues to augment with more and more rapidity. As regards workmen's trains, I think it is very doubtful whether it is to the pecuniary interest of the company to establish those trains; I doubt whether in most cases those trains can possibly be said to pay, and not only so, but they are extremely inconvenient. It is easy to establish an early train for workmen at 4 or 5 o'clock in the morning, but they have to be brought back again at all hours in the afternoon by the ordinary trains. The Great Eastern manager, for instance, complains, I think, of the serious disorganization of the ordinary traffic in consequence of the large number of workmen who return by the afternoon trains. Therefore in this case, no doubt some pressure is necessary, but if that pressure takes the form of an arbitrary hard and fast line, my opinion is that the railway companies will confine themselves strictly to that and will not go beyond it. As a matter of fact, I think owing quite as much to the pressure of public opinion as to their own interests, they have gone far beyond their legal obligations. The trains which they are required by law to run have been eleven in number over a mileage distance of 50 miles, while the railway companies have actually provided 107 trains over a mileage of 704 miles. Now, however, the circumstances are changed to some extent, as I say, by the passing of the Act of last session. What the Board of Trade have done is this: Immediately after the passing of the Act we issued a circular to all the railway companies, asking them what they were doing both in regard to "1d. a mile traffic," as it is called and also in regard to workmen's trains? We received replies, which

APPENDIX I.

showed generally that in every case the companies were doing a great deal more than they had previously been compelled by law to do, although perhaps not all that it may be desirable to press them to do. Then I have had my attention specially directed to the case of the three companies which were mentioned, I think, in Mr. Calcraft's evidence, and which at the present time do not run any workmen's trains from the metropolis. The companies which I understand to be specially referred to were the Great Northern, the Midland, and the London and North-Western.

12,428. The companies that do not run workmen's trains I understood to be the Midland, the London and North-Western, and the Great Western?—At all events, my attention was especially directed to those three companies, and I caused a letter to be written to each of those companies, calling their attention to the evidence that had been given and the questions that had been asked, and inquiring what they were doing, and what they had to say upon the subject. I have received a reply from the Great Northern, in which they state that they are now running workmen's trains from Palmer's Green, Barnet, and High Barnet, stopping at all intermediate stations, to Moorgate Street in the early morning, at fares from a farthing to a halfpenny per mile, and that the workmen are brought back by the ordinary trains in the afternoon. The London and North-Western say that they are not running workmen's trains from London, and that they have never had any application for them, but they expressed their willingness to give their favourable consideration to any application which might be made on the subject, either by a public authority or by any large body of workmen. The Midland Company say that they do not run workmen's trains, but they point out that they have done far more perhaps than any other railway company in the provision of cheap accommodation, since they attach third-class carriages to every train at fares of one penny per mile ; but they also express their willingness to give favourable consideration to any proposals which may be made to them.

12,429. This action is a mere second action on your part; you did take action in October of last year, did you not?—We took action in October last year; we sent out a preliminary circular inquiring what all the companies were doing, and we always intended from time to time to put additional pressure on. I should say now, in order that the particular case of those companies may be at once discharged, that I propose to request Major Marindin, who reported upon the subject some time ago, to make a special report upon the necessity of workmen's trains upon the Midland and the London and North-Western lines ; and if he reports in favour of such provision, I have not the least doubt in the world that the companies will at once agree to it.

The Rt. Hon. J. Chamberlain, M.P.

17 June 1884.

12,430. Certain suggestions have been made here upon various points as amendments of the law, and I should like to ask your opinion with regard to some of them. If there are any of them which you have not thought of, or as to which you do not care to answer, perhaps you will kindly say so at once, and answer only as to such as you may have considered, and as may have been brought before you. Some of them concern railways. One is that in every case where railway companies obtain statutory power to demolish houses, increased provision for workmen's trains should be made by law. That would be partly covered by the general answer which you gave just now, I suppose, in which you deprecated direct interference by law in laying down the number of trains ?—Yes, I think we have sufficient power now to enforce any provision which may ultimately be found to be expedient ; and I do not consider that it would be desirable to complicate the statute book with particular obligations which might seem to be unfair to particular companies.

12,431. (*Mr. Lyulph Stanley.*) Does that answer apply to the obligation to re-house ?—That is a different question altogether.

12,432. (*The Chairman.*) To come to that point to which reference has just been made, it has been proposed that what is known as the Shaftesbury Standing Order should be improved. The standing orders at the present moment, as you know, not always in the same terms, but in terms which resemble one another in the companies Acts, throw upon the railway companies what at first sight looks like the necessity to re-house the persons whom they displace ; but the language of the clause is such, taking its usual terms, that it can very easily be evaded, and it has been suggested that the standing orders of both Houses should be improved. At the present moment the duty of making a return of the number of persons to be displaced by any scheme is thrown upon the promoters, and it is often notoriously grossly incorrect. It has been suggested that the return should be made to the local authority ; that the local authority should report upon it ; and that it should go through the Home Office in the metropolis, or even through the

The Rt.
Hon. J.
Chamberlain,
M.P.

17 June 1884.

Local Government Board in the provinces, to the Committee of the House of Lords or the House of Commons, as the case may be, with a report upon it by one or other of those offices at the cost of the promoters. What would be your opinion as to that suggestion?—It would be necessary I think, in addition to indicate very definitely that the report was to state the number of houses inhabited by the working classes before the scheme was proposed; because the moment a scheme of this kind is threatened, the people voluntarily depart from their houses, knowing that if they do not do so they will be disturbed. In some cases they depart because they are bribed to depart by the body which requires the land.

12,433. That matter also arises in connexion with another suggestion. It has been said that the railway companies evade, as you have just suggested, the obligation to re-house by getting rid of the people before the scheme actually takes effect; and that, therefore, the obligation should be to re-house as many as were recently displaced?—Certainly it would be perfectly futile unless something of that sort were provided. Then there is another point which is equally important. You must not only require the railway company to re-house, but you must require them to give this accommodation permanently. Otherwise, what I am told in some cases railway companies have done, is to provide such accommodation, but six months afterwards to give all the tenants notice, and to turn the accommodation into warehouses or to some other purpose.

12,434. If you throw upon a railway company the obligation of actually themselves re-housing, should you think that the houses so built ought to be handed over to the local authority to manage?—I think that the railway company ought undoubtedly to be precluded from using them for any other purpose without the consent of the local authority.

12,435. It has been suggested that displacement and re-housing should be made compulsorily gradual; that is to say (of course this is a recommendation which specially applies to the case of London), that where, for instance, a scheme of metropolitan improvement, or a scheme under Sir Richard Cross's Act is adopted, the whole area should not be cleared at once, but that a portion only should be cleared, and that building should take place upon it before the people were completely driven out?—If you have a trustworthy local authority I should leave the discretion absolutely in them, because it is evident that in some cases it would be greatly to their advantage to make a partial clearance. That has been the case in Birmingham. On the other hand, it might seriously prejudice the success of a scheme if the new roads or streets required were not allowed to be carried out in the first instance. The making of a new street may be a necessity in order to develop the scheme. The circumstances vary so much in every case that you are not safe unless you leave a large discretion to the responsible authority.

12,436. The following clause has been suggested to us by Sir Sydney Waterlow :—"Provided always that the sites which may be acquired by the local authority under this Act for the erection of dwellings for the labouring classes shall be let or sold by the local authority before the houses have been pulled down, and where possible before the occupiers have been disturbed, and the lessor or purchaser, as the case may be, shall be required to erect new buildings on the site thereof in accordance with plans and specifications to be approved by the local authority; and shall be required to clear an area not exceeding one-third of the site and erect the said new buildings thereon fit for occupation before proceeding to remove the tenants and demolish the houses on the remainder of the area leased or purchased by him"?—That seems to be a suggestion based on the assumption that these schemes are to be very small schemes, which no doubt has been practically true in the case of the metropolitan schemes. If you are dealing with a small square block of very valuable land, it may be well to make such a limitation as is proposed by Sir Sydney Waterlow; but it would be an impossible limitation in the case of a great scheme such as ours, and I am convinced that these schemes will never be effective, and can never be conducted economically unless on a very large scale. I do not believe in these bit-by-bit improvements; I think that they are extravagant in cost, and a mere scratching upon the surface hardly worth undertaking.

12,437. Passing over one or two purely metropolitan suggestions that have been made, it has been suggested to us that the building byelaws of many urban authorities are unsatisfactory on one point as to which those of the Metropolitan Board of Works are satisfactory, namely, as regards the power to prevent *culs de sac*, or closed courts; has your attention ever been called to that point?—Yes, it is very important where possible to got through ventilation.

APPENDIX I.   105

12,438. Your own byelaws at Birmingham are satisfactory, as I understand from what you have said, as to the open space to be left in the rear of the houses?—I think so, entirely. It must be remembered that in Birmingham the houses are not lofty; as I have already said, there are no flats there.

12,439. Therefore that again must be looked upon as being mainly a metropolitan question?—I think so; and that also must be treated with great tenderness, because if you are going to require very large open spaces in London, of course you will enormously increase the cost of any improvements.

12,440. At the same time, your attention may have been called to the fact that in the Waterlow Buildings and in the Peabody Buildings the number of people to the acre is very large indeed; do you consider that that is dangerous to health?—The best answer I think to that question is that the death rate in those buildings is 14 per 1000.

12,441. The mortality, and especially the infant mortality, in one or two of the blocks has been very high?—Some time ago I looked into the subject, and I was then assured that the average death rate since the commencement of the Peabody Buildings was between 13 and 14 per 1000, the average death rate for London being, I think, 21 per 1000.

12,442. There has been one case of the Peabody Buildings where the death rate has been very high?—But it seems to me that if you can reduce the death rate to anything like that amount the improvement is so great that you need not consider it necessary to press for further improvement so as to make the work almost impossible.

12,443. I do not know whether your attention has been called to an Act which has been a dead letter; I refer to one of Lord Shaftesbury's two Acts of 1851. Lord Shaftesbury, in the year 1851, promoted the Lodging Houses Act, which has been a great success, and he also promoted an Act giving power to local authorities to acquire land for the purpose of artizans' dwellings, and to construct and work the dwellings?—I think that Act is sure to remain a dead letter, because the reasons which I have given why it is proved to be quite unnecessary in Birmingham to rehouse the whole of the people disturbed by the improvement scheme, would apply to any proposal that in any part of the town we should erect artizans' dwellings. If we do so, we must at once interfere with private enterprise, which is already doing more than we want.

12,444. A suggestion has been made (I do not know whether you are aware of it) for acting upon this principle by means of a private Act in the case of Liverpool?—I should think it was a most unwise thing to do. The only thing that I approve of is what has been done by the Glasgow Corporation, where they have erected lodging-houses which have been very successful.

12,445-6. (*Mr. Lyulph Stanley.*) Is not the Corporation of Birmingham now the direct landlord of upwards of 600 of those working-class houses that you have bought up and repaired?—Certainly.

12,447. (*The Chairman.*) Passing again to another subject, are you acquainted with the latter part of section 5 of the Artizans' Dwellings Act, which runs in the following words:—"It may also provide for such scheme or any part thereof being carried out and effected by the person entitled to the first estate of freehold in any property subject to the scheme, or with the concurrence of such person, under the superintendence and control of the local authority, and upon such terms and conditions to be embodied in the scheme as may be agreed upon between the local authority and such person?"—Yes.

12,448. That has been a dead letter, I think?—No, not in Birmingham. There are some very large plots of land with which we have dealt in that way. The whole of that piece, and all this piece (*pointing to the plan*), are under agreement with the trustees to be improved as soon as they get the freehold, and they were excluded from the scheme upon that understanding.

12,449. Do you think that there is ground for putting increased pressure by law upon ground landlords with regard to the state of their properties; for instance, has your attention been called to such a case as that which exists in one part of London, as to which we have had a good deal of evidence before this Commission, where a very large property lying together so declined in its condition for a great number of years, and towards the expiration of the long leases has come down into an extremely bad condition, that not being a case of merely a small patch which could easily be dealt with, but of a vast property consisting of 1000 or so of houses lying together so as to degrade a whole neighbourhood?—I do not understand from your question what the power of the ground landlord in that case is. The leases have not fallen in, as I understand.

The Rt.
Hon. J.
Chamberlain,
M.P.

17 June 1884.

P

APPENDIX I.

The Rt. Hon. J., Chamberlain, M.P.

17 June 1884.

12,450. Would you give the ground landlord any increased legal power?—Do you mean power over his leaseholders or tenants?

12,451. Would you give any increased power to the ground landlord to step in; would it be possible to give the ground landlord power of taking possession of bad dwellings with the view of carrying out the necessary work in the last years of long leases?—No, that does not commend itself to my judgment; I do not think I should deal with it in that way. I would rather that the local authority dealt with it if it were necessary.

12,452. There is another matter which has been raised before us, as to which I do not know whether you have any experience or not, and that is as to the power of ground landlords to let land on long leases on other than the best terms possible. In the Duke of Westminster's settlement there is now a clause enabling him to let land for the purpose of artizans' dwellings upon other than the best terms; that is to say, he may let upon such terms as are calculated to procure the erection of such dwellings, although they may not involve the highest possible rent that might be obtained?—It is an enabling clause to assist the life-owner to be philanthropic?

12,453. Yes?—I should think that that is a very good clause, but I should be disposed myself to carry the principle a good deal further. If only the proposals which I have made for securing a fair valuation, and which, I think are not very extreme, were adopted I think schemes would be proposed in sufficient quantity in the country to deal with the question. But my notion of the state of things in London is this: that in London the cost of re-housing, which is a necessary part of the scheme, is so great that something much more stringent is required; and it does seem to me that the principle which is adopted with regard to railways, and with regard to the Metropolitan Board of Works, under which they are not allowed to disturb any considerable proportion of the artizan population without seeing that they have provided accommodation for them elsewhere, ought also to apply to private owners, and that in fact the private owners should be held to have their land with certain incidents attached to it; that as a matter of principle at all events this land which is now occupied by artizans' dwellings should carry with it a special obligation, and that no such scheme should be allowed for what is called the improvement or reconstruction of this private property until the owner has shown that he, as a railway com-

pany are required to do, has provided for the artizan population upon his estate in close proximity.

12,454. When you say that no scheme should be allowed, you appear to be contemplating schemes which require Parliamentary sanction; but of course the commoner case is where the owner himself improves the property out of existence and drives the people away without any Parliamentary sanction?—Yes, I should not hesitate to prevent that.

12,455. Do you think that that could be done by a law, or do you not think that it is rather a matter for the pressure of public opinion and for the recommendation of such a Commission as this based upon moral rather than legal grounds?—I think the practical difficulties are very great, and I would perhaps not like to have the draughting of a law to give effect to my opinion; but if the principle were accepted I think you might find some way in which you could give it considerable operation. Probably it would be impossible to provide for its operation in every case; for instance, I do not see how it would be possible to deal with the case of a small owner who owned only one house, and who turned an artizan's dwelling-house into a shop, for instance. But in the case of very considerable improvements I think it would be much easier to deal with it, and to establish a kind of principle in reference to the matter which would have all the weight of public opinion.

12,456. As regards the moral consideration, and as regards the pressure of public opinion, I should gather from the questions which have been put here to witnesses who have been called that, generally, the Commission would agree with you; but I fancy you yourself rather point out that there would be enormous difficulty in putting that into the form of a legal obligation?—Yes, I have never considered how it could be put into legal form, and I see clearly, as any one must do, that it is a matter of very great difficulty and delicacy, but I do not think it is impossible.

12,457. (*The Prince of Wales.*) I think you said that at the commencement of the century the population of Birmingham was about 73,000?—Yes, Sir.

12,458. And that it had increased until, in the present year, it is nearly 500,000?—It is 408,000.

12,459. I think you also said that you did not consider that there was such serious overcrowding in the poorer districts of Birmingham as there is in London?—No, Sir, I do not think that overcrowding in Birmingham constitutes an important difficulty.

12,460. You also said, with regard to the water supply, that at one time it was not at all satisfactory, but that now it is considered as satisfactory as the supply of a great town can be?—I think it is thoroughly satisfactory now.

12,461. There is another important question about which I am anxious to ask you, with regard to the compensation that is given. In your opinion have not the arbitrators misread the Acts of Sir Richard Cross and Mr. Torrens?—I think so. I think that undoubtedly they have not carried out what I have always understood and believed to be the intention of Sir Richard Cross as the author of the Act, and of the Parliament which passed it.

12,462. Is it not necessary to alter the formula of compensation in those Acts as the old formula has been misrepresented?—I think so.

12,463. What modifications of the present law of compensation would be possible in the metropolis?—I fear that the alterations were not found in experience to be sufficient to carry out what I believe to be the intention of the promoters. The formula which I myself have put forward is, that in every case the fair value should be given as between a willing buyer and a willing seller in the open market, without any allowance for compulsory sale; and I believe that if that formula were adopted it would be impossible for the arbitrators to go beyond a fair value.

12,464. (*The Marquess of Salisbury.*) I understood that the scheme at Birmingham practically did not deal with overcrowding at all?—No, I think there was no overcrowding to speak of. To make my meaning clear, I should perhaps say there was a great overcrowding of houses, but not of persons.

12,465. And there was no provision made and none thought necessary for re-housing the population?—Yes, there was provision made in the original scheme, but experience has shown that it was unnecessary, and we have been relieved by the Local Government Board from the necessity of re-housing the population displaced.

12,466. I asked that question because it appeared to me that the Local Government Board would have had under the terms of the Act some hesitation in giving that power under the Artizans' Dwellings Act if there had been no provisions for re-housing in the scheme?—We were obliged by the terms of the Act to make provision for re-housing, and originally it was intended that the displaced people should be re-housed on or in close proximity to the area cleared.

12,467. You have been relieved of those provisions because they were found to be in practice unnecessary?—Yes, exactly.

12,468. There was a considerable destruction of unhealthy dwellings, was there not?—A very large destruction.

12,469. But the half a million which you have spent is mainly due to street making, because the destruction of unhealthy dwellings is not of itself an expensive operation, is it?—No, the cost is mainly due in the first place to the amount of space which has been thrown into new streets, and in the second place to the difference between the income which we can receive and the capital expenditure which we have been forced to make for the property.

12,470. But the result which the town has got from it consists of new streets; they cannot credit any part of it to the destruction of unhealthy dwellings, because that is an operation which they had a right to do without cost under the law; you do not require to buy a dwelling in order to destroy it if it is unhealthy?—No; according to the law we can destroy single dwellings.

12,471. Therefore none of the cost can be attributed to that, but the whole cost was really incurred (no doubt with a considerable sanitary result, on account of the draught through) on account of making the new streets?—No, not exactly. What you suggest would not be the practical operation. According to the law, no doubt if you can satisfy the authorities that a dwelling is in a state unfit for health, you may either require the landlord to put it into proper repair, or you may order it to be closed and pulled down; but no local authority in the world could go, as we have done, and in the course of the short space of two years require 500 dwellings to be pulled down. The thing would be practically impossible.

12,472. You mean that the pressure of public opinion would be too strong?—Altogether. It would appear like persecution. In many cases the people who own this property are very poor and very small people, and it is absolutely impossible for them to find money for the necessary repairs; and to take from them their property and to send them into the workhouse would be a kind of martyrdom which public opinion would not allow.

12,472a. Applying that to some extent with

The Rt. Hon. J. Chamberlain, M.P.

17 June 1884.

P 2

APPENDIX I.

The Rt. Hon. J. Chamberlain, M.P.

17 June 1884.

respect to your suggestion, that in cases where the local authority was the compulsory purchaser the customary 10 per cent. should not be admitted, do you not think that that would be subject to some of the inconveniences which you have just indicated, with respect to destruction where you were dealing with poor and multitudinous owners, that great unpopularity would be incurred, and that they would feel that they were not being fairly dealt with in not having the same compensation which they would have had if the railway or any other public work, not undertaken by the local authority, had taken their property from them?—But that is the law now. There is no allowance for compulsory sale when property is taken as part of an insanitary area under a scheme.

12,473. But I understood your suggestion to go further than that, and to be that wherever a local authority wanted a property it should have the power of taking it without paying the 10 per cent. for compulsory sale?—Quite so. I would carry it further; but the principle is already established, and established without opposition.

12,474. The principle is established where there is some default on the part of an owner who has allowed his property to get into an insanitary condition; but you propose to apply it to the most innocent and most immaculate owners?—I think you are a little mistaken. The Artizans' Dwellings Act went much beyond what you suggest. Wherever an area was declared to be insanitary, all the owners within that area were subject to the terms of the Act, whether their individual property was insanitary or not; so that I might have a property in the middle of an insanitary area which I had kept in perfect order, and as to which no possible blame could attach, and yet under the Act as originally framed I should have to sell my property on the same terms as my neighbours.

12,475. Not under the Act as it passed, I think?—Yes, under the Act as it passed.

12,476. Are you quite confident of that?—Yes, I am confident of it. The difference is this: We have got two districts, one of which was an insanitary district within which we bought all the properties without allowance for compulsory sale, no matter what the condition of the property was; we bought shops and warehouses on just the same terms as we bought unhealthy dwellings. But then we have another district called the improvement district, and it was there that we had to pay the 10 per cent. extra. It is a matter for argument, but I say that an owner in the improvement district should make the same sacrifice as the owners who were doing their duty in the insanitary area had to make for the public good; that is to say, they should be content with the full and fair value of their property without this excessive sum in the shape of 10 per cent., or very often more than 10 per cent. for compulsory purchase.

12,477. Do you not think that the weight of unpopularity which you would have to struggle against would be very much heavier than it is now when there is a certain consideration given to the owner in consequence of his being unwilling to sell?—I do not think that under any scheme that could be arranged the owners would be badly off. I think they would always get more than they would themselves value their property at supposing no scheme was in existence; and, therefore, I do not think a scheme would be very unpopular with the owners; it would be more unpopular with the ratepayers.

12,478. Your view is that the arbitration would to some extent make up to them for the fact of their property being compulsorily taken by giving them very high values?—Values are always speculative, and in the desire to do justice I think the seller has always the advantage.

12,479. Is there not always considerable sympathy with a private individual against a large public body?—I think there is never any sympathy for the public purse.

12,480. It is not only the public purse, because in contests between railway companies and private individuals the private individual has the best of it?—Yes, always.

12,481. Do you not think that the very fact that you had withdrawn this consideration would strengthen the argument in the mind of the arbitrator and of the jury, and that in the long run you would not be richer in purse though you would have incurred great unpopularity?—I do not think so.

12,482. Do you think that you would induce the public opinion of juries and arbitrators to fall in with your views as to the right of a local authority to take land at a specially cheap price wherever it wanted it?—I do not admit that I am claiming that they should take it at a specially cheap price; I am only claiming that they should not be forced to buy it when their needs require the acquisition of it, at a specially dear price.

12,483. But taking the word "special" as ap-

APPENDIX I. 109

plied to the various competitors for compulsory powers in land, it would certainly be the case that while railway companies and all other private undertakers would have to pay the 10 per cent. additional, the local authority would be spared that necessity ?—The railway companies stand on a totally different footing. The public authority has the public good only in view; the railway companies have private profit in view.

12,484. But the public authority only intervenes to enable the railway company to purchase, because it is assumed that the undertaking of the railway is for the public good ?—That there is a collateral public advantage is of course understood; but the distinction is still manifest between a public company which anticipates making a profitable investment for its shareholders, and the community at large, which is engaging in very heavy expense for the benefit of the whole public.

12,485. Would not the tendency of such a law as you propose be to discourage undertakings by private companies, and to concentrate works of all kinds in the hands of the local authority, as the local authority would be the only people who would be able to buy land cheaply ?—The railway company would not be any worse off than it is now. I do not see why railway enterprise should be discouraged by the fact that a corporation was enabled to buy at a lower rate than a railway company.

12,486. Would not the argument be a strong one that you should not allow this railway company to do it, because it can be done much cheaper by the local authority ?—But Parliament has not given a railway company authority to make an improvement scheme.

12,487. On the same principle should not the local authority undertake to make tramways and similar works ?—They do so now. The local authority of Birmingham now has the tramways very much to the advantage of the community. In all cases I am in favour of the public authority assuming the absolute control of its own roads, and that it can only do by taking possession of the tramways.

12,488. (*Mr. Broadhurst.*) Glasgow has its own tramways, has it not ?—Glasgow has its tramways, and so has Bristol.

12,489. (*The Marquess of Salisbury.*) You wish the local authority to undertake many of the works which are at present undertaken by private persons ?—I think that everything in the shape of natural or artificial monopoly should if possible be undertaken by the community.

12,490. You have no dread of the possibility that jobbing might result from putting so much patronage and expenditure in the hands of local authorities ?—Not the least. I have never seen the slightest sign of municipal jobbery or corruption. I know a great deal about municipal local government, not only in my own town, but in other towns, and I have never heard of one single case of municipal jobbery since the Reform Corporations Act was passed, although we have heard, of course, of individuals doing wrong things.

12,491. Have you never seen a case in which the expenditure has been unduly pressed by the influence of experts, and of the permanent officers of a municipal body ?—I do not think so, I cannot call to mind any such case. Such a thing is possible, but I do not remember it.

12,492. You will admit that in that respect the local authorities are very much more happy than the Imperial authorities ?—I think so. The control of public opinion and of public interest is very much more direct in the one case than in the other.

12,493. With reference to your formula, the price which a willing purchaser would give to a willing seller, do you think that is really a definition which a court of law could easily apply ? Is there not a great difference in willingness ? There is not an absolute willingness to buy on the part of the purchaser; it is a willingness to buy if he can get it at the price he likes. There is not an absolute willingness to sell on the part of the seller; it is a willingness to sell if he can sell at a price which he thinks sufficient ?—Yes; but I should think that the definition could be easily interpreted by a court of law, as they very often do by applying common sense to it. I should say, in the first place, that the price ought to be the price at which a willing seller would sell; but I want to meet the case in which there is no purchaser at all to be found. Is the property to be unduly depreciated because at the moment there is no purchaser, the Corporation or the local authority having intervened between the possible purchaser and the willing seller ?

12,494. If you go to a man and ask him to sell you some land, his answer may be, "I am anxious to get rid of the land, and I shall be glad to deal with you;" but his answer may be, "I have no objection to sell the land if I am tempted by a good price." Which of these two is the willing seller ?—The man who required to be tempted by a good price would not quite come within my

The Rt. Hon. J. Chamberlain, M.P.

17 June 1881.

APPENDIX I.

The Rt.
Hon. J.
Chamberlain,
M.P.

17 June 1884.

definition of a willing seller, that is to say, if he will not sell unless he can get a great profit, he would not be a willing seller. But there are many cases which would illustrate my meaning in our own experience in this scheme, where property purchased just before the Corporation came in was sold to us for immense advances upon the price which the then owner had paid. In one case a man had paid, if I remember rightly, 2500*l.* for a property three years before we had to buy it; we were compelled to buy it because it was a portion of the scheme which it was absolutely necessary that the Corporation should acquire. He asked us 8000*l.* for it, and we had to pay 6000*l.* I have not the least doubt that if that man had wanted for the purpose of any other investment to sell his property he would have been delighted to sell it for 3000*l.*, that is at an advance of 500*l.* upon the price that he had paid; and I look upon the extra 2000*l.* as being the sum which we were forced to pay him, because we were a public authority who were compelled to acquire this land.

12,495. But the market for selling land is a purely hypothetical term. When a valuation is put upon land, either by courts of law or elsewhere, it is usually in these terms: "We know from practice that such and such an income may be got from the land, and we take so many years' purchase in order to capitalize it." But the question of willing purchaser and willing seller never comes in; what comes in is the question of willing letter or willing tenant ?—Take the ordinary case of land : if it were proved that in any particular county or district the ordinary price of land was 30 years' purchase of the rental, that would be the price which a willing purchaser would give to a willing seller, and that is the price that I want to establish. What I object to is, 30 years' purchase being the ordinary price, its running up to 35 or 40 years' purchase when a public authority comes to buy.

12,496. Thirty-three years' purchase is the utmost that the Lands Clauses Act gives, with an addition of 10 per cent., is it not ?—In provincial valuations it is often 20 per cent.

12,497. Your objection goes not so much to the 10 per cent. additional as to that addition made by stress of habit or public opinion ; but I did not understand how you thought that any legislation would interfere with that ?—I think it is very much owing to the habit of the professional people employed, and I would try and break that habit by a new formula which they would be forced to observe. I want to mark for their benefit the intention of the legislature that in this case at all events those excessive prices are not to be given.

12,498. (*Mr. Lyulph Stanley.*) Have you not known cases of 50 years' purchase of the rental being often given under compulsion ?—Certainly.

12,499. (*The Marquess of Salisbury.*) But those cases, if they have happened, have been the result, not of any peculiar provision in the law or in the Lands Clauses Act, but of the idiosyncrasies of juries or of arbitrators ?—Yes, and of the exceeding practical difficulty of dealing with speculative values.

12,500. Do you think that if you made the normal conditions of the law more severe you would array against yourself in greater hostility this opinion under which you already suffer ?—No, I do not think so. I think that a jury is always a very bad tribunal for dealing with these cases ; but the arbitrators I should expect to do better if my formula were adopted, without at the same time the least fear of imposing unduly upon owners of property.

12,501. With respect to what is called betterment I understand your scheme to be, that if a street is made everybody within such and such a radius should pay higher rates than the rest of the rate-paying area ?—Supposing it can be shown that their property has been improved by the making of the street.

12,502. But would that be easily shown ? For instance, if you make a good street from the north of London to the south by the side of a bad street which exists already, you not only do not improve the value of that bad street, but you take away its importance and lower its rents ?—That may be so.

12,503. Would you still charge them for the making of the good street ?—Certainly not.

12,504. The greater benefit of making of the new good street would be to the people at each end and not to the people at the side ?—The circumstances would have in each case to be specially considered, but I will take a case in which the improvement is evident, the case in which a portion of property is taken in order to widen a street. Enormous compensations have been paid to landowners in those cases. Six feet has been taken off their frontage, and instead of facing, as they have hitherto done, a mean court, or a wretched side street, they find themselves on a great thoroughfare, and the remaining part of

APPENDIX I.

their property is worth twice or three times as much as the whole of it was worth before; and, yet, although nothing is taken from them by way of contribution, they have secured enormous compensation.

12,505. Would it not be necessary, in order to assess that extra rate, to make a special inquiry in each case?—Certainly.

12,506. (*The Chairman.*) I understood you to propose a Local Government Board inquiry?—Certainly.

12,507. (*The Marquess of Salisbury.*) Would not that swell the already monstrous bill of expenses under which the compulsory purchaser already suffers?—No, I do not think so. Local Government Board inquiries, which are on the whole exceedingly satisfactory to everybody concerned, are held on a great number of questions, and they are the cheapest of all local inquiries. They are much more satisfactory than parliamentary committees, and, as a rule, after one of those inquiries all parties feel that their interests have been fairly considered; and they cost very little. The inspector comes down, and he hears the people themselves, and if they require to be professionally assisted he makes no objection, but he endeavours to get, as far as he can, the truth from the people themselves; and although the inquiry is to some extent informal, justice is almost invariably done.

12,508. But can you beforehand say who will benefit by making a street and who will not?—Yes, I think so; not if it were necessary to ascertain the exact amount of benefit; but I have only proposed that those who are benefited should contribute in rather a larger proportion than those who are not benefited.

12,509. But it would be a benefit of a purely speculative character; it might easily turn out, might it not, without assuming the slightest want of ability on the part of the inspector, that the people who were extra taxed would be the people injured, and that the people who were lightly taxed would be the people benefited?—It is not a bit more speculative than the value of property; it is generally decided with a view to all sorts of prospective considerations.

12,510. It is decided after hearing with professional assistance, witnesses called, and so forth, all of which means cost, which must be borne either by the local authority, which would add very much to the cost of the improvement, or by the individual, which would impose great hardship?—An arbitration as to value is now the most expensive thing that can possibly be undertaken, and I am almost inclined to say one of the most immoral things too, because an immense mass of professional evidence is always produced on both sides, and there is a most extraordinary variation between the witnesses. I would like to see all that very much reduced; and one of my proposals is that there should be a limit to the costs allowed in any case, one effect of which would be that the claimant would not attempt to bring such an array of professional evidence. I do not think that he is benefited by it himself; it tends rather to confuse than to elicit the truth; but it enormously adds to the cost of the arbitrations. I am suggesting that the inquiry in the case of the proposed rate should not be conducted in that way by a professional arbitrator, with assessors and witnesses, but in the ordinary way in which a Local Government Board inquiry is conducted, which is much less formal and much less expensive.

12,511. Would such a tribunal be adequate for the purpose of dealing with so delicate and difficult a question as ascertaining what was the benefit to the property of an improvement in the neighbourhood? I believe that the decisions would be much nearer the truth than the ordinary decisions in an arbitration are.

12,512. You stated just now that the ground landlord escaped scot-free, and that you did not see why he should do so; who receives the benefit of a present improvement, the occupier or the ground landlord?—Both.

12,513. The ground landlord gets no increase of rent, does he?—No, not immediately; but he has a reversionary benefit, a future benefit.

12,514. And when his future benefit accrues he will have to take his share of the burden which is put upon him in the shape of a deduction from the rent?—Which may have been all cleared off before then, and very often is.

12,515. But then he will get no benefit?—Pardon me, he will get a benefit just the same. For instance, to take a very common case, take the case of a water company. A corporation buys a water company and is forced to repay the whole sum in 30 years. At the end of 30 years the water company is worth just as much as it was before, if not more, and the ground landlord may come into that property at that time with nothing to pay for it.

12,516. That would be a fair ground for charging

The Rt. Hon. J. Chamberlain, M.P.

17 June 1884.

The Rt. Hon J. Chamberlain, M.P.

17 June 1884.

the ground landlord with his share of the sinking fund, but none for charging him his share of the present interest?—He does not pay any part of the sinking fund at present.

12,517. You made a suggestion which I did not quite understand, that owners of town property were to be prevented from driving artizans away by making improvements in their houses; have you at all formulated to yourself in what detail you would carry out that idea?—I think the Chairman has suggested that it is rather a matter for moral pressure than for any very definite legislation. I should like, if possible, to see the sanction of the law given to the establishment of some obligation upon the part of landlords that where they have a large property of this kind they should not displace any considerable number of the working classes without seeing that some provision was made for them; but, as I have already said, I have not thought of the terms of an Act of Parliament which would carry that into effect.

12,518. Would you not rather be making the presence of artizans a very serious danger and burden to the landlord, so as to induce him to take every opportunity he can of getting the artizans off the place one by one?—If he wanted to evade the law, and did not recognise the obligation which the law sought to establish, I am afraid he would find a means of running a coach and six through it.

12,519. Is it not found that if you attempt to reinforce public opinion by statutory enactment you effect the opposite result and set public opinion to resist the enactment?—If you press the conclusion too far; but I should have thought that there would be no objection to something of this kind, that wherever in the process of any public or private improvement more than a certain number of artizans are displaced, the local authority shall be consulted, and in concert with the person making the improvement shall see that some sufficient provision is made for them elsewhere. That would not burden the landlord in ordinary cases with an improvement, and at the same time it would establish the kind of principle which we were seeking to establish with railways. I do not think that in the case of railways hitherto much good has been done by laws enacted to prevent them from disturbing the people, but they have made them a little careful of what they do; and I believe that as a matter of fact they prefer now to take property which is not inhabited by artizans where they can do so, where they have any choice, rather than property upon which artizans' dwellings exist.

12,520. That answer brings out exactly the difference which exists between a private owner and a railway company. The railway company is taking property which it has not hitherto possessed; you are proposing to interfere with property which a man already has, and to say that he shall not deal with it in a particular way when it happens to be tenanted by a particular class of tenants?—Yes, I am trying to establish some kind of obligation as an incident of land already occupied by artizans' dwellings.

12,521. Do you not think that the first instinct of an Englishman when he is interfered with is to resist that interference?—I think so. But still an Englishman has to submit to a great deal of interference now.

12,522. But if it becomes a struggle between an Englishman and the law, the Englishman very often gets the best of it. With reference to railways, I understand your definition of the position of the Board of Trade to differ in some degree from Mr. Calcraft's. I asked Mr. Calcraft this question: "Your theory of your position is that it is absolutely passive, and that you take no action until a stimulus is applied to you from without," and his answer was, "Exactly." I did not understand your view to be exactly the same as that; I understood you to say that the Board of Trade stood aside vested with great powers, but only intending to use them where manifest abuse called for them to do so?—I do not think there is any inconsistency. I understand Mr. Calcraft's reply to be rather directed to the past policy of the Board of Trade, that they would not think it their duty to interfere unless a representation came to them from some local authority or from some body of working people. On many occasions such representations have been made to us, and we have at once put some pressure upon the companies. But I think the situation is a little altered by the passing of the Act of last session, which gave us very much greater powers, and, therefore, may be said to have imposed upon us a greater obligation; and I should say now, although I would not take the initiative unnecessarily, yet I should not hesitate to do so if I had any reason whatever to believe from any information, however obtained, that the companies were not doing all that they ought to do.

12,523. You would not necessarily wait for a

formal representation from any particular individual?—No, not necessarily.

12,524. (*Mr. Lyulph Stanley.*) You are giving this property as the ground landlord for your great street improvements with the expectation of getting the reversion?—Yes.

12,525. The greater part of Birmingham is built on leasehold tenure, is it not?—A great part is.

12,526. In your judgment, is a leasehold tenure a good tenure for the healthy, substantial, handsome, and generally advantageous construction of towns?—I cannot say that in our experience we have found any disadvantage from it. There have been great improvements made in Birmingham in the last 20 years, all upon leasehold tenure. Splendid public buildings, banks, and warehouses have been erected on that tenure.

12,527. Then, in your judgment, you do not consider a leasehold tenure in the hands of private persons a disadvantageous tenure upon which to build a town?—I should myself prefer to build upon a freehold, but I do not think that leasehold tenure interferes with the improvement of a town.

12,528. In Birmingham it is very common for your workpeople to live in small houses in courts off the main street, is it not?—Yes.

12,529. You have greatly improved those courts, I think. I saw in one of the reports of the town council that there were felt to be some drawbacks, owing to their not being lighted, and pressure was brought to bear to introduce a gas lamp in every court; that has not been done yet completely, has it?—No, but it has been done in a great number of cases.

12,530. Do you consider that a system of building largely for the poor in courts is a satisfactory system of building?—Yes, I think so, decidedly.

12,531. You have never had brought under your notice any moral disadvantages arising from the isolation of people away from public opinion, and from the general eye of the world?—No, I do not think it applies to courts which are properly lighted and ventilated, and which are all in connexion with the main street.

12,532. Still, even if the courts have gas lamps in them, those courts, with a little colony getting into them, are quite apart from the general public opinion of the town; people do not go up into the court and down again?—I do not know any one in Birmingham that is apart from the general public opinion of the town, but my desire to see more lamps in the courts is dictated by a desire for cleanliness.

12,533. You are not aware that it has been found, in London especially, that the existence of a *cul de sac* in courts almost inevitably leads to moral degradation?—I should not be at all surprised to learn that. I know much more about Glasgow, and I know that in Glasgow, where the wynds are very narrow, dark, and dirty, and unhealthy, there was the greatest immorality, besides discomfort and ill-health, and all that I should expect naturally to follow from a bad system of building. But we are speaking now of courts which I assume to be properly built, and built in accordance with the model byelaws of the Local Government Board.

12,534. I was not considering a place which was badly constructed, but the experience of London is that even a street if it is built as a *cul de sac* has a distinct tendency, a certainty you may say, to become occupied by a worse class of people; the character of the people is lowered, and the rents are lower than if that street was a through street?—That is very interesting, but I did not know it before.

12,535. In Birmingham your town council would have no scruple in countenancing the further habit of building in the way of courts?—No; as I have already said in answer to the Chairman, I think it of importance that there should be through ventilation through all those courts, and therefore, they would not be *culs de sac* in those cases.

12,536. They would if there was not a thoroughfare?—There cannot be through ventilation without a thoroughfare.

12,537. You might have a railing at the end, and in that case there would be through ventilation, but no thoroughfare. It has not come under your notice in Birmingham that there is a drawback in a street not being a thoroughfare?—I have never heard it suggested.

12,538. You referred to a clause in the Artizans' Dwellings Amendment Act, 1882, which enables the owner of two properties, one of which is pulled down for the purpose of ventilating, and the other property is benefited, to have an apportionment made; and you think that in every case an adjoining other property, if it can be shown to be improved, should pay more than the general rate of the town towards that improvement?—Yes.

12,539. You are not prepared to say that there should be a mathematical adjustment, but you think that there should be a rough and ready

The Rt. Hon. J. Chamberlain, M.P.

17 June 1884.

Q

APPENDIX I.

The Rt.
Hon. J.
Chamberlain,
M.P.

17 June 1881.

method of levying rather more on the immediate neighbourhood than on the place which was outside ?—Yes, exactly.

12,540. Of course that might be partly met, might it not, in a rough and ready way by creating local sub-areas within the municipal area, and saying that the burden should fall upon one ward and not upon the whole town ?—That a greater burden should fall upon that ward.

12,541. It would work some injustice, but you think that it would work less injustice than there is at present ?—I think so.

12,542. You cannot apportion the burden exactly in proportion to the gain; but you think you would get nearer to making the burden fall comparatively equally if you had a variation of the incidence of taxation with the area ?—Yes. It would be extremely clear in the case of some properties; in others it would be more doubtful; and probably the tendency would always be to relieve large properties unless it was quite clear that they were benefited.

12,543. You said, in answer to Lord Salisbury, that you thought that any property, no matter how healthy, if it was within an area included under the Artizans' Dwellings Act, was bound to be taken in the same way, and subject to the same obligations; but I know it is the case in London improvement schemes that if there is a particular patch of sanitary property in a large scheme that patch is exempted from the operation of the scheme and has to be treated for separately. I know that in the case of the Whitechapel scheme you will find a certain school which lay in the middle of the Whitechapel scheme and, as appears on the map, there are patches left out. It would be obviously necessary in dealing with such a scheme as that to make some negotiation or to acquire that property; but I think you will find that if property was perfectly sanitary the owner could not get it excluded from the scheme except upon the terms of having special compensation ?—I think it is quite possible that they might get excluded; but as a matter of fact in Birmingham we were enabled to purchase the whole of the portion coloured red, or any portion of it that we chose to select under the Artizans' Dwellings Act.

12,544. But if you made a scheme in which the property was chequered in character you would probably find yourself compelled to give special terms and clauses to the people who had perfectly good property, though it was not necessary for your purposes, ringed up with bad property ?—I daresay you might, and if so, in my opinion, the Act would be rendered perfectly useless.

12,545. You stated that you estimated the loss on your new street to be half a million of money ?—Upon the whole scheme.

12,546. That I suppose I may take as a charge of about 20,000l. a year ?—Yes.

12,547. You think it advisable to hold your property for the reversion and not to sell the ground rents ?—Yes.

12,548. This amounts to a building speculation of the Corporation of Birmingham on the expectation that the prosperity of Birmingham will be as great or greater 80 years hence than it is now ?—I do not call it a building speculation because we do not build. You may call it a speculation in land.

12,549. Or in house property ?—Yes, but we do not erect any property.

12,550. But as holders of it it becomes a speculation in house property, based on the expectation that the prosperity of Birmingham will be as great or greater 80 years hence than it is now ?—Yes.

12,551. But, of course, in a decaying town at the end of 80 years the ground rents which are now being secured would not be secured on the reletting ?—Quite so, but I do not myself anticipate any speedy decadence of this country.

12,552. But still there is always that element of risk ?—If you think it is a risk.

12,553. Generally those improvements are made in prosperous times when there is a general wish to spend money, and not in times of great depression; do you not think that if when you had made these improvements you had sold the land off at once you would find, if a sinking fund were set apart, that the capital in the hands of the town at the end of the 80 years would be larger than the probable reversion of the ground rents ?—No, I feel absolutely certain that it would be the other way. I have no doubt whatever that we obtained almost exactly as much for our property upon these long leases as we should have obtained if we had sold it out and out, and that therefore the ultimate reversion whatever it is worth would be practically the profit to the community at the end of 80 years.

12,554. You found in Birmingham that the poor people who were displaced, in fact before they were displaced, re-housed themselves, and there was no need for re-housing, and your officials

APPENDIX I.

The Rt. Hon. J. Chamberlain, M.P.

17 June 1884.

ascertained that there were 5000 empty houses in Birmingham ?—Of the artizan class.

12,555. But still you know from looking at the census, that there are always a very large number of unoccupied houses even in towns where the building trade is very active and there is a pressure for dwellings; there seems to be a certain necessary margin of houses standing empty even in a town where really there is a great pressure for house accommodation ?—Certainly.

12,556. And taking the whole of England, town and country together, it works out to about 8 per cent.; but I noticed that in many active growing towns it is above 10 per cent.; so that though I do not dispute the local investigations of your authorities, yet I put it to you that the mere existence of empty houses in a borough does not prove that there ought to be no re-housing ?—I do not quote that as conclusive of the matter; I only quote it as one matter that bears upon the question. The conclusive thing in the case of Birmingham is that we have built houses for 40,000 at a time when the whole population has only increased by 35,000.

12,557. Building speculators may build houses in the wrong district, and there may be a greater pressure in one district than in another ?—It is about the same all over the town.

12,558. You said that your building byelaws greatly restricted the number of houses that the speculative builder could put upon a plot; and you said that there were nine where there might otherwise be twenty ?—I did not give that as the usual average, but as a particular case.

12,559. But the number put up is less than formerly, owing to your requirements for open space, and so forth ?—Certainly.

12,560. Have you considered whether that loss falls mainly upon the ground landlord, or whether the tenants have to bear the burden of the whole of the ground rent distributed over nine houses instead of twenty ?—It is a thing upon which it is impossible to do more than speculate. In my opinion both the tenant and the landlord have to contribute to the loss. The landlord gets rather less than he would otherwise have got for his land, and the tenant has to pay more for his house.

12,561. Then would you not have a great deal of unpopularity to contend against if, in introducing better sanitary regulations, the builders could go amongst the working classes and say, "You have to pay 5l. for a plot of ground where formerly you paid 2l., owing to these sanitary fads of the Town Council" ?—Not in the least. We have had the argument out, and we have never hesitated to meet any contention of the kind, and to urge upon our people that they must give a larger sum for rent, and even spend a larger proportion of their income upon their rent, and we have never found, amongst the better class of our artizans, the least reluctance to do that.

12,562. You would be inclined to concede that that argument was a true argument, and that the bulk of the cost would fall upon the tenant ?—Certainly, I think so.

12,563. (*Mr. Broadhurst.*) In the case of the property which the Town Council of Birmingham have let on lease, the only other alternative, of course, was to sell the freehold to any purchaser who presented himself ?—Certainly.

12,564. In that case the probabilities are that the purchaser would have let it on lease ?—Certainly.

12,565. Then the result would have been that the increased value, the unearned increment of this property, would have drifted into private pockets instead of, as now, drifting into the general treasury of the community ?—Certainly.

12,566. And under those circumstances it was thought justifiable to let it on lease ?—Yes.

12,567. (*Mr. Samuel Morley.*) On the question of the charge for money we have been advised that it would be a perfectly proper thing for the Government, having absolute security for the loans which they make, to charge for money as to which they have security, that it will be used in erecting buildings for the working classes at the lowest rate that they can get it for without profit; have you any opinion upon that subject ?—I do not think it would make any difference in the case of large towns. We can borrow already so well for ourselves that we do not want the Government to help us; but in the smaller towns no doubt it is a matter of considerable importance, and I think that the rate of interest should be put so low as to pay all expenses, provided that the Government do not lose anything.

12,568. (*Mr. Godwin.*) Taking you back for a minute to the present condition of Birmingham, you know the opinion that the Artizans' Dwellings Committee came to in their Report at page 14, that the dwelling-house accommodation for the artizan and labouring classes within the borough is, generally speaking, in a fairly sanitary condition, and that overcrowding does not exist to any great extent. I think you have yourself said that

Q 2

The Rt. Hon. J. Chamberlain, M.P.

17 June 1884.

you think there is no serious overcrowding in Birmingham ?—Yes.

12,569. I find in the evidence given by Mr. Councillor Middlemore an account of an entirely different state of things, which agrees, I am bound to say, with a condition known to myself. He describes places in which healthy life is quite impossible, where seven or eight people dwell, where there may be from five to ten residents in one room. In one house that he visited he found the bedroom occupied by a man and his wife and eight children ; there were two sons, aged 25 and 26 ; two daughters, aged 20 and 18 ; and four younger children. Then he mentioned the case of a man and his wife living in a kitchen 12 feet by 10 feet, where the woman had lately been confined, and where seven others also slept, and where the baby, to quote the poor mother's words, had " just died of the will of God and Dr. Jones." How do you reconcile these statements with the general assertion that there is no serious overcrowding in Birmingham ?—Because those are particular statements, and mine is a general statement. In my evidence-in-chief I mentioned that there were 2,082 cases in which persons were being overcrowded in Birmingham at the present time, and no doubt some of those 2,082 are the cases referred to by Mr. Middlemore, who made a report which was rather considered by most of the people who knew Birmingham at the time to be a little sensational in its character, and not altogether borne out by the evidence of other gentlemen who had long been acquainted with the circumstances of the ward which he visited. But the ward contains some of the worst streets in the town, and it would be quite possible to find some very heartrending cases in that particular district.

12,570. It would be hardly fair, I suppose, to ask you whether you know such a street as Balloon Street ?—Yes, I know it very well.

12,571. Is that still in existence ?—Balloon Street, I think, is wiped off the face of creation by the new scheme, if I remember rightly.

12,572. I have visited some courts in Brick Kiln Street ; does Brick Kiln Street still exist ?—Yes.

12,573. I am bound to say that I found a frightful condition of things in that neighbourhood, and I am therefore anxious to know how this downright assertion on the part, at any rate of the committee, can be borne out ?—I cannot say more than I have said, that undoubtedly in Birmingham, as in all other large towns, there are cases in which people are living under conditions which are very shameful and discreditable to all of us ; but at the same time the general condition of the population is very good.

12,574. It would not be desirable that too good a notion of the state of the town should get about if such things as these still remain, would it ?—I have said in my evidence that I should like to see two or three more schemes, similar to that which we are now carrying out, carried out in Birmingham alone ; and if they could be carried out I think there would be nothing that is practicable left to be desired in the state of the town.

12,575. Do you happen to know what effect upon the rateable value of the neighbourhood the new street has had ?—I cannot tell you that now, but I know that it has very considerably increased the rateable value.

12,576. That has not been taken into account in estimating the cost to the ratepayers ?—It was taken into account in the first proposal which I made to the council. I went into it very carefully then upon the estimate, and showed them that the nominal cost of the scheme might be considered to be reduced so far as the apparent burden upon the rates was concerned by the increase in the rateable value.

12,577. (Mr. Goschen.) When you gave your estimate that it would cost half a million was that taken into consideration in elucidation of the point raised by Mr. Godwin ?—No. In fact, I think that is fair, because the one is an actual loss of money, the other is an improvement for the purposes of rating which is not an improvement which all the owners of property appreciate, because it increases their burdens.

12,578. The receipts from the rates would be a source of income to set against the loss of 500,000l. ?—Yes, so far as the balance sheet of the corporation goes it will not lose the whole sum necessary to pay the interest on the 550,000l., because it will gain in the increased rateable value of the property all round.

12,579. (Mr. Godwin.) You have told us that with regard to Birmingham it has not been found necessary to provide for the persons who have been unhoused by knocking down houses, and so forth, and I rather think you expressed a somewhat similar opinion afterwards in respect to London ?—No, I said exactly the reverse with respect to London. I said that in London the difficulty was the necessity for re-housing the poor in close proximity to the places from which they

APPENDIX I. 117

are removed, and that that would immensely increase the expense of any London scheme.

12,580. You would be aware that after any unhousing of that sort the neighbourhood immediately becomes overcrowded in consequence ?—Yes.

12,581. So that it would be a very injurious impression to entertain, that it was not necessary to put up houses for those who were removed ?—Quite so.

12,582. (*Mr. Jesse Collings.*) I do not know whether you are aware that Mr. Middlemore's report was founded very largely on hearsay ?—I do not know that.

12,583. And that the committee themselves visited the places, and houses in the localities referred to in his report, and found that although it was correct in a few individual cases, yet it did not in any way represent the state of things generally ?—No, that is evident from the report of the committee.

12,584. I was present at the verification of his report, and I found that to be the case ?—

12,585. (*Mr. McCullagh Torrens.*) I think I understood that you indicated a decided preference for large and comprehensive schemes of demolition to bit-by-bit schemes ?—Yes, I did.

12,586. Does that apply distinctively to London and the country towns ?—It applies distinctively to the country. All my observations applied in the first place to the country; but I am inclined to apply it to London too, although deprecating my own want of knowledge about the particular circumstances of London.

12,587. Has it been brought to your attention that one of the great difficulties and subsequent losses arising from Sir Richard Cross's Act being put in operation is consequent upon the wholesale demolition of a great portion of the parish or district, and the consequent impossibility of getting building contracts made to rebuild there ?—Yes, and I have never been able to understand why that was done. I should like to see a very large scheme proposed, but I should think it was very imprudent to carry it all out at once. In such a case a wholesale demolition seems to me to be unwise.

12,588. With regard to the distinction which you drew, in answer to questions put by the Chairman and by Lord Salisbury, as to the amount of allowance to be made under a better system of arbitration, between the remuneration as I will call it, the sum to be given for what was taken away, and, on the other hand, the 10 per cent. for compulsory sale; should I be justified in calling that a compensation which you would not allow ?—I should not allow the 10 per cent. for compulsory sale in any case.

12,589. In the one case you would consider it remuneration for loss, and in the other case compensation for prospective value. The 10 per cent. I take it is the provision made for the possible deprivation for public purposes of an enhanced value ?—No, I have always thought that it was a compensation for a supposed unwillingness to sell. Supposing that I have got a house, and it suits me very well, and I am not satisfied that you should take it, even though you should pay me its full value; in order to compensate me for the inconvenience to which I am put, even if I get my full value, I am allowed 10 per cent. or something extra.

12,589*a*. The full value is to be paid, but the compensation is to be reduced ?—The full value, but nothing more.

12,590. In answer to a question which was put by Mr. Stanley, I think you expressed a guarded opinion as to the consequences of leaving *culs de sac* even of a respectable kind unopened. I do not ask you to pronounce an opinion about such instances in London, but I venture to suggest that you may take it from me, and others, that there are in London many instances of *culs de sac* that are not either degraded or depraved ?—I dare say that may be so.

12,591. For instance, Downing Street has now been opened, but it was for a long time a *cul de sac*; and Stratford Place and Carlton Gardens are instances of *culs de sac* that I never heard were particularly demoralised ?—But perhaps Mr. Stanley would consider that the population was very much isolated from public opinion in those cases.

12,592. (*Mr. Lyulph Stanley.*) I think you understood me to speak of districts that are occupied by the poorer class ?—Yes.

12,593. (*The Bishop of Bedford.*) A good deal of your evidence, and of other evidence which has been brought before the Commission, has been with regard to providing an equivalent for property destroyed; but that is a very small part of the work which, at any rate in London, would have to be contemplated if the labouring classes are to be provided with houses, because of the constant increase of the population and of the immense overcrowding at present existing. We want a great deal more than that, do we not ?—Yes, I take it so.

12,594. One remark of yours has suggested a way

The Rt.
Hon. J.
Chamberlain,
M.P.

17 June 1884.

The Rt.
Hon. J.
Chamberlain,
M.P.

17 June 1884.

in which space might possibly accrue in London; you spoke of factories that were removed in your large improvement scheme in Birmingham having gone elsewhere, I suppose into the suburbs?—Yes, and to parts of the town which are less populous at the present time.

12,595. Do you suppose that such a process might be carried out in London very beneficially; that is, that the factories and similar institutions in the crowded parts of the metropolis might be moved into the country with advantage to all parties, and so that large spaces might be obtained for workmen's dwellings?—I think the process is going on undoubtedly as regards the factories; but there will always remain, of course, a demand for artizans' and labourers' dwellings, and houses for them must be provided.

12,596. The labourers would follow the factories in large numbers, probably?—The workmen, of course, are attached to the factories; but what I mean is that there must always be a very large labouring class who are not attached to factories.

12,597. Did you find a great complaint on the part of the manufacturers themselves of being removed further from the centre of their market?—Not the least, except when they were coming forward for compensation; we found all sorts of complaints then.

12,598. Is it not true that in estimating compensation, not only has a possible prospective increase of value been taken into consideration, (whether from the improvement itself or from sanguine views of trade possibly,) but also that undue rents received from tenants misusing their premises either for immoral purposes or by overcrowding have been taken into consideration?—I think so, undoubtedly.

12,599. What would you suggest as a preventive of that?—I think that the arbitrator ought only to take into account the income which can properly be derivable from the property. As a matter of fact he does very often take into account the income only derivable, because the property is misused.

12,600. That should be prevented by legislation, if possible?—I think so.

12,601. Supposing that this matter of compensation were satisfactorily settled, so that arbitrators gave no more than the value which you consider Sir Richard Cross's Act contemplated, could you then leave the provision of workmen's houses very much to private enterprise?—In the country, absolutely.

12,602. But in London?—In London, I think not.

12,603. Do you not think that an improvement in the habits of the working classes through education, the influence of other classes, as, for example, in Miss Octavia Hill's plan, and especially, perhaps, the increase in the temperate habits of the people, would do more than legislation to improve their general condition?—I think it has done an immense deal already; but what is distressing is that whatever is done does not seem to touch the lowest. There is always a proportion apparently almost as great of people who are not improved at all by anything that is being done.

12,604. With regard to all schemes of improvement, I think the one practical suggestion as to legislative action is that of the Government lending on the lowest possible terms; that you thoroughly approve of?—Yes, providing they do not make a loss.

12,605. All other suggestions seem rather to point to the removal of obstacles than to the imitation of any practical action; is not that so?—I want to cheapen the cost. The secret is there; everything which will cheapen the cost will help to solve the question. The cost is the one thing that stands in the way. You have local authorities willing and able to do the work, but they cannot do it if the cost is excessive.

12,606. Even if the cost is lowered considerably, and buildings are provided for the working classes at cheaper rents, even then there will always be great difficulty in housing the lowest class on account of their destructive and disagreeable habits to their neighbours, and so on, will there not?—Yes.

12,607. There seems to be no scheme at present suggested to us for meeting the difficulty in the case of the lowest class of all?—No. I think you must rely upon the gradual spread of education more than upon anything else.

12,608. (*Mr. Goschen.*) With regard to compensation, have you had experience of compensation of weekly tenants?—Yes, we have a good number of weekly tenants. I do not in the least object to compensation there, because it is so small a matter. Some very trifling sum was given to them to sweeten the change, and although I do not think it was quite intended by the Act, yet it is not a thing to which I should take any exception.

12,609. It is of no real benefit to the tenants to have greater compensation than will enable them to move without much expense. Are there not great dangers in giving high compensation to weekly tenants?—I think so; I think that compensation

APPENDIX I. 119

should always be a moderate sum for the purpose that you name.

12,610. But you do them a greater service by rebuilding places where they can go to than by compensating them by the payment of a certain sum down?—Certainly.

12,611. With regard to the other point, namely, the loss to the corporation, could you state how much they have recouped by increased rates forming a set-off against their losses of half a million?—That was in the speech that I made to the council in the year 1875; it was only an estimate then. I said, "The rateable value of the property we are going to deal with is roughly 32,000*l*. Assuming it to be increased threefold we shall have an increased rateable value of 64,000*l*.; and assuming a rate of 2*s*. in the £, which I take as the normal rate, we shall have an annual increase in our revenue, to set against the cost, of 6,000*l*. per annum." That was an estimate which was based on the increase of rateable value of certain other improvements in the town.

12,612. The cost to you is practically the interest on half a million?—20,000*l*. a year.

12,613. From which you would have to deduct 6,000*l*. if that was a correct estimate?—Yes.

12,614. With regard to some questions that were put to you by the Bishop of Bedford, would you be in favour of a local authority providing house accommodation for the poorest class at less than the market rate?—No, I do not think I should; I should be afraid of it. I should be afraid that by so doing they would so much disturb the market that they would stop the supply, and would therefore do more harm than good, because the builders would be afraid of the competition of the public authority, and they would not come in and do what they are now doing voluntarily.

12,615. You would cheapen production as far as you could, in order to increase the supply; but when you had thus cheapened the production you would not give it cheaper to the working classes, except under fair competition?—No.

12,616. You would approve of cheaper buildings to increase the supply, and you would let them compete with the buildings provided by others, hoping that the aggregate rents might be less, but you would not take any legal steps to ensure a certain rent for the poorest class?—No, I would not; and I do not myself think that the question of rent is so important as some people suppose. I think that the better class of artizan does not grudge his rent at all; he does not grudge a rental which will give him a fair house; and I think that these very poor people spend, now, too little in rent, but the saving is not to their advantage. They waste the money they save in rent in something much less to their advantage. I would, therefore, not object to a system under which, practically, they would be compelled to attribute a larger proportion of their income to house rent than they do at present.

12,617. Your opinion is distinctly against any attempt on the part of the local authorities, or on the part of the State, to regulate a maximum of rent for the poorest class?—I think that is impossible.

12,618. It would be Utopian to try it?—I think so.

12,619. (*Earl Brownlow*.) Speaking of the arbitration, I understood you to say that if a satisfactory tribunal were instituted you would be in favour of abolishing the right of appeal?—Yes.

12,620. Can you suggest any tribunal which would command public confidence for that purpose?—I think so. If the Local Government Board would appoint an arbitrator and allow him to sit with one or more local assessors, who would know the circumstances of the town, I think that would be a perfectly fair tribunal and one which would command public confidence.

12,621. The Local Government Board would be a court of appeal?—There would be no appeal to them, but they would appoint the arbitrator.

12,622. You think that would be sufficient to command public confidence?—I think so.

12,623. Is it the custom in Birmingham for very large employers of labour to take a personal interest in the housing of their hands, or is it looked upon as entirely a matter of contract?—I do not think the employers of labour in any case in Birmingham interfere as to the housing of their people; I do not think the necessity has ever arisen. Of course there are cases where a factory is established in a country district; there have been cases where factories have been established in the outskirts of Birmingham where the manufacturer has been compelled to provide at the same time accommodation for his workpeople, but in the town itself the accommodation is provided by private enterprise always *pari passu* with the demand, and generally in excess of it.

12,624. Where an employer in the outskirts of the town has been compelled, as you say, to supply houses for his workmen, do you think that the result has been good?—I really cannot call to mind

The Rt.
Hon. J.
Chamberlain,
M.P.

17 June 1884.

The Rt.
Hon. J.
Chamberlain,
M.P.

17 June 1884.

any instance of that. I know there are several factories on the Worcestershire side of Birmingham where I think something of the kind has been done, but I do not know what the result has been.

12,625. The reason why I asked you that question is that we have had evidence that on the Metropolitan Railway they have housed their workmen to a large extent, and they say that the result has been very beneficial both to the railway and to the workmen?—I doubt whether there is any useful information to be obtained as to that in Birmingham. It has not been done on any large scale, and I should think you would get such information much better from Sir Titus Salt at Saltaire where there has been a very large operation of the kind.

APPENDIX II.

PRIZE COMPETITION FOR A GENERAL IMPROVEMENT PLAN OF THE CITY OF VIENNA.

1. The Civil Governor of the Royal and Capital city of Vienna herewith offers prizes for the preparation of plans for the general improvement of the whole parish of Vienna, and invites home and foreign architects and engineers to take part in the competition under the following rules and according to the appended programme.

2. The proposed designs will only be considered complete and have a right to the published prizes when they contain the following.

(a) A ground plan of the whole city of Vienna to the scale of $\frac{1}{10000}$ size, on which the proposed division of the city, arrangements of the principal streets and squares, and suitable access to the different means of communication, railways, &c., must be clearly shown.

(b) A plan to the $\frac{1}{2880}$ scale showing the proposals in more detail.

(c) As many longitudinal and transverse sections as may seem necessary to explain the new or altered streets and means of communication. These longitudinal sections are to be to the scale of $\frac{1}{2880}$ for the lengths, and $\frac{1}{720}$ for the heights. The transverse sections are to be to the $\frac{1}{720}$ scale for lengths and heights. In every case such sections are to be made for characteristic parts, such as Vienna Vale Street (Wienthalstrasse), the streets and parks along the Donau Canal, showing the improved water bed, and the lines of the city railway.

(d) A detail plan to a scale of $\frac{1}{1440}$ showing building plots in the district along the river Vienna from Schikaneder Bridge to the Donau Canal, including the neighbouring district Wollzeile — Dominikanerbastei — Ferdinand's Bridge. This plan is to be accompanied by longitudinal and transverse sections on the $\frac{1}{720}$ scale,

which must explain the arrangement in a technical and æsthetic manner; especially the parts, Elizabeth's Bridge, Charles Church, Black Mountain Place, Wollzeile public road, General Post and Customs Offices. In the transverse sections the position of the improved river Vienna and the city railway are to be shown. The plots proposed for building are to be given, with their measurements, in a special table.

(e) A description, in which the competitor explains and gives reasons for his designs and proposals.

3. Part designs * which do not contain the whole city, but only consider a few questions of the improvement or means of communication, will be received. Such designs have, however, no right to the prizes offered for the whole work, but there are special prizes of 3000 florins and under, placed at the disposal of the prize committee for specially good part designs. The part-designs are to be made to the same scales as the complete ones, and are also to be accompanied by similar descriptions.

4. The specified drawings (a)–(d) to required scale will be (for the purposes of dividing the prizes), sufficient to explain the intended proposals, and those drawings will form the basis on which the projects will be judged. Nevertheless each competitor may send in further drawings or models if he considers them useful in explaining his proposals.

5. The ground plans under (a), (b), and (d),† are

* The following designs will be considered as such, building and improvement proposals for the Vienna valley district under (d) in the internal city, and proposals regarding the railways and canals in connection with the dwelling and manufacturing districts, as well as quays, stores, business premises, &c., and their necessary detail drawings.
† The sheets of the drawing under (b) $\frac{1}{2880}$ are not to be pasted together in large sheets; various sheets may be pasted together, but only to such an extent as will allow the plans being easily examined and exhibited.

R

to be drawn on the plans which are given out from the city of Vienna for this purpose.

6. The competitors can, on payment of 100 florins in Austrian money, obtain from the Vienna City Building Office the offered plans and helps for the designs after the day this competition has been published. There, copies of this competition notice are also to be had gratis. The necessary plans for part-designs are to be had at the prices mentioned in the appendix. Single plans and helps can, if required, be had later on from the City Building Office on showing the certificate received with the first set, and on further payments.

7. As many further details and information as possible will be given by the Directors of the City Building Office.

8. For the best designs made according to the regulations the following prizes will be given :— 2 at 10,000 florins, 3 at 5000 florins, and 3 at 3000 florins. In addition, the sum of 20,000 florins is set apart for part-designs or those complete ones which have not received one of the above mentioned prizes, and which are considered good in some parts. Such prizes shall not exceed 3000 florins.

9. The division of prizes is to be made by a committee, which has the only and unlimited right of decision. No more prizes will be given than praiseworthy designs are offered. The prize committee, which has already been appointed, consists of the Lord Mayor of Vienna, and the following thirteen judges :—

1. Ferdinand Dehm, Architect (City Architect).
2. Raimund v. Gotz, Engineer.
3. Franz Ritt. v. Neumann, Architect, Royal Building Commissioner.
4. Georg Rosenstingl, Engineer.
5. Alois Wurm, Architect, Royal Building Commissioner (chosen by the Vienna Town Council).
6. Frederich R. von Bischoff, Royal Commissioner, Building Director of the State Railways (as representative of the Executive of the State railways).
7. Siegmund Taussig, Government Commissioner (as representative of the Donau Improvement Works).
8. Franz Ritt. von Gruber, Royal Commissioner, Professor in the Royal College.
9. Alexander Wielemans von Monteforte, Architect, Royal Commissioner (Delegate from the Austrian Architects' and Engineers' Club).
10. Franz Roth, Architect, President of the Liberal Arts Club, Vienna.
11. Julius Deininger, Architect, Professor in the Technical College (Delegate from the Liberal Arts Club, Vienna).
12. Franz Berger, Chief Building Commissioner (as Building Manager of the City).
13. Ignaz Kraus, Magistrate.

10. In addition the following have been chosen to insure the number of jurymen being complete :—
Heinrich Adam, Architect.
Johann Gschwandtner, Town Architect (from the City Council).
Alexander Kmosko von Bernicze, Chief Engineer of the Donau Improvement Works (from the Commission of the Donau Improvement Works).
Paul Klunzinger, Engineer (Architects' and Engineers' Club).
Otto Thienemann, Architect (from the Liberal Arts Club).

For those members of committee who are government officials, the Lord Mayor has to appoint a substitute, should any be unable to attend.

11. The Jury have bound themselves not to take part in the competition either directly or indirectly. All the plans and helps relating to the competition have been laid before and approved by these gentlemen.

12. The prize designs become the property of the city, and the Council has the right to use the whole or part of the designs or proposals without giving the designers any further notice or compensation. The designer has the right to publish his designs after the result of the competition is made known, although they have become the property of the City.

13. The designs are to be well sealed and delivered not later than 12 o'clock mid-day on the 3rd of November, 1893, at the Evidenzbureau des Wiener Stadhauamtes (1 Bezirk Rathhaus). The bearer will receive an official receipt for them. Designs which arrive later than the specified time are not eligible for competition.

14. After the deciding of prizes the whole of the drawings will be publicly exhibited for 14 days. The time and place of the exhibition will be announced.

15. The designs which do not become the

property of the City are to be called for within three months after the close of the exhibition, and will be delivered back on handing in the receipt for the drawings. Plans that have not been called for within the said term become the property of the City, and the designer has no right whatever to compensation.

16. The authors of unsuccessful designs can have the sum paid to the City of Vienna returned, if required, within three months after the prizes have been divided, provided that all the plans received have been used in the design, or the unused sheets are returned in good condition; and that the certificate received when the plans were bought is also returned. In as far as the designer does not return the plans delivered him, or has damaged them to such an extent that the City cannot accept them, the sum to be repaid will be reduced. The reduction will be made according to the plans which are missing or damaged.

PROGRAMME AND EXPLANATION.

The object of the general improvement plan is to define the disposition according to which the further building extension and improvement of the whole City is to be carried out. In the intended designs are not only to be considered the present requirements of the City extension, but also the organized and future destined extension * in a thorough manner.

The designs must also contain proposals for a systematic extension and completion of the City Railway and all parts of the general communication; also for building better dwelling-houses with social and sanitary improvements; and for the unlimited building of factories, by arranging separate districts for dwellings and factories; and proposals showing the character of the buildings and improvement, which are to be of a practical as well as an æsthetic kind. The general improvement plan must contain the whole county or parish of Vienna. All present vacant ground is to be utilized, and the streets, &c., are to be laid down across these spaces. In the parts already built and badly arranged, the present streets and squares are to be improved, as well as new ones proposed, so that the principal centres are defined. The old parts of the city are to receive special attention, especially for the purpose of improving the streets and the artistic arrangement. In consideration of this principle old and new buildings are to receive the utmost care. In working out the designs it is not to be forgotten that the general improvement plan is only to form the foundation of the future arrangement and extension of the city, and not a design worked out in detail. The detailed appearance of the streets, squares, and other places will be shown by the general building line plan which will be worked out after the general improvement plan is arranged.

CITY DIVISION.

The using of Special Districts for Special Purposes.

The now extended city district comprises large spaces of vacant ground, which on account of their position and arrangement are specially suited for various purposes, and consequently permits the dividing of the city into districts suited and intended for definite uses. Such a division is allowed by law, because the City Council reserve the right (through pars. 71 and 82 of the Vienna Building Regulations) of retaining certain strictly defined city districts specially for dwellings or factories.

In consideration of present necessities and previous circumstances, the city division is to be so laid out that special districts are set apart for the dwelling and family houses, as well as for factories and public works.

In connection with this may be mentioned that the western periphery of the district from Kahlenberge to Hetzendorf is specially suitable for dwellings and family houses, while the factories, which with the noise of machinery, the smoke, and smell are unpleasant, should principally be confined to the X. and XI. districts, the Brigittenau and the Donau river improvement ground on the right

---

* The word "sizibewussten" is not easily translated; it means "with an object in view;" probably they mean the extension is to be shown so that it would be advantageous to the commerce or industry that may in later years be drawn to the city. One of the principal objects they no doubt have in view is the commerce and the shipping on the Donau and Vienna. Austria is trying hard to get forward in that just now.

and left bank of the river. The parts generally intended for family and dwelling houses are intended to be built up with semi-detached villas or blocks of houses with a definite number of stories, and with or without front gardens. In addition, the planting of trees in these streets is recommended.

In these districts the streets are also to be amply relieved by public gardens and other open spaces.

In the districts preferred for factories, &c., the streets are to be arranged so as to form blocks of suitable number and size for laying down large public workshops. In a similar manner the size and shape of the blocks for dwelling houses is to be arranged with proportionately large gardens or courts.

The designs to show, according to the use of the districts, suitable proposals for railway connections, coaling stations, arrangements for general business (markets, offices, and shops), railway and shipping stations, sheds, stores, workmen's houses, baths, hospitals, children's houses, &c.

Arrangement of Streets, Squares, Public Markets, &c., and Places, Churches, Public Buildings, Barracks.

The old street system is to be modernized in such a manner as to promote the sanitary and convenient arrangement of the city, by improving the present principal streets and important connections, as well as by proposing new thoroughfares. Much attention is to be given to the æsthetic requirements. That is not to be wanting in any district. For the already developed parts of the city, where historical monuments and memorial buildings form welcome landmarks, the laying out of squares and street openings or widenings is to be considered, so that the present buildings and monuments are seen to better advantage. The characteristic and artistic variety of the streets and squares is to be retained, and the new buildings to be placed with that object in view. In the unbuilt districts a distinct connection of main and side streets is to be made, in which the main ones are to be broad, and not contracted with a thought of saving space, while the side streets may be narrower, but always bearing in mind the intended purposes of the district and the sanitary arrangements. Generally, the aim is to make the new streets and squares, &c, in proportionate breadth to the height of the highest block of buildings. The new streets are to be projected as much as possible in correspondence with existing ones, and the harmonious connection with present buildings to be considered.

Consideration is to be made in the plans, where necessary, for new and for renovating buildings, for the clearing of the ground round churches, and for public buildings, schools, market halls, theatres, baths, &c. In addition, certain spaces are to be reserved for future uses in those districts which are not yet or only partly built upon. For sanitary reasons public gardens, children's playgrounds, and garden squares are to be kept intact, and possibly new ones made in the older districts.

In the as yet unbuilt parts grounds are to be reserved of sufficient number and size for laying out such places.

The woods are not to be cut down except for the continuation of the principal thoroughfares, and at good and suitable points for the laying out of villas.

In the laying out of gardens and squares, the placing of fountains and monuments is especially to be considered, and proposals regarding such are to be made.

The Royal Prater (Public Park) is not to be built upon. Where houses are designed to overlook same, the villa style is preferred.

The continuation of the streets in the district near the Royal Zoological Gardens, from the boundary mark 19 at Speising to the boundary mark 20 at Aufrof, in the Royal Zoological Gardens outside Vienna.

In the designs for the street system in the District I., and in the Districts II. to XIX., the main thoroughfares and the principal side streets are to be shown. In districts which are intended for a special use, the style of buildings is to be roughly sketched on the plan. Important changes in the old building plans for the already built-up districts are not to be made except when they are necessary or of great advantage. Also, those districts which have been given over for building purposes, although they are not yet built upon, are not to be subjected to great changes, except for the laying down of main streets and continuation of important thoroughfares.

In all designs the expense, and the protection of private interests is to be considered.

The Royal Military Drill Ground on the Schmelz (City Plan, Sheet VI., 4, and VII., 4) must remain vacant. However, the following military barracks and buildings in the general district of Vienna are to be pulled down and proposals are to be made for the cleared spaces :—

1. The Kaiser Franz Josefs-Kaserne (Emperor Francis Joseph's Barracks) in I. District, Dominikanerbastei.
2. The Cavalry Barracks in VIII. district, Josefstadterstrasse 46 and Florianigasse 43.
3. The Gumpendorfer-Kaserne Barracks in VI. Gumpendorferstrasse 76, Kasernengasse 1.
4. The Fuhrwesen-Kaserne (Army Service Barracks) in III. District, Ungargasse 49.
5. The Holzhof-Kaserne in IV. District, Favoritenstrasse 26.
6. The Reitschulgrunde (Riding School Ground) near the Military Bed-store in VIII. District, Josefstadterstrasse 73.
7. The Military Provision Stores in VIII. District, Florianigasse 70.
8. The Ararische Ground on the Turken-schanze (Turk's Tail) in Wahring.

Cemeteries intended to be utilized are chiefly to be laid out as gardens, free squares, or for church building. Those closed and those to continue as cemeteries are as follows :—

(a) The St. Marxer Cemetery in III. District, close to the Aspang railway.
(b) The Matzleinsdorfer Cemetery in X. District, close to the South railway.
(c) The Hundsthurmer Cemetery in V. District, am Margarethener Gurtel.
(d) The Schmelzer Cemetery in front of the West railway line.
(e) The public Wahringer Cemetery, along with the adjoining Jewish Cemetery in Wahring, between the main street and the Gymnasiumgasse.
(f) The old Wahringtown Cemetery, between the Schulgasse and the main street.
(g) The old Dollinger Cemetery on the Grinzingerstrasse.
(h) The old Hernalser Cemetery between the Dorotheer and Rosensteingasse.
(i) The old Dornbacher Cemetery in the Friedhofstrasse.
(k) The old Nussdorfer Cemetery in the Heiligenstadterstrasse.
(l) The old Sievringer Cemetery in the main street at Sievring.

MEANS OF COMMUNICATION.

City Railways, Improvement of the Donau Canal and the River Vienna, and the building of Branch Canals.

The carrying out of the Vienna communications will be controlled by a special bill from the Cabinet and Parliament, in which the constituency of Vienna is represented, and sanctioned by the Crown. This work is to be done in the manner mentioned in this programme, and in accordance with the corresponding plans (plan help 8). The costs are to be divided proportionately between the State, Lower Austria, and the Town of Vienna, specified and the amount of money available is in the propositions. Modifications or extensions of the proposed work which do not exceed the specific sum are allowed, while alterations that require additional cost must first be approved by the three constituencies, and consequently would only be carried out in the most urgent cases. The designer of the general improvement plan is thus given the necessary directions for probable intended changes. Such changes in the already divided programme proposals will only be used when they do not increase the cost.

Projects for completing or altering those programme proposals which are only indefinitely arranged, or reserved for private speculation, or for future uses, are allowed.

Special value will be given to those detail propositions which, bearing in mind the immediate surroundings, provide means of communication in an artistic manner.

In working out the general improvement plan, the programme proposals for the means of communication are to be little changed, only suitably detailed and completed.

(A) *Railways.*

The following are guiding principles for completing the railway system and the laying down of the City railway :—

(a) The completion of the passenger traffic by joining up the present lines of railways for the distant and through traffic, but especially for the suburban districts. Improvement of the traffic from great distances to within the city by a city railway: connection of those lines with the communication to the Prater (Public Park) and Central Cemetery. Suitable proposals how the traffic in and through the city can be laid out. Proposed direction of streets and tramways to the railway stations, so that the communication with all parts is equally advanced without much loss of time.

(b) The extension of the goods traffic, suitable railway connection with the factory district, and also those parts set apart for commerce, &c. Projects for connection with the landing-places with consideration of the Donau Canal and the Winter Harbour.

It is taken for granted that the city railway will be constructed at high or low level according to the circumstances of the ground. In those districts where the building of a high railway from an æsthetic point of view is not advisable, and artistic effect cannot be produced, an underground railway is to be chosen.

In working out the details care is to be taken to promote the æsthetic appearance, the through traffic, and the utilization of the ground over which the railway runs.

(B) *Donau Canal and Side Canals.*

The Donau Canal is, according to the accepted programme, to be turned into a commercial and winter harbour, which is to be protected against high water, ice, or indrifts, by a means of stoppage on the right bank, closing at Nussdorf, and by building locks and breakwaters.

The proposed low level city railway runs along the right bank from the Brigittabrücke to the Aspernbrücke (Donau Canal line).

Quay walls are being built at present on both sides of the canal, from the Augarthbrücke to Franzensbrücke.

Gathering sewers for carrying away dirty water from the sewers, which previously ran into the Donau Canal, will be built in both banks of the canal.

The above are the arrangements of the approved programme, and the following directions for the detail working of the remainder are suggested to the designer.

The landing places along both quays, between the Augarten and the Franzens bridge, are specially suitable for provision arrangements, markets, &c., and for the city and passenger traffic.

The remaining parts of the banks of the Donau Canal are to be reserved for goods traffic, packing, supply of coal, building material, wood, petroleum, spirits, &c., and suitable landing stages, stores, sheds for the coming and going traffic, are to be considered. In addition, are desired suggestions for the laying out of ship-yards or wintering places, as well as other necessary arrangements.

With reference to the expected building of the Donau-Oder, and Donau-Elbe Canals, whereby Vienna will form one of the principal junctions of the European Waterways, the future necessities are to be considered in the proposals, by reserving spaces suitable for probable necessities. The designer may combine other proposals for the promotion of any industries.

(C) *Vienna River Improvement.*

According to the projected improvement of the river Vienna for navigation, some of the overflow water will, when required, be kept back in reservoirs, while the rest is allowed to flow away in a channel enclosed in quay walls. Within the boundary of the city these reservoirs are to be formed in such a way that they can be partly or completely built over at any time.

With reference to building over the Vienna river there are as yet no arrangements, therefore the designer is free to make whatever proposals he thinks best. Still, it is considered that in the near future the river cannot be built over from the Schikaneder bridge upwards, and that if it is at all agreed to build over it, the district from the Schikaneder bridge to the Schwarzenberg bridge, and possibly to the Tegetthoff bridge, would be the first, as also the district Ungargasse to the Donau Canal.

The necessary connection of the streets from the neighbouring districts is to be made by bridging, where the river is left open.

With reference to the track of the river bed the designer is allowed to make some small alterations, but no sharp turnings are to be proposed, such as are in the old bed.

DETAIL PLAN OF BUILDING PLOTS FOR THE DISTRICT FROM SCHIKANEDER BRIDGE TO THE DONAU CANAL ALONG THE RIVER VIENNA.

The complete design must include a detail plan for building in the district from the Schikaneder bridge to the Donau Canal, including the

APPENDIX II.

neighbouring district I: Wollzeile Dominikanerbastei to Ferdinand's bridge.

In this design the improvement of the river Vienna, as well as the use to which the ground thus gained is to be put, are to be shown.

The memorial buildings such as the Charles Church, the Schwarzenberg Palace, the parts of the City with the City Park, and the unbuilt parts of the Ring Street, require that special attention is given to the artistic appearance when laying out these streets and squares.

The low position of the Polytechnic (School of Science and Art) opposed to the high positions of the Charles Church and the Summer Palace of the Prince Schwarzenberg and the rising ground near the Dominikanerbastei are to be specially considered and artistically laid out.

In working out this plan, care is to be taken to lay out the reclaimed ground in an economical and useful manner, without injuring the artistic or technical aim.

With the object of gaining a better arrangement and shape for the blocks of buildings, as well as a suitable fulfilment of the scheme, in addition to the houses along the Vienna river, those older ones further away may be included in the improvement. At all events in this sense are to be included in this detail design the old fruit market (so-called Nasch market); the district of the so-called free houses between Margaret Street, Schleifmuhlgasse and Vienna Street; the parts close to Charles Church; the part of the city from the City Park to the Donau Canal (whereby the skating ground is proposed for shops, stores, or markets); also the ground belonging to the Francis Joseph Barracks, with the Dominikanerbastei to the Ferdinand's bridge. A calculation of the spaces to be built upon is to accompany the building plan; actual buildings upon the arches over the river Vienna, and the underground city railway are not, as a rule, to be allowed. How far the buildings are to be placed from the improved river bed is not specified: still it is to be taken as a rule that the foundations of the houses are to be separate from the quay walls and abutments. The quay walls may, however, form foundations for light halls, &c.

The space of the city reserved garden, and children's park on the right-hand bank of the Vienna river are, as far as possible, to be preserved. If any change a suitable substitute is to be provided.

Closing Remarks.

In working out the design of the improvement plan, the competitors are generally to adhere to the directions and arrangements of this prospectus. However, if a design, by following a certain artistic idea or practical useful purpose, changes one or more of the arrangements of this prospectus, it will not be excluded from the competition.

List of the Plans and Helps which may be had for the specified prices.

1. A ground (position) plan of the whole parish of Vienna, with the nearest part of the adjoining districts, scale $\frac{1}{10800}$ in size.

In this plan (25 sheets) the boundaries of the parish and each district are shown in red, the present buildings in red, the gardens and fields in green, the woods in grey, the railways in black, and tramways blue.

The figures of altitudes marked ✧ are the altitudes above the Adriatic Sea, the full surface lines represent a surface 10·00 metres high, and the dotted lines a surface height of 5·00 metres.

If ordered afterwards, a price of 9 florins for a complete plan, and 70 kroners for a single sheet will be charged.

1a. A ground plan of the whole parish of Vienna the same as I., but in fainter lines and lighter colours, and without writing, on which the plans under A. (paragraph 2, prospectus) are to be drawn.

If ordered afterwards, 7 florins 75 kr., or single sheets, 55 kr.

2. A general plan of the whole parish, like plan I., but in the $\frac{1}{28800}$ scale.

This plan gives a general idea of what is to be done. Price later on 1 florin.

3. A city plan of the old city district, with the old suburbs, scale $\frac{1}{2880}$.

This plan contains the whole district for which (under b, paragraph 2, prospectus) a detailed scheme of improvement is wanted.

In this plan the already defined building lines are shaded, and the normal breadth of the streets shown.

The public buildings, monuments, and other buildings remarkable either for artistic or historic reasons are shown shaded.

In the districts I. to X., the age (building year) of all the newer houses, as well as many of the old ones, and their alterations are given.

In the street-crossings the present altitude is given from the nothing point on the measuring post* at the Ferdinand's bridge on the Donau Canal, written inside a circle.

The said nothing point has a height of 156·77 metres above the Adriatic Sea.

Along with the plan notes of the most useful statistics and the most frequent strength and direction of the wind will be given. If ordered later the prices are, for the sheets marked IV/6; V/5, 6, 7; VI/5, 6, 7; VII/5, 6, 7; and VIII/5, 6; per sheet, 4 florins, and all the others, per sheet, 3 florins.

4. A ground plan of the city district on the River Vienna, from the Schikanederbrücke to the Donau Canal, including the districts Wollzeile, Dominikanerbastei, Ferdinandsbrücke, scale $\frac{1}{1440}$ in size. This plan contains, in addition to the old extent of the city, the up till now defined building lines, the proposed Vienna river improvement and altitudes, &c. Price 5 florins.

* The nothing point on such posts is generally in Germany about one-half between high and low water-mark.

5. A ground plan as above, but in brown colour, in which the detailed building plan is to be drawn as under d (in paragraph 2, prospectus). Price 3 florins.

6. A pamphlet on the detail project for the improvement of the River Vienna, from the City Building Office, with 4 plates, according to the programme of the means of communication for Vienna, officially decided at that time, as well as discussed and altered in an appendix in reference to the extension of the parish).

7. The law from 26th December, 1890, by which the rules of the building arrangements for Vienna were changed (Law and Order sheet of 31st December, 1890, No. 48).

8. The programme of the means of communication, with the plans belonging to it. Price 15 florins.

9. A copy of this prize prospectus, along with the correct programme and the explanation belonging to it.

INDEX.

	PAGE
ACCIDENTS in streets	7
— from steps	59
Advantages of comprehensive scheme	38
Æsthetic reasons for comprehensive plan	47
— — for improvements	76
Albert Gate	68
Ancient buildings	13, 47, 63
— roads	74
Anderson, J. Macvicar	58
Annual number of new buildings	44
— Report of London County Council	3
— — of police	7
Application of suggested principles	65
Arbitration in future	37
Arc de Triomphe, Paris	18
Archæology	13, 47, 63, 76
Architects, Institute of	32, 58
— standing council of Parisian	17
— training of Parisian	32
— want of qualifications in London	70
Architectural difficulties	70
Art schools, Kensington	68
Arteries (see Streets)	
Artizan dwellings	5, 6, 9, 41, 43, 54, 70
Assessment of land at municipal value	82
— — London	85
— — — inequalities in same	86
Asylums	40
— Bethlehem	32, 40, 41, 76
— Chelsea	41
— St. Luke's	41
Attraction of labour to London	8
Austrian Emperor's decree	19
Automatic system in improvements	44, 47, 74
Avenue de l'Opéra, Paris	56
Avenues across parks	50, 53

	PAGE
BAEDEKER's Guide	12
Bank of England	67
Bankruptcy buildings	72
Barriers	66
Barristers	67
Bayswater Road	42, 57
Belgrave Square	82, 83
Bedford, Bishop of	87
Benchers	39
Benefits from commons	53
— from improvements	3, 9, 87
Berlin	4, 19, 22
Bethlehem Lunatic Asylum (see Asylum)	
Bethnal Green death rate	3
— — market	63
Betterment	90
— from railways, gas, and water companies	89
Birmingham, death-rate	4
— improvements	25, 30, 91
— municipal spirit	48
Blackfriars Bridge	69
Blocks to traffic	6
Board of Trade and of Agriculture, offices for	11, 12
Bond Street	18, 47
Booth, "General"	88
Borough High Street	57
Borrowing money unnecessary	45, 77
— — extravagance of	78
Boulevards in Paris	18, 56
Bow, rates in	86
— Street Station	69
Bridge over Ludgate Hill	70
Bridges over river	61
Brighton	12
British Museum	69, 76, 89

s

	PAGE
Bromley	86
Brompton Oratory	68
— Road	68
Brussels	4, 11, 19
Buckingham Palace	75
Building estates, laying out	36, 43, 47
— frontages, revised	36, 43
— land adjoining commons	53
— laws in France	14
Buildings, annual new in London	44
— historic	63
— v. land, for taxing	84
Burns, John	87
Bye-laws for future improvements	36
CAB PASSENGERS, statistics	89
Cabs, delays to	6
— tax on	89
Cadogan estate	11, 46, 55, 68
Camberwell	68
— New Road	58
Cambridge, Duke of	41
Cambridge Circus	46
Capitalists, benefit to	8
Central London	41, 54, 66
Chamberlain, J.	5, 26, 35, 45, 48, 91
Champs-Élysées, Park and Avenue	50, 56
Chancery Lane	7
Chaos of London Government	27
Charing Cross	7, 68, 69, 75
— Road	10, 57
Charity money, amount of	88
— — waste of	87
— Organization Society	88
Chatham	12
Cheapside	7
Cheerless streets	10
Chelsea, asylum and schools	41
— rateable value	46
Children living in slums	6
Circuses, designs for	60
City	6, 10, 80
— delay to traffic	6
Clapham Common	53
Clerkenwell	41
— Road	7, 57
Coal and Wine dues	77, 78
Columbia market	63
Commission des Artistes	14
— Housing Working Classes (see Royal)	

	PAGE
Commissioner of Police reports	7
Commons and open spaces	53, 66
Compensations, present	33, 34
— proposed	37
— in Paris	17
Competition for good shops	10, 64
— for improvements in Vienna	22
Comprehensive plan of improvement, draft	65
— — — — reasons for	30
— — — — in Paris	17
Consolidated stock	77
Constables regulating traffic	7
Continuous arteries	42
Control over buildings, Paris	14
Convex curves	60
Corporation of London	80
— tax	85
Costermongers	11, 64
Cost of parliamentary procedure	29
— — present improvements	45
Council Broadway, proposed	44, 60, 71
— of Architects in Paris	17
Covent Garden market	7, 69
— — theatre	60
Craven Hill	42
Cromwell Road	68
Crowded districts, open up	54
Culs-de-sac	43, 60
Current income for improvements	78
DEATH DUTIES	82, 83
— rate in London	3
— — other cities	4
— — ideal	5
Deaths from street accidents	7
Debt, municipal	77
— of Paris	18
Delays to traffic from narrow streets	6
— from parliamentary procedure	30
Depression of trade	8
Destruction of ancient buildings	13
"Devil's own" estates	39
Devonshire House	47
Difficulties, engineering	70
— present, cause of	38
Dilke, Sir Charles, on London	54
Direct routes	7, 75
District councils	32
Disturbance to trade	37
Docks, surplus from	79

	PAGE		PAGE
Donations for beautifying London	12	Fleet Street	7, 57, 70, 72
Draft improvement plan	65	Forced improvement schemes	74
Drury Lane	39, 42	Foreign criticisms	9
— — theatre	69	Foundling Hospital	40, 41
Dublin, death rate	4	France, Northern	12
Dwellings, Artizan (see Artizan)		Free travelling	41, 42
		Freedom of contract	10, 64, 75
EAST LONDON, charity in	87	French building laws	15
Economic reasons for comprehensive plan	45	— frontage laws	14, 17
— uses of land	40, 47	— improvement schemes	36
Economy in reconstruction	45	— technical schools	17
Edgware Road	43, 57	Frontage lines, new	36, 43
Education of Architects, English	32	Fulham	68
— — French	17	Furnishing trade benefited	8
— Technical, in Paris	17	Future improvements, arbitration	37
Embankments of Thames	69	- - traffic	75
Emperor's decree in Vienna	19		
Encouragement of trade	8, 12, 75		
Engineering difficulties	70	GAIETY THEATRE	64
Engineers, Institute of	32	Gardens, public	40
English Opera House	46	Garrick Street	60, 72
Enthusiasm, municipal	26, 48	Gas Companies to contribute	89
— — in Birmingham	26	— supply, surplus from	78
— — in Glasgow	24	— -works	41
Epidemic diseases	3	General benefit	9
Equalization of rates	81, 86	— plan of improvement	31, 65
Estates, laying out building	36, 43	— Post Office	74
— — — — adjoining commons	53	Gifts to London	12
Examination in architecture	32	Glasgow, absence of pride in streets	24
Example of metropolis	9, 12	— City Chamberlain's statistics	4, 24, 26, 29
Excessive compensations	33, 34	— death rate	4, 24
Exeter Hall	47	— enlightened policies	24, 70
Exorbitant rents	10, 64, 75	— financial position	25
Expenses of parliamentary procedure	29	— George Square	24
— — street improvements in past	33, 78	— improvements	23
Expert committees	32	— insufficiency of width of streets	24
Extravagance of borrowing	78	— municipal buildings	24
		— — undertakings	79
		— parliamentary expenses	29
FARRER, Sir THOMAS	85	Government buildings wanted	11
Farrow, F. R., on Vienna	19	— — benefit to	89
Ferguson, Mr. Munro	84	Gower Street	74
Fetter Lane	39	Gradients in streets	59
Filter beds	32, 41	Graduated death duties on buildings	85
Financial arguments for improvements	8, 11	— — — land	82
— — for order in carrying out improvements	76	— improvement rate	86
— position of Glasgow	25	Grand Hotel	61
Fire Brigade headquarters	68	Gray's Inn Road	60, 69, 72
Fire of London	55	Great Peter Street, Westminster	35
Fish market	70	Green Park	50, 75
		Grosvenor Place	75

s 2

INDEX.

	PAGE		PAGE
Grosvenor Square	83	Industries benefited by improvements	8
Ground landlords	81	Infant mortality in Glasgow	24
Ground values, tax on	39	Inns of Court	39, 53, 66
— tax or rent	81, 82	Institute of Architects	32, 58
Guildhall	40	— of Engineers	32
Gutters, water in street	59	— of Surveyors	32
		Irregularity of streets	58
		Islington	43, 69
HAGUE, death-rate in	4	Isolation of important buildings	63
Hamerton, P. G.	9, 18		
Hammersmith	68		
Hampstead, death-rate	5	JUNCTIONS OF STREETS	45, 60
Harrison, Frederick	54, 72		
Hatton, Edward	2	KENNINGTON PARK ROAD	69
Health	5, 75	Kensington	7
— of children in slums	6	— High Street	68
Height of modern buildings	57	— Museum	43
High-class shops	10	— Road	68
Historic buildings	63	— Schools of Art	68
Holborn	7, 39, 66	King's College	64, 72
— Viaduct Station	70	— — Hospital	72
Home rule for London	27, 28	— Road, Chelsea	63
Hooper, Francis, on Paris	14-18	Knightsbridge	57, 68
Horse Guards Parade	51		
House of Commons	86		
Houses of Parliament	68, 89	LABOUR CRIMES	8
Housing working classes (see Artizan)		Labourers' dwellings (see Artizan)	
— — — Commission (see Royal)		Labouring classes, benefit to	8, 87
Hunt, Sir Henry	33	Lambeth	41
Hyde Park	50, 53	— Bridge	68
— — after dark	52	Lampson, Sir Curtis M.	35
		Lancaster Gate	43
		Land, death duty on	82
IMPEDIMENTS to traffic	6, 40	— laws in France	15, 18
Imperial revenue to contribute	89	— — in Prussia	22
Improved Dwellings Act	23	— value, London v. Paris	57
Improvements already executed	78	— v. buildings	84
— benefits from	8	Lands Clauses Act	33
— best	40	Lanes of City	6
— economical	45	Law Courts	31, 72
— future arbitration for	37	Laws of building in France	14
— in Glasgow	23	— for future improvements	36
— in other towns	5	Laying out building estates	36, 43, 47
— plan, draft	65	— — — — adjoining commons	53
— produced rapidly	43	Leasehold system	80
— rates and duties	82, 85, 86	Leather Lane	39
Income for improvements	78	Legal expenses, present	33
— from special sources	78	Length of streets	60
— — visitors	11	Lincoln's Inn Fields	53, 66, 71
— — minor sources	88	Little Coram Street, Bloomsbury	35
Inconveniences, reasons for present	38	— Queen Street	7

INDEX. 133

	PAGE
Liverpool death-rate	4
Local councils	32
Loch, Mr.	88
Lofty buildings	55
Loi d'Alignement	14
London, backwardness of	19
— Bridge	68
— County Council and commons	53
London, death-rate	3, 4
— example of	12
— existing streets	42, 57
— foreign critics on	9
— government, chaos of	27
— in 1700	2
— increase in rateable value	46
— land value of	85
— like a pit	54
— of to-day	1
— position of	11
Louvre, gardens of	50
Lowther Lodge	47
Ludgate Hill	7, 44, 74
Lunatic Asylums	40, 41, 76
MAP of Central London	70
— of improvements, draft	65
— of London	31
— of Paris	73
— of Vienna	22
Market, Bethnal Green	63
Markets, fish	70
— retail	11, 64
— surplus from	78
Marlborough House	47
— Road, Brompton	40
Marylebone	41, 43
Merchandise forbidden in City streets	6
Metropolitan Board of Works	77
— Police reports	7
— railways	70
— Streets Act, 1867	6
Military Schools, Chelsea	41
Minimum width of future streets	58
Mint	40
Model city	3
Money waste from delays to traffic	6
Monopolies	81
Monotonous streets	9, 10
Monumental buildings	13, 47, 63
Mount street, Grosvenor Square	68

	PAGE
Muir, Lord Provost of Glasgow	25
Municipal Corporations Act	28
— debt	77
— enthusiasm	26, 48
— — Birmingham	26
— — Glasgow	24, 26
— Government	28
— improvements	36, 44, 74
— Offices, Glasgow	24
— — London	11
— rates	81
— socialism	27
— undertakings	78
— value of land	82, 83
Municipalization of town lands	35, 80
Munificence of Englishmen	12
Museums	89
NAPOLEON III. in Paris	14
Narrow streets, present	6, 9
Nation to contribute	89
National benefits from improvement	11, 89
— buildings benefited	89
— dignity	9, 12
— exchequer to contribute	89
— Gallery	63, 64
Nationalization of land	80
Natural increment	81, 84
New Bond Street	10, 80
— Inn	67
Nicol, James	4, 24, 26, 29
Night in the parks	52
Nine Elms Lane	7
Northumberland House and avenue	83
OBSTRUCTIONS, present iniquitous	39
Occupiers' improvement rate	86
— poorer	81
Offices, public, Glasgow	24
— — required in London	11
Official plan of London	31
— — of Paris	17
Old Street, St. Luke's	11
Omnibuses, delays to	6
— statistics of passengers	89
— tax on	89
Open spaces	32, 53, 66
— — in Paris	73
Opera House, English	46

	PAGE
Opera House, Paris	69
Order of carrying out improvements	74
Ordnance survey	31, 70
Owners v. occupiers	81
Oxford Circus	58, 61
— Street	10, 18, 57, 68
PALL MALL	60
Parks	40, 49, 53, 66
— Parisian	50, 73
— v. streets in Glasgow	24
— v. wide streets	55
Parliament, interference of	27, 29, 30
— costly procedure	29
— Street	75
Paris	13
— bridges	73
— building laws	14
— Champs-Élysées	50
— Commission des Artistes	14
— Council of Architects	17
— death rate	4
— debt	18
— embankments	50
— improvements, principles of	13
— in old and present times	9, 18
— in 1750	1
— income from visitors	11
— map of	73
— model modern city	18
— municipal spirit	48
— Opera House	69
— parks	50, 73
— pioneer of improvements	13
— Place de la Concorde	71
— proportion of space to buildings	57, 73
— technical schools	17
— width of streets	56
Passengers in London, statistics	89
Peabody trustees	33, 42
Perpetual leases	81
Piccadilly	7, 52, 68, 75
— Circus	75
Pimlico Road	68
Plan, draft improvement	65
— formation of general	31
— of Paris	17, 73
— of Vienna	22
Police statistics	7
Pollard, James	22

	PAGE
Poorer ratepayers	77, 81
Poplar, rates in	86
Portland Place	43, 60, 72
Portsmouth	12
Post offices	89
Praed Street, Paddington	43
Prince's Gate	68
Principles of street improvement	49
Profits from municipal undertakings	78
Projecting buildings	36
Prominence of public buildings	60
Property on trust or corporate	85
Proposed improvements	66
Proportion of taxation of land to buildings	84
Public buildings	11, 63
— — hemmed in	40
— — suitable sites for	64
— — meeting halls	64
QUADRANTS	45
Quaintness in streets	58
Quays	70
Queen Victoria Street	10, 57
Quinquennial valuations	81, 82
RAILWAY COMPANIES to contribute	85
— passengers, statistics	89
— termini	62
— traffic	62, 69, 72
— viaducts	39
Rateable value, increase of	11
Rates, equalization of	86
— existing	81, 86
— new	86
Reasons for improvement	1
— for comprehensive scheme	38
Record Office	40, 63
Recreation spaces	32, 49, 53, 66
Red Lion Street	39
Regent Street, width of	57
Regent's Park	51
Registrar General's death-rate	3, 4
Re-housing of poor	41
Relief of occupier	81
— of poor, amount of	88
Rents, present exorbitant	10, 64, 75
Reservoirs	32
Re-survey of London	31, 41
Retail markets	11, 64

INDEX. 135

	PAGE		PAGE
Retail shopkeepers	10, 64, 75	Sources, various, for improvement fund	88
Re-valuation of land	81	Southampton Row	7
Reynolds, Sir Joshua	47	South Kensington Museum	63, 68
Richmond	12	Southwark	41
Roads (see Streets)		— Bridge	68
Rome, death-rate	4	Spaces for recreation	32, 53, 66
— income from tourists in	11	Special sources of income	78
Rosebery Avenue	7	Speculators in land	35, 45
Rotten Row	51	Spirit, municipal	24, 27, 48
Rouen	19	Squares	54
Royal Commission Housing Working Classes	5, 7, 33, 45, 48, 91	Staple Inn	67
		Stations, railway, approaches to	62
— Institute of British Architects	32, 58	Statistics of city travellers	6
Rue de Rivoli, width	56	— — passengers annually	89
Russell Square	52	— — police constables	7
		— — London	89
		— — Glasgow	4, 24, 26, 29
St. George's, Hanover Square	46	— — new buildings in London	44
— James' Park	50, 69, 75	Steamboat passengers, statistics	89
— — Street	60	Steps along footpaths	59
— Luke's Asylum	41	— to shops	59
— Martin's Parochial Offices	61	Straight streets	58
— Marylebone	46	Strand	7, 10, 39, 66, 72
— Mary-le-Strand	47, 72	Street accidents	7
— Paul's Cathedral	7, 68, 69, 74	— comparison, London to Paris	18
— — Station	70	— designing	42, 55, 60
— Peter's, Bloomsbury	69	— gradients	59
— Stephen's Club	61	— ideal	18, 43
Salisbury, Lord, at Glasgow	30	— junctions	45, 60
Salmon, James	6	— new business	64
School Board Visitors	6	— picturesque	58
Schools, military, Chelsea	41	— tortuous	43
— of Art, Kensington	68	— widths in Glasgow	24
— Technical, Paris	17	— — London	57
Scotland Yard, new	63	— — Paris	56
Seats in streets	18	Sunshine, absence of	6
Secrecy of present schemes for improvement	35	Surplus from municipal undertakings	79
Separate valuation of land	82	Survey of London	31
Seven Dials	10	Surveyors	32
Shaftesbury Avenue	10, 18, 46	Swansea	12
Shaw, Albert	3, 13, 25, 27, 42		
Shaw Lefevre, Right Hon. G. J.	33		
Shopkeepers	10, 64, 75		
Sight-seers, income from	11	Tables, graduation of death duties, land, and buildings	85
Sites for retail shops	10		
Sloane Square	43, 68	— — of improvement rate	87
Slums	5, 9, 22, 39, 41, 54, 66, 71, 75	Taste, public, in Paris	17
— effect on health of children	6	Tax on ground values	39, 82
Snow Hill Station	70	— — omnibuses and cabs	89
Soho	10	— — retail traders	10
Somerset House	69, 72	— — vacant ground	39

INDEX.

	PAGE		PAGE
Tax on wealthier occupiers	86	Unsuccessful improvements, reasons for	38
Taxation, extinguish	79	Utilization, proper, of land	40, 46
Technical schools in Paris	17		
— training of architects	32	VACANT LAND	82, 83
Temple	66	Value, land v. buildings	84
Termini of railways	62	— London and Paris land	57
Thames	40	Vans, delay to	6
— bridges	61	Vauxhall Bridge	61
— Embankment	39, 69	— — Road	60, 72
— Street	10	Viaducts for railways	39
Theobald's Road	39, 66	Victoria Station, Westminster	68, 75
Thoroughfares (see Streets)		— Street, Westminster	68, 75
Time wasted from delay to traffic	6	Vienna	19
Tooting Common	53	— competition for improvement	121
Tottenham Court Road	57	— death-rate	4
Tourists, income from	11	— extension in 1857	19
Tower Bridge	68	Vienna maps	22
Town Holdings Committee	84, 85	— visitors, income from	11
Town lands, utilization of	40	Visitors, income from	11
— parks	40, 49, 53, 66	Voltaire on Paris	1
Trade, future disturbance of	37		
— stimulus to	8, 12	WALWORTH ROAD	7
Tradesmen, retail	10, 64	Wandsworth Road	53
Trafalgar Square	51	War Office	11
Traffic, delays to	6	Waste from delays to traffic	6
— east to west	68	— in charity	87
— to stations	62, 72	Water companies to contribute	89
Tramps in park	52	— filter beds	32, 41
Tramways	7	— in street gutters	59
— no further tax on	89	— supply, surplus from	78
— passengers, statistics	89	Waterloo Bridge	69, 72, 76
— surplus from	78	— Station	69, 89
Transformation of Birmingham	25	Westminster Abbey	51
— of Glasgow	23	— Bridge	61
— of Paris	14	— — Road	7, 69
Travellers, London, statistics	89	— estate	11, 55
Trees in streets	18	— Town Hall	40
Tunnel under Thames	70	Whitehall	7
Turin, death-rate	4	Wholesale traders	10
Typical modern city	13	Width of future streets	55, 57
		— of Glasgow „	24
		— of London „	57
UGLINESS of London	1, 9	— of Paris „	56
Uncertainty of Parliamentary decisions	29	Winchester House	68
Undeveloped estates	36, 43, 47	Working classes, benefit to	9, 54, 87
Undulating streets	59	— — Commission (see Royal)	
Unearned increment	84	Workmen's dwellings (see Artizan)	
Unemployed	8	Wren, Sir Christopher	55
University Hospital	74	— — plan of London	56

LONDON: PRINTED BY EDWARD STANFORD, 26 AND 27 COCKSPUR STREET, CHARING CROSS, S.W.

www.ingramcontent.com/pod-product-compliance
Lightning Source LLC
Chambersburg PA
CBHW031813220426
43662CB00007B/624